Consumer Credit Law

A guide for money advisers

GUY SKIPWITH and KAREN DYSON are both trainers at the Birmingham Settlement's National Money Advice Training Unit and also carry out casework for the Birmingham Settlement's Casework Centre.

Consumer Credit Law

A guide for money advisers

Guy Skipwith and
Karen Dyson

Legal Action Group
1997

Birmingham Settlement
1997

This edition published in Great Britain 1997
by LAG Education and Service Trust Limited
242 Pentonville Road, London N1 9UN

Reprinted 1999

British Library Cataloguing in Publication Data
A CIP catalogue record for this book is available from the British Library

ISBN 0 905099 72 9

Phototypeset by RefineCatch Limited, Bungay, Suffolk
Printed in Great Britain by Bell and Bain Ltd, Glasgow

Preface and acknowledgements

Many people have helped in the preparation of this book. In particular, we are indebted to John Buckley at Staffordshire Money Advice Services and Laurie Elks for their invaluable comments on the text at various stages. Special thanks are due to Jennifer Jones, Ros Wright and all at the Birmingham Settlement, as well as all the staff at the Legal Action Group.

To the best of the authors' knowledge, the law in this book is stated as at 1 January 1997, although account has been taken of the County Court Fees (Amendment) Order 1996 SI No 3189 at proof stage, which came into force on 15 January 1997.

Contents

Table of cases

Table of statutes

Table of statutory instruments

Table of abbreviations

Agreement Regs	Consumer Credit (Agreements) Regulations 1983 SI No 1553
APR	annual percentage rate
CCA 1974	Consumer Credit Act 1974
CCA 1984	County Courts Act 1984
CCR	County Court Rules
CLSA 1990	Courts and Legal Services Act 1990
CNC Regs	Consumer Credit (Cancellation Notices and Copies of Documents) Regulations 1983 SI No 1557
Consumer Protection Regs	Consumer Protection (Cancellation of Contracts Concluded away from Business Premises) Regulations 1987 SI No 2117
Crowther Report	Crowther Committee, *Report on Consumer Credit* (Cmnd 4596, HMSO, 1971)
D–C	debtor–creditor
D–C–S	debtor–creditor–supplier
DG of FT	Director General of Fair Trading
DTI	Department of Trade and Industry
Early Settlement Regs	Consumer Credit (Rebate on Early Settlement) Regulations 1983 SI No 1562
Enforcement, Default and Termination Regs	Consumer Credit (Enforcement, Default and Termination) Regulations 1983 SI No 1561
Exempt Agreements Order	Consumer Credit (Exempt Agreements) Order 1989 SI No 869

Goode	R M Goode, *Consumer Credit Legislation* (Butterworths, looseleaf)
HP	hire-purchase
HPA 1964	Hire-Purchase Act 1964
MA 1967	Misrepresentation Act 1967
OFT	Office of Fair Trading
Quotations Regs	Consumer Credit (Quotations) Regulations 1989 SI No 1126
SG(IT)A 1973	Supply of Goods (Implied Terms) Act 1973
SGSA 1982	Supply of Goods and Services Act 1982
SOGA 1979	Sale of Goods Act 1979
SSGA 1994	Sale and Supply of Goods Act 1994
the Act	Consumer Credit Act 1974, unless otherwise stated
UCTA 1977	Unfair Contract Terms Act 1977
UCT Regs	Unfair Contract Terms Regulations 1995 SI No 3159

Table of figures

CHAPTER 1

Introduction

1.1 History of consumer credit legislation

Before 1974, consumer credit law developed in a piecemeal fashion. Indeed, before 1854, there was very little credit legislation per se, the focus being upon usury and more particularly pawnbrokerage. The following is a summary of the main provisions and their effects.

1545 *'An Acte Concerning Usurie'* – under Henry VIII, all medieval usury laws were repealed and interest was permitted to be charged up to 10%.

1551 *'An Acte Against Usurie'* – under Edward VI, the medieval view was reimposed and usury (ie, charging of interest) again became illegal. This led to a reappearance of the various ways of avoiding usury perfected by the merchant community, eg, loans as sale of goods that were vastly overpriced, heavy penalties for failing to repay at an impossible early date. The motivation of the legislation was religious and artificially distinguished between the gains of finance and those of commerce and industry. The effect was unfavourable to the financial industry in that debtors could repudiate their agreements by invoking anti-usury laws against creditors who sought to enforce.

1571 *'An Acte of Elizabeth I'* – this act restored the position under Henry VIII and allowed 10% interest. Social and economic realities won the day and attitudes were changed permanently. No longer was usury a sin – a violation of Christian charity and brotherly love – rather, consumer credit was equated with business credit. It was no longer a private issue between neighbours, but an economic rather than a moral problem and thus properly subject to laws to prevent oppression and suffering.

As a result, from the 17th century onwards, there were two   1 forces at work in the development of credit. One was an attempt to lay down protective legislation setting out the rules for the granting of credit, the other the gradually improving standard of living of the population that led to a move away from credit as a way of staving off misfortune to a method of anticipating improving income and a better lifestyle.

1603   *'An Acte Against Brokers'* – pawning first became important in the late 16th century. As a result of this, parliament sought to prevent sale before the redemption date or the use of broking to cover for the disposal of stolen goods.

1624   The maximum permissible interest was 8%.

1654   Cromwell reduced the legal rate to 5%.

1672   Charles II increased the rate to 6%.

1713   Queen Anne reduced the legal rate to 5% on all consumer and business loans. This level remained until 1854. As a result, evasion and avoidance increased during the period of industrial and economic expansion up to the date of repeal.

1784   *Pawnbrokers Act* – allowed interest of over 6% on short-term loans.

1785   *Pawnbrokers Act* – introduced the licensing of brokers in order to protect the poor rather than prevent fraud. From this date, pawnbroking was highly regulated.

1854   *Bills of Sale Act* – abolished existing usury legislation and, as a result, moneylenders became very prosperous in their new-found freedom.

1869   *Debtors Act* – the final reform limiting the power to imprison for debt which halted abuses of the system by moneylenders and shops selling on credit.

1872   *Pawnbrokers Act* – amended and extended previous laws requiring the licensing of businesses.

1900   *Moneylenders Act* – in the 17th and 18th centuries, the main business of moneylenders was with needy gentlemen – loans to the impecunious middle and upper classes. The poor used pawnbrokers. In the 19th century the profile of business shifted to the lower classes and parliament's concern with the plight of the poor, faced with very costly credit and ruthless enforcement, resulted in this Act. It required registration, created criminal offences and allowed the rewriting of 'harsh and unconscionable' agreements. The Act did not cover banks or building societies and control of lenders depended on the initiative of aggrieved borrowers.

1927   *Moneylenders Act* – in order to tighten up the law to control the continuing abuses of extortion and harassment, this Act substituted annual licensing for registration, restricted the seeking of business (eg, outlawed canvassing), required certain documentation and restricted interest to 48%.

1938   *Hire-Purchase Act* – hire-purchase was first developed in France in the late 18th century. It was introduced into England in the mid-19th century to assist the growing sales of items like furniture, pianos and sewing machines to the middle and working classes. Abuses of the system, such as 'snatch back' (termination and repossession without compensation) led to the first statute to regulate this mode of retail. Further Acts followed in 1954, 1964 and 1965.

1967   *Companies Act* – the other way around the strictures of the 1927 Act was to create a banking company. As a result, a system of finance houses involved in secondary banking developed. These institutions' status was ambiguous until s123 of the 1967 Act required them to apply for a certificate confirming their banking status.

Thus it can be seen that the law developed in a piecemeal way, largely as a response to advances in retail practice. Coupled with this was an artificial separation between the regulation of lending and the regulation of security.

As a result of these problems, in 1968 a committee was appointed under Lord Crowther to examine the whole legal framework of credit granting and security. The committee's brief was to investigate the need for reform in the legal system, and the social and economic implications of the growth of credit.

With regard to the former area, it was acknowledged that the existing law was 'gravely defective'. The most serious weaknesses were seen to be:

– Regulation of transactions according to their form rather than their substance or function.
– Lack of distinction between consumer and commercial transactions.
– Artificial separation between the laws on lending and security.
– Excessive technicality.
– Irrelevance to modern requirements and failure to solve common problems.
– Lack of consistent policy in relation to sanctions for infringement – no distinction between technical and major breaches of contract.
– Inadequate protection of consumers – it was not clear where a

person's rights lay. For example, in the case of loan credit, nine different acts were involved and 23 different institutions loaned money, each covered by its own legislation.

The committee's report (Cmnd 4596, HMSO, 1971) recommended a sweeping revision rather than the amendment of existing statutes, leading to total repeal and replacement. It suggested the main principles of the new law be:

– redress of bargaining equality;
– control of trading malpractice;
– regulation of default remedies.

This was to be achieved by two statutes: a Lending and Securities Act dealing with all credit bargains and a Consumer Sale and Loan Act specifically regulating consumer credit.

The Crowther Committee's recommendations included a credit commissioner, licensing, regulations controlling advertising and seeking business, documentation and cancellation rights, use of the APR, early settlement rebates and the exclusive jurisdiction of the county court.

The committee's report led to a White Paper in 1973 accepting the majority of the recommendations. This was followed by the passing of the Consumer Credit Act (CCA 1974) with all party support. Its title embodies the committee's belief that the status of the lender should become irrelevant and that what mattered was the nature of the business conducted and the amount of credit advanced, with the interests of the consumer paramount. The American principle of 'truth in lending' runs throughout the Act.

The Act was designed to provide a comprehensive code regulating the supply to individuals of credit and hire not exceeding £15,000 and ancillary credit matters. The previous piecemeal and fragmentary legislation was replaced by a unified Act dealing with consumer rights and protection, all stages of credit and hire transactions, general credit regulations and enforcement.

1.2   Scope and structure of the Act and its relevance to money advisers

The use of credit over the last 30 years has played an increasingly important role in the financial lives of individuals and small businesses. Berthoud in *Credit, Debt & Poverty* (Policy Studies Institute (PSI), Social Security Advisory Committee, Research Paper I, HMSO,

1989) found that three-quarters of UK households used consumer credit, and a further PSI report, *Credit & Debt in Britain* (Berthoud & Kempson, PSI, 1992), found, breaking credit use down to different income groups, that 78% of households on incomes of £300 per week and above were users of consumer credit, with a figure of 68% for those on incomes of less than £150 per week.

The increased use of credit, particularly in the 1980s, saw levels of consumer commitment, or 'gearing ratio', increase dramatically. This, exacerbated by the recession of the late 1980s and early 1990s, unsurprisingly resulted in greatly increased levels of credit default and multiple debt, not only in the areas of consumer credit but also in the areas of housing, local tax and utility debt. The OFT estimated in 1989 that over two million householders were struggling to meet their commitments, without having fallen into arrears (*Over indebtedness*, a report by the Director General of Fair Trading, OFT, 1989). The National Consumer Council reported in 1990 that default on consumer credit agreements had increased 400% over ten years (Young, *Debt Provision in the UK*, National Consumer Council, 1990), and the PSI indicated in 1992 that 2.5 million households (12%) suffered from debt problems with 560,000 households facing serious multiple debt problems (*Credit & Debt in Britain*, above).

The money advice approach to multiple debt envisages an overall approach to a client's debt problems involving in-depth advice, assistance and advocacy. As many of a multiple debt client's liabilities will be regulated by the Consumer Credit Act 1974, it is necessary for advisers to be aware of the scope, structure and detail of the Act, and understand the relevance of its provisions to their work.

Advisers need to be able to:

- assess which of a client's agreements are covered by which part of the Act;
- understand the rights and obligations that are imposed on creditors and consumers;
- be aware of the provisions of the Act that may be invoked to assist and protect consumers, and the powers available to the court in relation to regulated agreements.

It is useful, therefore, briefly to outline the structure of the Act to illustrate its wide ranging scope and its relevance to money advice work, with references included to the relevant sections of both the Act and this text.

1.2.1 *Part I*

Part I of the Act (ss1–7 and 2.1) deals with the duties and functions of the Director General of Fair Trading (DG of FT).

1.2.2 *Part II*

Part II of the Act (ss8–20 and 2.2) defines the agreements to which the Act applies, ie, those that are 'regulated' by the Act, those which are excluded from regulation, and includes definitions of a number of new concepts introduced by the Act.

It is important that advisers can clearly identify different types of agreements to enable them to ascertain whether, and in what way, they are regulated.[1] To do this it is necessary for advisers to understand, eg:

- the basic requirements that will lead to agreements being regulated (ss8 and 15, 2.2.2 and 2.2.9);
- the definition of 'credit' (s9 and 2.2.3), 'fixed-sum' and 'running-account' credit (s10 and 2.2.4), 'restricted-use' and 'unrestricted-use' credit (s11 and 2.2.5), 'debtor–creditor' (D–C) and 'debtor–creditor–supplier' (D–C–S) agreements (ss12 and 13 and 2.2.6/7);
- which agreements are exempt from regulation (s16 and 2.2.10);
- what constitutes a small agreement (ss17 and 2.2.11) and a non-commercial agreement (2.2.12).

1.2.3 *Part III*

Part III of the Act (ss21–42 and 2.3) covers licensing matters. As unlicensed agreements are, by and large, unenforceable, and involve the creditors concerned being liable to criminal prosecution, it is necessary for advisers to understand the different licence categories, which category of licence particular creditors (or debt collectors) are required to have and how checks can be made.[2]

1.2.4 *Part IV*

Part IV of the Act (ss43–54 and 2.4) deals with the seeking of business: advertising, canvassing and circulars. General awareness of these

---

1 See also Flowchart 1 in Appendix 1 (p202) which may assist in the identification of agreements.
2 Wholesale revision of the licensing requirements are planned with the abolition of the different licensing categories (see 6.1.3).

provisions is useful in order to give advisers a more complete view of the Act's scope. Although breaches of the requirements will often leave a creditor liable to criminal prosecution under the Act or other legislation, eg, the Trade Descriptions Act 1968, they will rarely be of assistance to an indebted consumer. However, where misleading advertising is concerned, a remedy may lie in misrepresentation (7.2.1) or under the Consumer Protection Act 1987 which deals with misleading price indications.[3]

1.2.5   Part V

Part V of the Act (ss55–74 and 2.5) covers two aspects: (a) pre-contract preliminaries, ie, the form and content of the agreement, signature and copy requirements, and cancellation; and (b) agreements which, while regulated, do not fall under the greater part (ss57–73) of Part V.

Part V is of particular relevance to money advice work as breach of its provisions may lead to agreements being unenforceable, or unenforceable only with the leave of the court on such terms as the court thinks fit. The detailed rules are to be found in the regulations made by the Secretary of State under the Act (see 2.5.7), and will often require advisers to be able to define the exact nature of an agreement (see Part II above, 1.2.2) in order to be able to assess and advise on the applicability of the relevant technicalities. While it is not particularly commonplace to find agreements with mainstream creditors that do not comply with Part V requirements, it occurs frequently enough to make the proper checking of the formalities of entry into agreements and their form and content a basic but essential requirement (see 2.5 and Appendices 1 and 2).

1.2.6   Part VI

Part VI of the Act (ss75–86 and 2.6) covers matters arising during the currency of agreements. Of particular relevance are the provisions concerning 'connected lender liability', ie, situations where creditors are liable for breaches of contract by suppliers of goods and services, which can provide consumers with a defence and/or counterclaim against the creditor (s75 and 2.6.1). Also of importance are the requirements on creditors to supply account information and copies

---

3 Where misrepresentation by a broker or supplier is alleged, the possible liability of a creditor under ss56 or 75 must be considered (see 2.5.1 and 2.6.1).

of agreements (ss77–79 and 2.6.3), failure to comply with which can lead to an agreement being unenforceable and possible criminal prosecution of the creditor.

1.2.7 Part VII

Part VII of the Act (ss87–104 and 2.7) deals with issues of default, the necessity for and the form of default notices, restriction on the use of remedies available to creditors on default, early settlement rebates, the termination of agreements, particularly hire-purchase agreements, and liability on such termination.

Advisers need to be aware of the technical requirements regarding the service and contents of default notices, as these must be adhered to if a creditor is to be able to enforce an agreement, eg, by taking court action (ss87–89 and 2.7).

Of considerable importance are the provisions which protect hire-purchase (HP) and other goods and/or land from being repossessed without a court order, and the remedies available to consumers should creditors repossess in breach of these (ss90–93 and 3.2.2/3). The restrictions on default interest are also important (s93 and 2.7.5).

It is necessary to be able to advise when consumers have an option to terminate HP agreements, what their liability will be on such a termination (ss99, 100 and 3.1.1), and how liability will be assessed following a creditor terminating and repossessing (3.1.2).

In addition, advisers need to be aware of when early settlement rebates are available to consumers who are in a position to settle agreements in full before their due expiry date, and how to calculate (or obtain) early settlement figures so as to be able to give clients accurate information about their available options (ss94–97 and 2.7.6).[4]

1.2.8 Part VIII

Part VIII of the Act (ss105–126) is concerned with matters relating to security, pledges, pawnbroking and the enforcement of mortgages regulated by the Act, which requires that this can only happen on the order of the county court (s126).

---

4 It is proposed to make substantive amendments to the early settlement regulations in order to make them more equitable to consumers (see 6.1.4).

1.2.9 Part IX

Part IX of the Act (ss127–144) deals with judicial control of enforcement in cases where a creditor is in breach of CCA 1974 requirements (s127 and 2.5.10) and on the death of an indebted consumer (s128 and 2.6.10). It also deals with time orders (ss129–136 and Chapter 4), extortionate credit (ss137–140 and Chapter 5), and gives exclusive jurisdiction in consumer credit matters to the county court (s141 and 2.8).

This part of the Act is of considerable relevance to advisers' work. It is essential that they are aware of the effects of improperly executed agreements, creditors' rights to enforce these and the role of the court (ss65, 127 and 2.5.10), together with the effect of unenforceable agreements on goods purchased or money borrowed on credit, or goods subject to HP agreements (2.5.10).

The time order provisions are of importance to multiple debt cases as they provide for a way of dealing with HP debt, can be used where creditors under regulated agreements will not negotiate and/or refuse to freeze accruing interest, and may be the only option for borrowers who are in difficulty with second (regulated) mortgages. The interpretation and application of time orders has been a confused and uncertain area of the law. Some clarification has now been given by the Court of Appeal which, although answering some of the uncertainties, raised new questions (see Chapter 4).

The extortionate credit provisions, which apply to *all* credit agreements with 'individuals', are potentially of great assistance to borrowers, especially given the very high APRs that are often seen at the 'high risk' end of both the secured and unsecured market. Historically, however, they have been of little practical benefit to consumers, a fact which has been recognised by the government which has proposed amending the law to make it more effective in protecting consumers from excessively expensive credit (see Chapter 5).

1.2.10 Part X

Part X of the Act (ss145–160) covers ancillary credit business, the licensing thereof, seeking business, etc, largely relevant in relation to credit-brokers and the operation of credit reference agencies.

1.2.11 Part XI

Part XI of the Act (ss161–173) is concerned with the authorities whose duty it is to enforce Consumer Credit Act provisions, ie, the DG of FT, and local 'weights and measures' authorities, ie, trading standards or consumer protection departments, their powers, their liability to pay compensation, and offences, defences and penalties under the Act.

Two sections are of particular relevance to money advisers. Section 172 makes certain statements made by creditors binding upon them in relation to details of accounts supplied on request to consumers under ss77–79 (2.6.3), early settlement statements under s97 (2.7.6), termination statements given under s103 (2.6.4) and account details provided on request to sureties under ss107–109 (2.6.3/4).

Section 173 provides that any term or statement of a regulated agreement is void to the extent that it is inconsistent with a requirement of the Act, ie, contracting out of the provisions of the Act is forbidden.

1.2.12   Part XII

Part XII of the Act (ss174–193) deals with a number of miscellaneous matters including the duties of agents, requirements as to the service of documents, matters of interpretation, etc.

1.2.13   The schedules

Schedule I to the Act lists the criminal offences established and the penalties. Schedule II contains examples to illustrate the terminology of the Act. Schedule III covers the commencement of the provisions of the Act and transitional matters. Schedule IV deals with the consequential effects of the Act on other UK legislation.

1.2.14   Conclusions

Advisers may, once they are reasonably familiar with the scope of the Act, if not with the details, wish to devise a list of consumer credit checks to enable them to ensure that no areas of enquiry are overlooked. The flowcharts and checklists provided in the appendices to the text may be of practical assistance to advisers dealing with multiple debt cases, although they are not intended to be exhaustive. They should be useful, however, in directing the adviser to the relevant legislative provision and the relevant section of this publication.

CHAPTER 2

The Act in detail

References to 'the Act' are to the Consumer Credit Act 1974, unless otherwise stated.

2.1 The Director General of Fair Trading and the OFT (ss1–7)

The main duties of the DG of FT are to:

- administer the licensing system and make adjudications in relation to licensing matters;
- supervise the working and enforcement of the Act;
- enforce the Act and regulations where necessary;
- keep under review and advise the Secretary of State on social and commercial developments relating to the provision of credit, etc, and on the working and enforcement of the Act;
- disseminate information and advice to consumers, advisers and financial organisations;
- make annual reports to parliament under the Fair Trading Act 1973, and make public any directions given by the Secretary of State.

2.2 Credit and hire agreements, exempt agreements, multiple agreements, linked transactions and the total charge for credit (ss8–20)

There were a number of new concepts and much new terminology introduced by the Act. An understanding of these is fundamental to an understanding of the working of the Act. Examples are given in Schedule 2 to the Act and s189(1) contains definitions of terms used in the Act, alphabetically, from 'advertisement' to 'working-day'.

2.2.1   A consumer credit agreement

A consumer credit agreement is defined as a personal agreement between an individual ('the debtor') and any other person ('the creditor') by which the creditor provides the debtor with credit of any amount up to but not exceeding £15,000 (s8(1) and (2)).[1] This includes credit provided to firms and partnerships but not credit provided to companies.

It is not necessary that the creditor is a person carrying on a consumer credit business, except in relation to the provision of credit-tokens (s14(1)) (see 2.2.8), although if s/he is not carrying on such a business, the agreement may be a non-commercial one under s189(1) and (2) (see 2.2.12) and parts of the Act will not apply (s74(1)(a)). Thus the only requirements are that the debtor is an individual and that the credit is granted 'in the course of a business carried on' and within the monetary limits. The private or 'trade' status of the debtor is not relevant (other than where there are non-commercial agreements), nor is the use to which the credit is put.

2.2.2   Regulated agreements

Most of the Act applies only to agreements which are 'regulated'. A consumer credit agreement will be regulated unless it is exempt under s16 (see 2.2.10). Certain types of agreement, however, although regulated, are exempt from some of the provisions of the Act, eg, 'small agreements' (s17 and see 2.2.11), other forms of agreement are exempt from the documentation rules of Part V of the Act under s74 (see 2.5.1/2), and certain provisions of the Act, eg, the provisions as to extortionate credit under ss137–140 (see Chapter 5), apply to all agreements with 'individuals', whether regulated or not.

2.2.3 Definition of 'credit'

'Credit' is defined to include any 'cash loan or other form of financial accommodation' (s9(1)). This is an extremely wide definition, is

---

1 It is proposed that the consumer credit monetary limit of £15,000 be raised to £25,000 and that all business lending and hiring (ie, including sole traders and partnerships) be deregulated, although no time-scale has been detailed for these changes (see 'Consumer Credit Deregulation – A review by the DG of Fair Trading of the scope and operation of the Consumer Credit Act 1974' (OFT, June 1994) and 6.1.1 and 6.1.2).

unlimited in its form and is intended to cover all existing forms of consumer credit facility and any new forms that may be devised. In addition to the common forms of instalment credit relating to cash loans and transactions relating to goods, such as hire-purchase (HP) and credit sale, the definition covers *any* agreement where credit is extended or payment is deferred beyond the 'normal' date.[2]

The definition of credit does not require that a charge be made for the provision of credit, although certain 'low rate' agreements are excluded from regulation under the Act under s16(5)(b) (see 2.2.10).

It is important to note that under s9(4) any item forming part of the total charge for credit is not treated as credit. It is only the principal sum advanced that is 'credit' and it is this amount which determines whether an agreement falls within the monetary limits of the Act (see 2.2.1). For example, if part of a loan is withheld by a creditor in respect of a valuation fee which should be included in the total charge for credit, it will not form part of the credit advanced. Such charges include all interest payable under the agreement and 'other charges at any time payable under the transaction by the debtor . . . whether to the creditor or any other person' (see 2.2.15).

Thus, in practice, loans in excess of £15,000 which include charges such as broker's fees, valuation fees, maintenance charges and/or legal costs which form part of the total charge for credit may, after those items have been deducted, result in an agreement for credit of £15,000 or less, whether an amount to cover such charges was withheld or retained by the creditor or time allowed for their payment. If this is the case, the loan should have been made in the correct 'regulated' form (see Part V of the Act and 2.5) and, if not, the agreement may have been improperly executed and may possibly be unenforceable (see 'Consequences of improper execution' at 2.5.10). It would also give the debtor the right to apply for a time order (see Chapter 4). In *Huntplast Ltd v Leadbeater* [1993] CCLR 15, the Court of Appeal adopted a wide construction of these charges in order to avoid evasion. The first premium of an insurance policy on mortgaged property subject to the agreement was deducted from a broker's fee (which at the time did not form part of the total charge for credit). It was

2 Debit-cards, such as Switch, Delta or Connect do not per se involve the offer or granting of credit since the accounts to which they relate are assumed by the terms of the cards' issue to be in credit. The agreement to issue a debit-card is not, therefore, a credit agreement. Where, however, a debit-card is used to overdraw, the current account becomes a credit-token agreement and the card a credit-token under s14 as credit is provided in 'connection' with the card's use (see 2.2.8).

held that the insurance premium was part of the total charge for credit, with the result that the agreement, when the premium was deducted from the sum advanced, fell within the monetary provisions of the Act.

EXAMPLE 1

A finance house lets a car on hire-purchase to an individual at a total price of £22,985, composing:

	£
Cash price excluding VAT	17,000.00
VAT	2,975.00
Total cash price	19,975.00
Compulsory credit insurance	500.00
HP charges	2,500.00
Option to purchase fee	10.00
TOTAL	22,985.00

Calculation of credit advance must include the deduction of all advance payment and all items forming part of the total charge for credit, ie:

$$
\begin{aligned}
&£22,985.00 \\
\text{less} \quad - \quad &500.00 \text{ insurance} \\
- \quad &2,500.00 \text{ HP charges} \\
- \quad &10.00 \text{ option fee} \\
- \quad &5,000.00 \text{ deposit} \\
\hline
&£14,975.00
\end{aligned}
$$

The agreement is therefore regulated.

Note: For details of what charges are included in the total charge for credit, see 2.2.15.

2.2.4   Forms of credit

Two forms of credit are provided for in the Act: running-account credit and fixed-sum credit. Generally, running-account credit is revolving credit, ie, an umbrella facility under which the debtor can draw on credit on an ongoing basis, within any limits imposed by the creditor, so long as any specified credit limit is not exceeded. Fixed-sum credit provides an amount which is either fixed at the beginning of the contract or is determinable under its terms.

Technically, running-account credit is a series of different contracts, a separate one each time the credit facility is used under the umbrella or 'master' agreement. One of the effects of this is that the APR actually paid by a debtor cannot be determined in advance, as the pattern of credit use and repayment is not predetermined. The rules governing the content of running-account credit agreements are simpler and more flexible than for fixed-sum credit, and do not require separate documentation for each separate transaction and supply of credit under the 'master' agreement.

Under fixed-sum credit agreements, no further credit is available, so repayments will inexorably bring the credit to an end and discharge the agreement, whereas running-account credit can continue indefinitely, within any specified credit limit, and is thus 'open-ended'. From the creditor's point of view this encourages an ongoing and indefinite relationship with a customer.

These two forms of credit are defined by s10:

– *Running-account credit* is where a debtor is able to receive from time to time from a creditor or a third party cash, goods, etc, to an amount or value up to a specified credit limit (s10(1)(a)). Examples of this form of credit include authorised bank overdrafts, even where the overdraft level is exceeded, shop budget accounts, credit cards and option accounts.

Running-account credit will be regulated by the Act if the credit limit does not exceed £15,000. Certain anti-avoidance provisions are included to ensure that fictitiously high credit limits are not set. Under these provisions a term of an agreement which permits a debtor to exceed a credit limit merely temporarily will be disregarded in calculating the credit limit (s10(2)) and any running-account credit agreement with a credit limit in excess of £15,000 will be regulated if the credit charge increases when the debit balance rises above a given amount below £15,000 (s10(3)).

Unlike fixed-sum credit, running-account credit customers are only entitled to contractual information which is relevant at the inception of the contract. Accruing interest can be calculated on a daily, monthly or annual basis. Credit cards, for example, although they quote an annual and a monthly rate, will calculate interest on a daily basis (see p16 for different methods and p18 on compound interest). For illustrations of running-account credit agreements see CCA 1974 Sch 2 Examples 15, 16, 18 and 23.

It is important to identify running-account credit agreements because of the ongoing accrual of interest which can seriously exacerbate levels of indebtedness in short periods of time.

- *Fixed-sum credit* is any other facility under a personal credit agreement whereby the debtor is enabled to receive credit (s10(1)(b)). A fixed-sum is usually borrowed over a fixed period of time and often at a fixed rate although this is not necessarily the case. Variations are permitted subject to the terms of the agreement, for example, variations in the rate of interest. This is often the case with regulated secured agreements (second mortgages). The best examples include HP, credit sale, pawnbroking loans, fixed personal and bank loans, check and voucher trading, etc. Credit given by way of a drawing facility will be fixed-sum credit if the debtor's right to draw is exhausted when the facility has been fully utilised, as repayments by the debtor will not 'restore' the drawing facility. Also, an unauthorised overdraft will amount to fixed-sum credit, ie, where a debtor, without prior agreement, draws a cheque in excess of the credit balance available and the bank honours it (see CCA 1974 Sch 2 Example 17). If, however, a debtor exceeds an authorised overdraft, the whole overdraft, including the unauthorised element, is deemed to be running-account credit as the two 'elements' are not treated as 'multiple' agreements under s18 (s18(5)) (see 2.2.13).

Interest can be charged to credit agreements in a number of different ways:

- *Pre-computed interest with no specified rate or amount per charging period, ie, no specified period rate:* a pre-computed charge is one which is fixed at the outset of an agreement, is specified as an amount and included in the total repayment figure. Pre-computed charges are used in fixed-sum credit agreements where the period, the amount of credit and the mode of repayment are specified in the contract. Typical examples include HP, conditional sale, credit sale and loan agreements.

  With fixed-sum agreements it is common for agreements to provide for 'default' interest on any payments which are late or in arrears, although such default interest cannot exceed the rate charged on the principal (s93 and see 2.7.5). In practice, however, although HP, conditional sale, credit sale and money-lenders' agreements (eg, the Provident) provide for default interest, it is rarely charged.
- *Period rate applied to outstanding balances without pre-*

computation: interest is charged on the application of a percentage rate (which may be variable under the terms of the agreement) at specified charging periods on the balance owing. This method is used in running-account credit agreements or other agreements (eg, a drawing facility) where the amount and the timing of the use of credit (and sometimes of its repayment) is at the debtor's discretion. Typical examples include bank overdrafts, budget accounts and credit cards.

The method of charging may vary both as to the frequency of the charge and as to the account taken of drawings and repayments made during the charging period. Interest may be debited monthly, as with credit cards, quarterly, half-yearly or annually. It may be applied to a debit balance outstanding at the end of a charging period regardless of movements on the account during the charging period, may reflect drawings and purchases made during the period but not payments into the account or may be calculated on the daily balance outstanding. With many building society mortgages, for example, interest is calculated annually at the beginning of the year on the debit balance outstanding at the end of the previous year without regard to subsequent repayments of capital.

– *Fixed fee combined with period rate interest:* many running-account agreements provide for a fixed fee, eg, an annual credit card fee, together with period rate interest on outstanding balances.

– *Pre-computed interest based on a period rate:* interest is expressed to accrue periodically, but as the agreement is for a fixed term, the interest is pre-computed on the assumption that the agreement runs its full term. The rate can be subject to variation where the agreement provides so. This is the typical method of charging interest on second mortgages.

Such agreements will often include accelerated payment clauses which may be automatically invoked on default (s87 and see 2.7.1), or on the issue of a calling-in notice (s76 and see 2.6.2) or termination notice (s98 and see 2.7.2) in non-default cases. These can require the debtor to repay the whole outstanding balance that would have been payable had the agreement run its course, subject to an early settlement rebate where the debt is paid before the date the agreement was due to expire (s94 and see 2.7.6). A demand for early payment normally only occurs on the debtor's default although ss76 and 98 can give a creditor an unfettered right to call in or terminate an agreement, ie, be 'at large', or may be related to a specific event, eg, the levy of distress on the debtor's goods or the commission by the debtor of an act of bankruptcy. Where the debtor cannot, in these circumstances, repay the accelerated balance owed, the whole of the balance, now being in arrears, can be subject to default interest. This can cause the debt to escalate at an alarming rate. Where the agreement is regulated an application for a time order under s129 and a freeze or reduction in the rate of accruing interest under s136 may be appropriate (see Chapter 4).

These are the principal ways in which interest is charged on credit agreements although there are other possible methods, eg, an agreement may require part of the interest to be paid in advance as a commitment fee, so that there would be a partial pre-computation, which in this particular case would not depend on the agreement being for a fixed-term.[3]

Interest can be calculated in different ways:

— *Compound interest:* where interest is charged on a period rate basis on outstanding balances, as in the case of running-account credit, and is capitalised. This has the result of interest being chargeable on interest. Unpaid overdraft or credit card interest, for example, will be capitalised at specified periods, usually monthly, thus increasing the debit balance owing and escalating the accrual of future interest.

The frequency of compounding is independent from the way in which interest is accrued. A credit card or overdraft balance is likely to accrue interest on a daily basis yet be added to the debit balance on a monthly basis.

Compound interest can lead to a rapidly escalating debt, with debtors often unable even to cover the accruing interest, never mind repay the principal. If negotiations fail to resolve this problem an application for a time order under s129 and reduction or freeze in the interest under s136 should be considered (see Chapter 4).

— *Flat-rate interest:* where a rate is applied to the original credit advanced, even when the loan is repaid by instalments and will,

---

3 It should be noted that some creditors, particularly those specialising in second mortgages, have two rates of interest in their agreements: a 'standard rate' and a 'discount for prompt payment rate' (which may also require payment by standing order). If a payment is late by only one day, the lender will be entitled to change the interest rate from the lower to the higher rate, increasing it by as much as 10%.

therefore, be reducing throughout the period of the agreement. Flat-rate interest can be an 'add-on' or a 'discount' rate:

– *Add-on rate* is a flat rate applied to the amount of credit actually received by the debtor. For example, where the debtor borrows £100 and repays £110 by 12 monthly instalments, there will be a flat rate of 10%.

– *Discount rate* is a flat rate applied to an amount from which a discount has been deducted from the outset and never paid to the debtor. For example, where a loan of £100 is repayable by instalments over 12 months at a discount rate of 10% deducted from the advance, the debtor only actually receives £90. The equivalent add-on rate would be 11.1% (10/90 × 100) since the true amount of the loan is £90 and not £100.

 The term 'discount rate' is particularly misleading as it implies a discounted rate when it in fact disguises a higher rate.

Both add-on and discount flat rates are misleading as to the real cost of the credit as they take no account of the payments made by the debtor during the period of the loan. The actual annual rate will usually be approximately double the flat rate.

2.2.5   *Restricted- and unrestricted-use credit*

Restricted-use and unrestricted-use credit are defined by CCA 1974 s11 which distinguishes between agreements under which the creditor controls the use of the credit by the debtor and agreements under which the credit is provided in such a way (eg, cash) as to be in fact at the free disposal of the debtor.

Restricted-use credit
Restricted-use credit is credit provided in such a way that the creditor can ensure its application to a purchase or other transaction in relation to which the credit is extended, that is credit to:

– Finance a specific transaction between a debtor and a creditor (s11(1)(a)).

 This type of restricted-use credit covers situations where the creditor is also the supplier. Typically, the credit will take the form of a deferment of the price, or part thereof, of land, goods or services, etc, the subject of the supply. In effect, the supply and credit agreements become one. Common examples are HP, conditional sale, credit sale, the sale of land where part of the price

is left outstanding on mortgage and the supply of services on credit.
- Finance a specific transaction between a debtor and a third party supplier other than the creditor (s11(1)(b)).

This category of restricted-use credit is where the supplier is a third party and the creditor controls the application of the credit to the intended supplier by either making direct payment to the supplier or by furnishing the debtor with a credit token (see 2.2.8) which can only be used at suppliers designated by the creditor (eg, a credit card, voucher or trading check). In these situations, there are two distinct contracts, the supply contract and the credit agreement. The nature of the supply contract is not relevant. The most common examples are the purchase of goods or services by credit cards (but not cash advances, which are unrestricted-use credit), voucher and check trading (eg, Shopacheck), loan agreements financing specific purchases under which the supplier is paid directly by the creditor, eg, the typical finance house loans and budget account where the creditor is a person other than the retailer. An example of the latter is 'in store' finance provided by a third party creditor (see CCA 1974 Sch 2 Example 12).
- Refinance any existing indebtedness of the debtor's, whether to the creditor or another person (s11(1)(c)).

The third category of restricted-use credit covers both the refinancing of agreements with the creditor and agreements the debtor has with third parties.

An example of the former would occur where a creditor agrees to make a new loan to a debtor who has fallen into arrears and needs more time to repay. A new credit agreement will be entered into which will discharge the original loan and give longer to pay, usually with lower monthly instalments. A request by a creditor for a debtor to enter a new agreement is not uncommon where money advisers are negotiating reduced payments under HP agreements. The terms of such new agreements should be checked carefully. Alternatively, a debtor may owe a creditor sums under several credit agreements which may be consolidated into one new agreement to be discharged by agreed instalments.

An example of the latter would be where a debtor owes money to a number of third parties and a 'consolidating' creditor enters an agreement with the debtor enabling him/her to discharge liability to the third parties. This can be advantageous to debtors where short-term high APR loans are discharged, but many creditors offering such loans will only do so on a secured basis, and it is a generally accepted principle of money advice that a secured loan (a priority debt) should not be entered into to repay an unsecured loan (a secondary debt).

Unrestricted-use credit

Unrestricted-use credit is the contractual method of providing credit which does not enable the creditor to control its application and is any regulated consumer credit agreement that is not restricted-use credit (s11(2)).

In practice there would appear to be only two types of unrestricted-use credit possible: typically, where credit is provided in the form of cash to the debtor (or at the debtor's direction and not under a pre-existing or contemplated arrangement between the creditor and the supplier) and, secondly, where the credit is advanced for the benefit of a third party, even where the creditor makes payment directly to the third party's supplier. Although the creditor would, in these circumstances, control the application of the credit, it would not be restricted-use credit as s11(1)(a) is confined to transactions involving only the debtor and not a third party.[4]

The distinction between restricted-use and unrestricted-use credit is relevant in relation to:

- the definition of debtor–creditor–supplier agreements and debtor-creditor agreements (ss12 and 13 and see 2.2.6/7);
- linked transactions (s19 and see 2.2.14);
- the withdrawal from prospective land mortgage agreements (s58 and see 2.5.4);
- the cancellation of agreements (s67) and notices of cancellation (s69) (see 2.5.11);
- agreements exempt from Part V of the Act (s74 and see 2.5.2).

---

4 An agreement will *not* be for restricted-use credit if *in fact* it allows the debtor free disposition of the money loaned, even where this would be in breach of a term of the agreement (s11(3)). This would occur, for example, where a creditor makes an advance for a particular purpose (s11(1)(b)) or to refinance debts owed to third parties (s11(1)(c)), but instead of paying the supplier or third party directly, provides the credit to the debtor who, albeit in breach of the agreement, uses it for another purpose. An agreement can be for restricted-use credit under s11(1)(b) even where the identity of the supplier is not known when the agreement is made (s11(4)), eg, credit card agreements for the purchase of goods or services. The use of a credit card for cash advances, however, would give rise to unrestricted-use credit as it falls within none of the categories specified in s11(1).

2.2.6   *Debtor–creditor–supplier agreements*

The distinction between debtor–creditor–supplier (D–C–S) and debtor–creditor (D–C) agreements arises from the Crowther Committee's distinction between credit which is 'connected' to a supplier and credit which is not.

> Where goods are bought for cash provided by an independent lender there is no reason to regard the sale as any different from a normal cash sale, or to treat the loan as other than a normal loan. Where, however, the price is advanced by the seller or a connected lender the sale and loan aspects of the transaction are closely entwined. The connected lender and the seller, where not the same person, are in effect engaged in a joint venture to their mutual advantage, and their respective roles cannot be treated in isolation (Crowther Committee, *Report on Consumer Credit* (Cmnd 4596, HMSO, 1971) at 6.2.24).

Broadly, credit falls into the 'connected' category when:

– the creditor acts as a supplier of goods or services, the credit normally taking the form of deferred payment;
– an advance or loan is made under the terms of a regular financial arrangement (a 'pre-existing' arrangement) between a creditor and a supplier for the purpose of financing a purchase by one of the supplier's customers.

Credit takes the form of an 'unconnected' loan when it falls into neither of the above categories.

Sections 12 and 13 aim to put these distinctions into a statutory form, although different terminology is used.

It should be noted that the term 'D–C–S agreement', replacing the term 'connected' loan, does not imply that there will be three distinct parties involved, let alone that there are three parties to the credit agreement itself. A regulated consumer credit agreement can be a D–C–S agreement even though there are only two parties involved, eg, credit sale or HP agreements with suppliers who finance their own transactions (see s12(c) below). The term D–C–S merely serves to state the crucial distinguishing feature of this form of credit, ie, that there is a business connection between the supply of credit and the supply of goods or services which is financed by that credit.

D–C–S agreements exist where agreements are made to facilitate the purchase of goods or services which are:

– *Restricted-use credit agreements to finance a transaction between the debtor and the creditor (s12(a))*. This covers situations, as noted above, where there is restricted-use credit, in this case to finance a specific transaction between the debtor and creditor, under which the creditor is also the supplier. The credit will almost invariably take the form of a deferment of some or part of the debtor's payment for the supply. Typical examples of this include hire-purchase and instalment sale contracts which finance the transaction by which the debtor acquires the goods from the creditor. It makes no difference whether the contract is a 'two party' agreement, ie, a dealer acting as creditor by supplying goods from stock on credit terms or a 'three party' or 'tripartite' agreement, ie, a finance company supplying goods on credit having itself acquired the goods for that purpose from the original dealer. In each case the creditor is financing a transaction with the debtor. Virtually all HP agreements and instalment sale agreements fall within this category. Retail budget accounts and 'in store' running-account agreements under which retailers provide their own line of credit also come under s12(a).

– *Restricted-use credit agreements to finance a transaction between the debtor and another person (the supplier) made under a preexisting arrangement or in contemplation of future arrangements between creditor and supplier (s12(b))*. Section 12(b) covers credit used to make purchases from a supplier, eg, a retailer or dealer, who has a 'pre-existing' arrangement with the creditor or where such an arrangement is 'contemplated'.[5]

Credit covered by s12(b) includes trading checks and vouchers, goods and services purchased with a credit card and retailers' budget accounts financed by a third party. Many finance house personal loans will also fall within this category since the advance is generally made to finance a purchase from a supplier who has an arrangement with the finance house under which the supplier introduces to the finance house customers who require credit. The fact that the supplier has been provided with application forms by the creditor will usually be sufficient to show that there is an arrangement between them.

To be covered by s12(b) the arrangement must involve credit, ie, the postponing of the debtor's obligation to pay and not just be a

---

5 'In contemplation of future arrangements' would cover a typical agreement between a credit card issuer and a card holder where the creditor contemplates future arrangements with a supplier who is not at that time within the creditor's scheme to supply goods, etc, against that card. Whether an arrangement is in fact 'contemplated' would seem to depend on the state of mind of the creditor.

convenient way of ensuring that the supplier is paid immediately, eg, direct debiting of the customer's account when the purchase is made. In any event, the most common way of doing this, the use of electronic transfer via debit-cards, such as Switch, Delta or Connect cards cannot, under s187(3A), give rise to a D–C–S agreement, even where they involve the *de facto* granting of credit, ie, purchasers exceeding their credit balance and incurring over-drafts or where they are used in connection with an authorised overdraft. The position is the same with regard to the use of cheque guarantee cards (s187(3)) (see also 'Credit-token agree-ments' at 2.2.8).

– *Unrestricted-use credit agreements made by creditors under pre-existing arrangements between creditors and suppliers in the knowledge that the credit is to be used in a transaction between the debtor and the supplier (s12(c)).* Section 12(c) covers a simi-lar situation to s12(b) but is different in two ways. First, it involves unrestricted-use credit, ie, the creditor does not control the application or use of the credit; and secondly, it only relates to pre-existing arrangements between creditors and suppliers which are made in the knowledge that the credit is to be used to finance a supply contract, and not where arrangements between creditor and supplier are merely contemplated. It should also be noted that under s12(c) it is necessary that the creditor knows where the credit is to be used. This will often be the case under s12(b), eg, with credit sale and HP agreements but is not necessarily the case. The use of a credit card, for example, is at the discretion of the debtor. For an agreement to fall under s12(c) actual knowledge of where the credit is to be used is necessary.

An example of an agreement which would fall under s12(c) is where a finance company has an arrangement with a supplier to finance the supplier's customers who require credit and the loan is made to the customer and not paid directly to the supplier. It is unlikely, however, that creditors would normally adopt such a prac-tice, and it may be that s12(c) was inserted to prevent the avoidance of s12(b).

2.2.7   *Debtor–creditor agreements*

Debtor–creditor (D–C) agreements, which represent 'unconnected' lending, comprise all regulated credit agreements which do not fall within s12. Although it would have been sufficient to define D–C agreements in such terms, three types are specified:

– *Restricted-use credit to finance a debtor-supplier transaction not made under pre-existing arrangements or in contemplation of future arrangements, ie, not under s12(b) above (s13(a)).* An example of an agreement falling under this category would be a loan paid directly to a supplier where the creditor does not have a pre-existing or contemplated arrangement with the supplier.

– *Restricted-use credit to refinance existing indebtedness (s13(b)).* Agreements falling under s13(b) are those where existing indebtedness, whether to the same creditor or to a third party, is refinanced by a new agreement. A rescheduling of a debt under an existing agreement would not be covered as it would merely be the variation of an existing agreement. It is necessary that a new agreement is entered.

Typical agreements within this category include 'consolidating' loans, 'roll over' loans and new HP agreements entered following negotiations by a debtor or money adviser to reduce monthly payments and extend the time for payment. 'Add-on' agreements whereby further goods are added to an existing HP or instalment sale agreement, with a revised repayment arrangement covering both the original and the new purchase would, as with the rescheduling of an existing agreement, be a variation not a new refinancing agreement.

– *Unrestricted-use credit not advanced under a pre-existing arrangement, ie, where the loan is at the debtor's free disposal, thus not covered by s12(c) above (s13(c)).* Examples of agreements falling under s13(c) include bank overdrafts, cash advances obtained on credit cards and personal loan facilities or money-lenders' loans where the money is at the free disposal of the debtor.

The distinction between D–C–S agreements and D–C agreements is important in a number of areas:

– the criteria for exemption from regulation is different (s16(2) and see 2.2.10);
– transactions linked to cancelled D–C–S agreements are automatically cancelled (s19 and see 2.2.14);
– consumer credit licences need to be endorsed to specifically allow canvassing off trade premises of D–C–S agreements (s23 and see 2.3.6);

- the canvassing of D–C agreements off trade premises is absolutely prohibited (s49 and see 2.4.2);
- the offence of sending unsolicited credit-tokens does not apply to 'small' D–C–S credit-token agreements (s51 and see 2.2.11);
- the provisions in relation to 'antecedent negotiations' and a creditor's responsibility for a supplier's or credit-broker's representations (s56 and see 2.5.1);
- the provisions concerning the cancellation of agreements (ss69–74 and see 2.5.11);
- there is no connected lender liability under s75 in relation to D–C agreements (see 2.6.1).

2.2.8   Credit-token agreements

A credit-token, as defined by s14(1) is:

> a card, check, voucher, coupon, stamp, form, booklet or other document or thing given to an individual by a person carrying on a consumer credit business, who undertakes–
>
> (a) that on the production of it ... he will supply cash, goods and services (or any of them) on credit, or
> (b) that where, on production of it to a third party ... the third party supplies cash, goods and services (or any of them), he will pay the third party for them ... in return for payment to him by the individual.

Paragraph (a) covers two-party or in-house credit cards where the creditor is also the supplier. Paragraph (b) covers three-party credit cards where the issuer is a separate party who undertakes to pay the supplier. Voucher or check trading is also covered.

Examples of credit-tokens include bank credit cards, cards which allow the holder to draw cash from dispensing machines (s14(4)), debit-cards (but see note below), checks and vouchers issued by trading companies and in-store credit cards.

Cheque guarantee cards are not credit-tokens as the banks in paying the supplier are not paying for goods or services but merely honouring a guarantee of the cheque (*Metropolitan Police Commissioner v Charles* [1977] AC 177; [1976] 3 All ER 112), although where the card holder is authorised to obtain credit, ie, overdraw, it will give rise to a D–C agreement whether credit is actually obtained or not. It should be noted that the use of a cheque guarantee card to obtain unauthorised credit is an offence under Theft Act 1968 s16(2)(b) of obtaining an overdraft by deception, although it is not theft from the bank (*R v Navrambi* [1986] 3 All ER 102; [1986] 1 WLR 1311). Use of a credit card to obtain unauthorised credit, ie, exceeding a credit limit without authority, constitutes the offence of obtaining goods or services by deception.[6]

2.2.9   Consumer hire agreements

Three agreements are defined by s189 and are agreements under which:

– possession of goods is transferred by the owner to another person, the hirer;
– the hirer promises to pay the owner money (or money's worth) for possession of the goods and permission to use them;
– the hirer undertakes to redeliver the goods to the owner (or as otherwise agreed) at a fixed or determinable time.

A *consumer hire agreement* is an hire agreement made with an individual which:

– is not an hire-purchase agreement;
– is capable of lasting longer than three months;
– does not require the hirer to make payments exceeding £15,000 (s15(1)).

A consumer hire agreement will be regulated if it meets the above criteria and is not exempt under s16 (see 2.2.10.5 at p35).

The purpose of the provision requiring hire agreements to be capable of lasting more than three months is to exclude short-term hiring (eg, DIY tools) arrangements which bear no resemblance to credit agreements. An agreement for an initial period of less than three months will, however, come within the definition of a consumer hire agreement if it provides for the possibility of renewal or extension beyond a three-month period as it will be 'capable' of lasting for more than three months. The agreement would fall outside the statutory

---

6 For cash-cards and debit-cards to be credit-tokens they must be issued with the authorisation to obtain credit. Where they are used to obtain unauthorised credit, they will not be credit-tokens (see Goode I (549.4) and III (188)). The reasoning is based on a distinction between de facto credit and authorised credit and Goode speculates that CCA 1974 Sch 2 Example 21 is probably incorrect (Goode III (15)). It should be noted that where a debit-card is used in connection with an authorisation to overdraw, although there will be a credit-token agreement, under s187A no debtor–creditor–supplier agreement will be created.

definition, however, if it required a completely new agreement to extend it beyond the three-month period.

A contractual term permitting the hirer to terminate the agreement without incurring liability in excess of £15,000 will bring the agreement within the statutory limit as the hirer would not be 'required' to make payments in excess of £15,000. Where rentals are variable, eg, indexed to a fluctuating rate, it may be uncertain at the outset of the agreement whether the hirer's required outlay will exceed the statutory limit. In these circumstances, the level of payment required must be calculated by reference to the hire charges payable at the inception of the agreement. If the amount payable cannot be stated at all, eg, because of the uncertain duration of the agreement, the agreement will be within the statutory definition of a consumer hire agreement since it cannot be said to 'require' the hirer to pay in excess of the statutory limit.[7]

2.2.10   Exempt agreements

In addition to agreements which are unregulated, eg, because they involve credit in excess of £15,000 or are made with limited companies, s16 provides for the exemption of certain agreements by reference to the nature of the creditor and/or the type of loan concerned.

2.2.10.1   Local authorities

Agreements with local authorities are automatically exempt under s16(1) provided they meet one of the criteria as to the type of loan specified in s16(2):

– *Secured D–C–S agreements financing the purchase of land or the provision of dwellings on any land providing that the loan is secured on the land being purchased or on which the dwelling is being erected (s16(2)(a))*. This exemption applies where credit is extended by the vendor of land, eg, by leaving part of the purchase price outstanding on mortgage, or by a house builder, eg, by deferment of the obligation to pay for the dwelling, or by a third party pursuant to arrangements made with the vendor or builder. It does not apply to unsecured loans or to advances which are not secured on the land being purchased or on which the dwelling is being erected.

---

7   It is proposed to deregulate all hiring to businesses and to raise the financial limit to £25,000, see 'Consumer Credit Deregulation' (OFT, June 1994) and see 6.1.1 and 6.1.2).

- *D–C agreements secured by any land mortgage (s16(2)(b))*. Where the agreement is a D–C one, eg, a cash loan at the free disposal of the debtor, and secured by mortgage, it is not necessary that the advance was made for the purchase of land or the provision of a dwelling. Thus, a further loan from a local authority for home improvements would be within this exemption.
- *Certain D–C–S agreements financing linked transactions which relate to the purchase of land or the provision of a dwelling and secured on the land in question, or in relation to D–C agreements secured on land (s16(2)(c))*. Goode comments that this subsection is 'obscure to the point of unintelligibility' with 'no guidance as to what the provision is aimed at or, indeed, why it is there at all', but speculates that it would cover situations where a local authority makes a further advance, eg, over and above 80% of the value of the property, on the security of an insurance company mortgage indemnity policy, the premium for which is advanced by the local authority lender (Goode I (626)).

In practice, all secured local authority loans encountered by money advisers are likely to be exempt from regulation.

2.2.10.2   *Other secured lenders: nature of lender*

Consumer credit agreements secured on land and entered by local authorities are distinctive in that they qualify for automatic exemption where they fall within the categories prescribed by s16(2).

Secured agreements entered by other creditors can be exempt by order of the Secretary of State provided that the lender comes within the general categories covered by s16(1), but in contrast to local authority agreements, must meet the criteria laid down by the Consumer Credit (Exempt Agreements) Order 1989 SI No 869 art 2 (see 2.2.10.3).

- *Authorised building societies* (under the Building Societies Act 1986) are exempt providing the agreements satisfy the requirements of Exempt Agreements Order art 2(2)(3).
- *Authorised institutions* (under the Banking Act 1987) are exempt providing the agreements satisfy the requirements of Exempt Agreements Order art 2(2) and (3).

  This exemption will cover all the major clearing banks. Checks will have to be made with the OFT in relation to 'secondary' banks, although as they are normally only involved in second mortgages, their loans are unlikely to have been in relation to the original purchase of land or provision of dwellings and, therefore, not exempt (Exempt Agreements Order art 2(2)).

Both categories above have been given class exemptions 'as a body ... of a description specified in an order made by the Secretary of State' (s16(1)(g) and (h)). Other exempt bodies have to be named specifically in the schedules to the Order.

– *Bodies named in the Exempt Agreements Order Sch I Pt I* providing the agreements satisfy the requirements of art 2 of the Order.

Numerous *insurance companies* are listed, as are some 50 or more *friendly societies* together with nine church-related *charities* and the Timber Trades Benevolent Society.

– *Bodies named in the Exempt Agreements Order Sch I Pt II* providing the agreements satisfy the requirements of art 2 of the Order.

Bodies listed under Part II include one land improvement company, the various regional electricity companies, the Commission for New Towns, the London Docklands Development Board, the Sea Fish Industry Authority and various Northern Ireland Health and Social Service Boards.

– Bodies named in the Exempt Agreements Order Sch I Pt III, being bodies named or specifically referred to under the Housing Act 1985, provided the agreements relate to the advance of money on the security of a dwelling and providing the agreements satisfy the requirements of art 2 of the Order.

Bodies listed include Abbey Life Executive Mortgages Limited (and other Abbey Life mortgage companies), Alliance & Leicester Mortgage Loans Limited (and other A & L companies), Bradford & Bingley Home Loans Limited (and other B & B companies) and approximately 50 other companies of a similar nature.

2.2.10.3   *Non-local authority secured lenders – category of agreements exempt*

Where a creditor is an authorised bank or building society or a body specified in Part I, ie, an individually listed insurance company, friendly society or charity, etc, the agreement will be exempt where it meets the requirements of Exempt Agreements Order art 2, ie, is a:

a) D–C–S agreement falling within s16(2)(a) above, ie, a secured agreement financing the purchase of land or the provision of dwellings, secured on the land purchased or on which the dwelling is erected, or falling within s16(2)(c) above (art 2(2)(a)).

b) D–C agreement secured by any mortgage for the purchase of land (art 2(2)(b)(i)).
c) D–C agreement secured by any mortgage for the provision of dwelling or business premises on any land (art 2(2)(b)(ii)).
d) D–C agreement secured by any land mortgage for the alteration, enlargement, repair or improvement of any dwelling or business premises (art 2(2)(b)(iii)) providing the creditor also financed or refinanced the original loan for the purchase of the land or the provision of the premises and the loan was secured on the land in question (art 2(3)(i)).
e) D–C agreement secured by any land mortgage for the refinancing of any existing indebtedness, whether to the creditor or to a third party, such indebtedness having been for the purchase of land, the provision of premises or improvements, etc (art 2(2)(c)).

In the case of refinance of an 'improvements' loan, the creditor must also have financed or refinance, as in d) above, the original loan for the purchase of the land or the provision of the premises and that loan must have been secured on the land in question (art 2(3)(i)).

The exemptions in relation to improvements are very complex. The reasoning behind them is to distinguish a further advance or a refinancing loan from the original mortgage lender from advances from 'new lenders'. It aims to exclude from exemption loans from the typical 'second mortgage lenders', an area of lending that 'has generated a considerable volume of trading malpractice over the years' (Goode I (629.4)).

Bodies listed in Parts II and III (see 2.2.10.2 above) have similar requirements in relation to the type of agreement exempted but these creditors are most unlikely to come within the areas of money advice work.

2.2.10.4   *Conclusions*

While the exact nature and detail of the agreements exempt under s16(1)(2) and the Exempt Agreements Order is complex, it will usually be sufficient for money advisers to know that the following agreements are likely to be exempt from CCA 1974 regulation:

– all secured loans from local authorities;
– secured loans from major banks, building societies and major insurance companies which are for the purchase of land, or for the provision of dwellings, provided the agreement is secured on the land purchased or on which the dwelling is to be erected;

– D–C agreements from banks, etc, for the purchase or the provision of dwellings or business premises on land secured by any mortgage;
– secured D–C agreements from the above lenders for the alteration of dwelling or business premises provided the lender made the original loan for the purchase of the land or the provision of the dwelling or business premises;
– secured refinancing loans from major banks, building societies and insurance companies, providing the original loan was for the purchase of land or the provision of dwelling or business premises, and the secured refinancing of improvement loans where the creditor also financed the original purchase of land or provision of premises.

2.2.10.5   Other exempt agreements

Other categories of agreements are exempt solely by virtue of the nature of the agreement.

Agreements exempt due to the number of instalments payable under the agreement (s16(5)(a)).

Fixed-sum D–C–S agreements which involve no more than four payments in 12 months.   This exemption would cover, *inter alia*, ordinary fixed-sum credit, eg, 28-day trade credit, but not cash loans or payments to suppliers not made under pre-existing arrangements. These are D–C agreements (Exempt Agreements Order art 3(1)(a)(i)).

Running-account D–C–S agreements which provide for the debtor, in relation to specified periods, to repay the credit in one instalment (Exempt Agreements Order art 3(1)(a)(ii)).   This exemption will cover running-account trade credit such as coal, newspaper or milk bills and charge cards, such as American Express, Diners Club and 'Gold' cards, where the full outstanding balance is repayable at the end of each statement period.[8]

D–C–S agreements for the purchase of land where there are no more than four payments (including payments of interest) (Exempt Agreements Order art 3(1)(b)).

D–C–S agreements for fixed-sum credit to finance a premium under certain contracts of insurance relating to land 'or any thing thereon' (Exempt Agreements Order art 3(1)(c)).   For such an agreement to be exempt the creditor must also be a creditor under a secured agreement which is exempt from regulation, the amount of credit (in rela-

---

8 Neither of the above exemptions apply to agreements to purchase land.

tion to the premium) must be repaid in the period to which the premium relates (which must not exceed 12 months) and there must be no charge for the credit other than interest at a rate not exceeding that under the principal secured agreement.

The intention is to exempt (*inter alia*) agreements under which a creditor, eg, a building society, advancing money on a mortgage for the purchase of a house, also arranges building insurance and pays the annual premium and collects this from the borrower by way of the borrower's monthly repayments (although in practice the premium is sometimes repaid in a single payment).

D–C–S agreements for fixed-sum credit to finance a premium under a mortgage protection policy (Exempt Agreements Order art 3(1)(d)). For such an agreement to be exempt the creditor must also be the creditor under a secured agreement which is exempt, the amount of the credit (in relation to the premium) must be repaid in no more than 12 payments and there must be no charge for the credit other than interest at a rate not exceeding that under the principal secured agreement.

The intention is to exempt (*inter alia*) agreements under which a creditor, eg, a building society advancing money on a mortgage for the purchase of a house, takes an assignment of a mortgage protection policy arranged by the borrower, pays the premium on behalf of the borrower and collects this from the borrower by way of one or more (but not exceeding 12) of the borrower's monthly payments.

Agreements exempt by virtue of the rate of the total charge for credit
CCA 1974 s16(5)(b) and Exempt Agreements Order art 4(1) exempts three categories of 'low-cost' credit agreement. It should be noted that there is one overriding criterion for the three categories of exemption: that an agreement cannot be exempt where it provides for indexation of the *principal* sum repayable by the debtor (art 4(4)). For example, where a loan of £4,000, repayable at interest of 10%, provides that the amount repayable in respect of *principal* shall be £5,000 plus a percentage increase equal to that shown in the RPI between the date of the loan and the date of repayment, this loan cannot be exempt, even where such an increase is limited to the maximum allowed under art 4(5). Subject to this provision, the following are exempt:

– D–C agreements where the total charge for credit does not exceed the specified maximum (Exempt Agreements Order art 4(1)(a)), that specified maximum being the highest of 13% or 1% above the highest base rate published by the clearing banks (art 4(5)).[9]

The maximum rate chargeable is based on the base rate in operation 28 days before the agreement is made. The rate becomes established, therefore, on entry into the agreement and subsequent changes in base rates can have no effect on the exempt status of the agreement.

In general, an agreement will not be exempt where it contains provisions for the rate of charge to increase, whether automatically or upon notice by the creditor, after the date of agreement (art 4(2)), although there are two exceptions to this under art 4(3):

- Where the debtor is an employee of the creditor, the agreement may provide for an increase in the rate of charge on the termination of employment (art 4(3)(a)).
- Where the rate of charge is to be ascertained throughout the period of the loan by reference to the level of an index or formula specified in the agreement (art 4(3)(b)).

    Where the rate chargeable at the outset of the agreement can fluctuate, eg, in relation to Finance House base rate, the agreement will be exempt provided it fixes as a ceiling a rate no higher than the maximum permissible, eg, 'no higher than the lowest of 2% above Finance House base rate or 13%' (see Goode I (637)).

- D–C–S agreements for fixed-sum credit to finance a premium under a mortgage protection policy where the creditor is the creditor under an agreement exempt under the Act or which would be so exempt if the credit did not exceed £15,000 (art 4(1)(b)).

    This exemption is similar to the exemption under art 3(1)(d) (see p33 above), except that instead of the requirement that the number of the debtor's payments must not exceed 12, art 3(1)(d) provides that there should be no credit charge other than interest and that that interest should not exceed the highest of 13% or 1% above the highest base rate.

- D–C agreements where the only amount included in the charge for credit is interest limited to the specified maximum of the highest of 13% or 1% above the highest bank base rate (art 4(1)(c)).

    This exemption only applies where there are no items other than interest included in the total charge for credit, eg, maintenance

9   It is important to note that the 'total charge for credit' percentage rates relevant to the exemption are APRs which are somewhat higher than standard annual rates. For example, for an agreement paid monthly, a 13% APR is the equivalent of a period rate charge of 12.28 % per annum or an annual flat rate of 6.78%

charges or insurance premiums. No agreement can be exempt under this article where any such charges are included.

It should be noted that for this exemption the relevant bank rate is not the highest prevailing 28 days before the agreement but the highest of the latest rates prevailing 28 days before any given time in the agreement at which interest is chargeable. A creditor is not, therefore, tied down to a bank base rate effective 28 days before the agreement was made. It will be necessary, however, that it can be seen from the outset, at the time the agreement was made that the maximum rate permitted will not be exceeded. It will have to be shown that the maximum rate was not excceded at the time the agreement was made and will, under the terms of the agreement, be automatically adjusted within 28 days of a fall in bank rates to prevent it exceeding the maximum allowed. Provision for such an automatic adjustment must, therefore, be built into the agreement at the outset.

Agreements with a foreign element

Under CCA 1974 s16(5)(c) and Exempt Agreements Order art 5, certain agreements that involve a connection with a non-UK country are exempt from regulation:

- Where the agreement is in connection with trade in goods and services between the UK and a non-UK country or within a country or between countries outside the UK.
- Where the agreement is between a creditor listed in Part IV of Schedule I to the Order, that is, a (US) Federal Credit Union, American Book Distributors Inc and National City Bank, Indiana, and a member of the US armed forces, an employee of the US armed forces not habitually resident in the UK or any member's or employee's wife, husband or other person wholly or partly maintained as a child (art 5(b)).

Exempt consumer hire agreements

Under CCA 1974 s16(6) and Exempt Agreements Order art 6, consumer agreements with utility companies for the hire of metering equipment are exempt from regulation.

Lending to limited companies: the monetary limit: extortionate credit

It should be remembered that agreements with limited companies (as debtors or hirers) can never be regulated (see 2.2.1), although it is proposed to deregulate *all* business lending and hiring (see 6.1.1).

It is also important to remember that lending or hiring in excess of £15,000 can never be regulated, although it is proposed to increase this figure to £25,000 (see 6.1.2).

In addition, it should be remembered that the extortionate credit provisions apply to all lending to individuals, whether regulated or not (see Chapter 5).

2.2.11   Small agreements

Small agreements (s17) are mid-way between regulated agreements and exempt agreements and are exempt from some provisions of the Act. Small agreements are:[10]

- regulated consumer credit agreements for credit not exceeding £50, excluding interest and other charges (s17(1)(a));
- regulated consumer hire agreements which do not require payments exceeding £50 (s17(1)(b)).

There are *anti-avoidance* provisions which cover situations where a number of small agreements are made but it appears probable that they would have been made as a single agreement but for a desire to avoid the provisions of the Act (s17(3)).

Small agreements are not in principle exempt from the provisions of the Act although a number of the important parts of the Act do not apply:

- provisions relating to unsolicited credit-tokens (s51(1));
- for small D–C–S restricted-use credit agreements, all of the provisions of Part V of the Act excepting ss55 and 56 (s74(2) and see 2.5.2);
- provisions relating to the duty to give regular account information on small running-account credit agreements (s78(7) and see 2.6.3);
- provisions relating to the documentation required on the issue of credit-tokens (s85(3)).

It should be remembered that small agreements *are* subject to the provisions of Part IV of the Act relating to seeking business, the

10   HP/conditional sale agreements are not covered, neither are agreements secured on land – agreements secured *only* by guarantee or indemnity can be. Running-account credit agreements will be small agreements if the credit limit does not exceed £50. It is proposed to raise the 'small agreement' limit to £150 ('Consumer Credit Deregulation' (OFT, June 1994) and see 6.1.2).

provisions requiring the creditor to supply information on request other than under s78(7) above (Part VI), and the provisions restricting remedies on default (Part VII).

2.2.12   Non-commercial agreements

Non-commercial agreements are similar in category to small agreements. As the Act is primarily aimed at traders and professional credit granters, many statutory provisions do not apply to these agreements.

A non-commercial agreement is one made by a creditor not in the course of a business carried on by him/her (s189(1)). It is important to note that the business carried on does not have to be a consumer credit business. To be non-commercial, a loan must not be in the course of *any* business, eg, a solicitor who regularly makes loans to clients or an employer who regularly makes loans to employees *will* be lending in the course of business, even where the granting of credit is purely ancillary to the main function of the business. If, however, the granting of credit is only occasional it will not be deemed to be in the course of business (s189(2)), ie, an isolated loan not made as an integral part of a business (*Hare v Schurek* [1993] CCLR 47). At what point an occasional activity becomes a regular one is a matter of fact and degree to be decided in each case (*R v Marshall* (1989) 90 Cr App Rep 73, CA; (1991) 23 *Adviser* 19 and see 2.3.3).

Exemptions enjoyed by non-commercial agreements include:

- exemption from Part V of the Act, other than s56 (liability for negotiator's antecedent representations) (s74(1) and see 2.5.1), ie, there are no formal documentary requirements, cancellation rights or a cooling-off period;
- exemption from the connected lender liability provisions of s75 (s75(3) and see 2.6.1);
- exemption from the provisions relating to the duty to supply information under ss77–79 and 107–110 (ss77(5), 78(7), 79(4) and see 2.6.3);
- exemption from the licensing provisions; non-commercial lending is not 'carrying on a consumer credit business' within s21(1) (see 2.3.3) and an unlicensed lender can enforce a non-commercial agreement without leave of the court (s40(1));
- exemption from the provisions relating to giving notice of variations of agreements (s82(7));
- exemption from the provisions relating to pawn-receipts (s114(3)(b)).

2.2.13   Multiple agreements

Multiple transactions are defined as those which fall within more than one category of agreement (s18(1)(a)). Examples of these include agreements where part of the agreement is for fixed-sum credit and part for running-account credit, where a credit card involves cash advances (unrestricted–use D–C credit) and the purchase of goods (restricted-use D–C–S credit) or where part of an agreement is regulated and part is not.

Under s18(2) each separate part of a multiple agreement is treated as a separate agreement. Each separate category must, therefore, be looked at individually in terms of the application of the Act. Part of the reasoning behind this approach is anti-avoidance, eg, to prevent the combining of a number of different categories in one 'multiple agreement' in order to exceed the £15,000 limit. An exception to this is where a debtor under a running-account credit agreement is temporarily allowed to exceed the credit limit. This would cover exceeding the credit limit on a credit card or exceeding an authorised overdraft. The 'excess' would not become a separate 'multiple' agreement (s18(5)).[11]

There are a number of difficult legal complexities relating to the interpretation of this section and the operation of s18 has been subject to an OFT discussion paper ('Multiple Agreements and Section 18 of the CCA '74' (OFT, June 1995)).

2.2.14   Linked transactions

It was thought necessary to extend the controls imposed by the Act to agreements which might not themselves be regulated agreements but which are closely associated with them. This was partly to prevent evasion of the Act and exploitation of consumers, eg, by disguising high credit charges as payments to be made under ancillary agreements to service or maintain goods, under contracts of insurance or by inducing consumers to enter further commitments over and above those incurred in the principal (regulated) agreement.

Linked transactions are agreements entered into by debtors with creditors or third parties, excluding those secured on land, by indemnity or by guarantee, *in relation* to actual or prospective regulated

11 The provisions do not apply to an agreement which relates to goods if, under the agreement, payments are to be made in respect of those goods by way of rent, eg, furnished tenancies (s18(6)).

agreements of which they do not form any part, in three situations which cover three types of transaction:

- *Compulsory transactions,* ie, a transaction entered into in compliance with a term of the principal agreement (s19(1)(a)), eg, a maintenance agreement compulsory under an HP agreement.
- *Financed transactions,* ie, where the principal agreement is a D–C–S agreement and the transaction is financed by the principal agreement, eg, the purchase of goods by credit card. The purchase of the goods is a transaction linked to the debtor-credit card company-supplier agreement (s19(1)(b)).
- *Suggested linked transactions,* ie, where a creditor or broker initiates a transaction by suggesting it to a debtor who enters into it:
    - To induce a creditor to enter a principal agreement (s19(1)(c)(i)), eg, where a broker suggests a life policy and the prospective debtor takes out the policy to induce or persuade a creditor to lend money.
    - For any other purpose related to the principal agreement (s19(1)(c)(ii), eg, an insurance policy taken out to cover repayments.
    - Where the principal agreement is for restricted-use credit, for a purpose related to a transaction financed by the principal agreement (s19(1)(c)(iii)). The example put forward by Goode is where frozen food is supplied for a deep freeze which the debtor is acquiring on credit.

Whether a transaction is linked or not will depend on the facts of the case and the nature and relationship of the agreements themselves. Time lapse may be important and it will often be difficult to decide if two transactions are linked or not. Goode argues that it would be fanciful to say that a debtor who is acquiring a car on credit enters into a transaction 'for the purpose related to' the acquisition of the car when he decides to acquire a caravan and states that 'the line is a very difficult one to draw' (Goode III (20)).

By s19(3) a linked transaction entered into by a debtor *before* the making of a principal regulated agreement has no effect until such time as the principal agreement is made. This could be important where goods are acquired and, eg, the principal agreement is not signed and, therefore, inoperative. Problems could arise where goods are damaged in these circumstances as neither the title nor the risk will have passed to the 'buyer'. Linked transactions will also be affected, ie, cancelled, by the cancellation of the principal agreement (s69(1)(c)(i)) and early settlement of a principal agreement will discharge most linked transactions, although this will not affect already accrued liabilities (s96).[12]

2.2.15 Total charge for credit

CCA 1974 s20, and the regulations made under it (see below), is one of the most important parts of the Act, introducing the recommendations of the Crowther Committee that creditors should be required to disclose the true cost of credit to debtors and prospective debtors (Cmnd 4596, HMSO, 1971, paras 6.5.12–21).

This is achieved by requiring creditors to disclose the 'total charge for credit', specifying what must be included therein and formulating how the rate is to be calculated (the APR).

Elements to be included in the 'total charge for credit'
If disclosure of the APR is to be meaningful it is necessary to include the whole of the borrowing costs, whether interest or other charges and whether payable under the credit agreement or under ancillary contracts. If this were not the case and the APR computed solely by reference to interest, it would be open to abuse by creditors who could apply a low rate of interest under the credit agreement itself and impose other non-interest charges or 'load' charges on ancillary agreements. Even where other charges on credit or ancillary agreements are bona fide and reasonable, they need to be included in the total charge for credit, and thus the APR, to enable a debtor to make comparisons with the different cost of different agreements. This does not mean, however, that the comparison of APRs always provides a true comparison as different services may be being offered under different agreements, and different people will have different requirements and different views as to whether a higher rate better meets their requirements.

The charges to be included in the total charge for credit are specified in Consumer Credit (Total Charge for Credit) Regulations 1980 SI No 51 reg 4, as amended by SI 1985 No 1192, and subject to the exclusions of reg 5, are:

a) the total interest payable on the credit which may be provided under the agreement; and

---

12 Linked insurance contracts are exempted from automatic cancellation where the principal agreement is cancelled (s69(5) and the Consumer Credit (Linked Transactions) (Exemptions) Regulations 1983 SI No 1560 *but will be affected,* ie, cancelled, if the principal agreement is not carried through for any other reason, eg, is withdrawn from.

b) other charges at any time payable under the transaction by or on behalf of the debtor whether to the creditor or any other person.

'Transaction' in b) covers not only the credit agreement itself but will also include any contract which is a 'linked' transaction under s19 (see 2.2.4), any contract for the provision of security relating to the credit agreement, any credit-broker agreement and any other contract which the debtor is required to enter as a condition of the granting of credit (reg 1(2)).

'Other charges' can include survey fees, land registry fees, brokers' fees, legal costs, stamp duties, installation charges and charges in relation to ancillary contracts that the debtor is required to pay, such as installation, maintenance or the insurance of the subject matter of the credit agreement. Ancillary charges will also be included where they relate to matters extraneous to the credit agreement (subject to reg 5 below) or will last beyond the expiry of the agreement. For example, if a credit agreement requires an item purchased on credit to be insured, the cost of general household contents insurance taken out to cover the item would form part of the total charge for credit, even though it covers other items and will continue after the expiry of the credit agreement itself.[13]

Items excluded from the total charge for credit
Various charges are excluded from the total charge for credit. These are charges which fall outside of the scope of reg 4, eg, a maintenance contract entered voluntarily with the creditor by the debtor and, in addition, those which would fall within reg 4 but are excluded by reg 5(1). The following are excluded:

- Default charges, whether incurred under the credit agreement or an ancillary contract, whether payable by the debtor or the creditor (reg 5(1)(a)).
- Charges payable by both credit and cash purchasers, eg, installation or delivery charges (reg 5(1)(b)).
- Charges payable for incidental services or benefits, other than those payable to credit-brokers, incurred under a contract entered prior to the debtor's application for credit (reg 5(1)(d)). These would include, for example, an insurance contract or a general maintenance agreement for household electrical goods entered into prior to the credit agreement and independently of it, even if it later covers

---

13 Under reg 5 many types of insurance are excluded from the total charge for credit, see below.

an item bought on credit. Regulation 5(1)(d) should be contrasted with ancillary contracts, eg, insurance or maintenance agreements entered after the application for credit, which also cover extraneous matters which continue after the expiry of the credit agreement (see above).

For the exclusion of insurance contracts, see below.

− Certain maintenance charges are excluded where they relate to the care, protection and maintenance of goods or land and will only be incurred if such services are *actually* performed (reg 5(1)(e)). Where, however, charges for maintenance or service are imposed whether the maintenance is actually performed or not, these will not be excluded. For example, it is often a requirement under HP agreements that a maintenance or service contract is entered, and the charge for this payable whether or not any maintenance is actually undertaken: this charge would not be excluded and would form part of the total charge for credit.

− Charges payable for the operation of a current account (reg 5(1)(f)).

− Premiums under a 'prior' insurance contract, ie, an insurance contract that the debtor entered prior to making an application for credit (reg 5(1)(g)). Such premiums will be excluded even where the policy subsequently fulfils a requirement of a later credit agreement. An example would be premiums under a general household insurance policy which at a later date meets the requirement under a credit agreement to insure the item purchased.

− Motor vehicle insurance premiums (reg 5(1)(h)). This will exclude premiums under policies covering all types of motor vehicle risk, including loss or damage to the vehicle itself, even where such insurance is a requirement of the credit agreement which finances the purchase of the vehicle.

− Premiums under a life assurance policy, where the policy monies are to be used to repay credit or the credit charge (reg 5(1)(i)). This exemption includes premiums under life policies where the balance outstanding on a credit agreement is to be discharged on the death of the debtor, premiums under endowment policies assigned to a creditor to secure the advance of a non-exempt mortgage (see 2.2.10) and premiums payable under an accident, sickness and/or unemployment policy for the payment of instalments in the event of the debtor's sickness, etc, where such a policy also covers the debtor's life.

− Premiums payable under voluntary insurance contracts (reg 5(1)(j)).

− Premiums under policies to insure property which are required by a third party (reg 5(1)(k)), for example where money is advanced to purchase leasehold property and under the lease the lessor requires the lessee to insure the property with a designated insurer.

– Other insurance premiums are excluded where the choice of insurer is left to the debtor, even where the debtor enters an insurance agreement with the creditor, providing 'comparable' insurance is available elsewhere and the creditor cannot reasonably withhold consent to alternative insurance under the terms of the credit agreement (reg 5(1)(l) and 5(2)(b)). 'Comparable' is not defined but if there is no alternative source of insurance, the exemption cannot apply.[14]

Credit and the total charge for credit

It should be noted that the definition of credit excludes any element of the total charge for credit (s9(4) and see 2.2.3).

Calculation of the APR

The APR is the yardstick against which, in principle, the cost of any credit facility can be measured. It represents the cost to the debtor of credit on the assumption that it is repayable at the end of one year. Its disclosure is required in some advertising (s40), in quotations (s52) and in contract documents (s60).

The methods of computing APRs are covered in regs 6–11 and in the 'Credit Tables'. The tables are used where an agreement applies exactly to one of the entries, otherwise one of the two formulae in regs 7 and 8 is used.

The method for calculating the APR on the basis of a true annual percentage rate can be extremely complex and would not be considered a normal part of money advice case-work. However, most trading standards departments have the appropriate computer programmes, and queries concerning APRs on agreements should be directed to them. Assistance should also be available from the OFT.

For further information, including details of the formulae, examples of calculations and extracts from the Credit Tables, see Goode I (1151–1189), III (860–889) and VII (1–800).

---

14 As a result of the various exclusions above, few types of insurance now form part of the total charge for credit. Those that do are policies that are required under a credit agreement which cover accident, sickness and unemployment insurance but do not include life cover, and the mandatory insurance of property and goods financed by the agreement other than motor insurance (reg (5)(1)(b) above) and insurance required by a third party (reg 5(1)(k) above).

2.2.16   Examples

The definitions discussed above are the ones most relevant to money advice work. To assist with understanding them, extensive practical examples are given in Sch 2 to the Act and it will be useful if advisers have these to refer to.

2.3   Licensing (ss21–42)

Prior to the CCA 1974 there was no unified licensing system and the provisions relating to consumer credit and hire licensing were to be found on a piecemeal basis in a variety of statutes, eg, the Moneylenders Acts, the Pawnbroking Acts and the Hire-Purchase Acts.

HP legislation provided no mechanism for enforcement of the licensing requirements and it was left to aggrieved individuals to take the initiative in invoking the Act's provisions. The Moneylenders Acts were theoretically stronger as they included a licensing system with a number of criminal sanctions. The provisions were, however, largely ineffective as a method of control because the system was decentralised and there was no specific authority with an overall duty of enforcement. Prosecutions were infrequent and often left to individual police officers. Revocations and suspensions of licences were virtually unheard of. A survey conducted by Goode in 1968 found that among 170 licensing authorities, only one had a record of any court order made during the previous ten years forfeiting a moneylender's certificate. During the same period there was found only one recorded instance of a suspension of a licence being notified to a licensing authority.

Following the Crowther Committee's recommendations, the CCA 1974 remedied the inherent weakness of the previously fragmented legislation by entrusting the overall administration and enforcement of the Act, and of any regulations made under it, to the Director General of Fair Trading, and by making enforcement at a local level the responsibility of local trading standards departments.

There are now powerful sanctions available where there are breaches of the Act's licensing provisions with offenders not only risking the loss of civil debt recovery actions or fines of up to £5,000, but also the more drastic sanction of up to two years' imprisonment and loss of their consumer credit licences.

While the centralisation of the licensing system has benefits in terms of the consistency of the standards required of licensees and the approach to enforcement, it has resulted in practice in a licence monitoring system which is slow, unwieldy and somewhat ineffective, partly because the OFT does not have ready access to local complaints about licensees. The OFT can, therefore, sometimes seem to be reluctant to warn licensees, or to suspend or revoke licences.

By the summer of 1990, approaching three million licences had been issued by the OFT, with credit brokerage by far the most popular category. By April 1992 a total of 3,048 creditor organisations had received notices warning that the DG of FT was not satisfied by their fitness; 1,339 of these had sanctions applied to them and a further 349 voluntarily surrendered their licenses or withdrew their applications.

2.3.1   Responsibility for licensing matters

The issue, variation, renewal, suspension and revocation of licences is the exclusive responsibility of the DG of FT, subject to rights of appeal. All licensing matters are dealt with by the Consumer Credit Licensing Branch of the OFT, Government Buildings, Bromyard Avenue, Acton, London W3 7BB (tel: 0171 269 8616).

2.3.2   Licence application

All licence applications must be on prescribed forms with the appropriate fee. Standard applications are made on form CC1/96, normally at a cost of £80 for a sole trader and £175 for others. Group applications are made on form CC3/75. The cost depends on the number of people to be covered. There are no fees for debt counselling, credit union or friendly society licences, or for licences for other non-profit-making organisations. Applications not made on the correct forms will not be considered.

2.3.3   Persons requiring a licence

Subject to the exemptions below, a licence is required to carry on:

- any business so far as it comprises or relates to the provision of credit or the hiring of goods under regulated agreements (s21(1));
- any ancillary credit business (s147(1)), ie, any business that comprises or relates to credit brokerage, debt adjusting, debt collecting, the operation of credit reference agencies and debt counselling (s145(1)).

For a business to require a licence it is not necessary that the provision of consumer credit be carried on as a business. It is sufficient that it is an activity regularly carried on in the course of some other business which does not have to have the granting of credit as its objective, eg, a company which regularly makes loans to employees even where this is the limit of its involvement in the granting of credit.

Agents and employees of licensed creditors will not need individual licences as a creditor's licence covers all lawful activities done in the course of a licensed business (s23(1)). Such individuals will require a licence if they carry out a licensable activity on their own account.

Occasional transactions will not be treated as 'carrying on a business' under ss21(1) and 189(2) and no licence is, therefore, required, but the Act gives no specific definition of 'occasional'. At what point an occasional activity becomes regular is a matter of fact and degree to be decided in each case (*R v Marshall* (1989) 90 Cr App Rep 73, CA; (1991) 23 *Adviser* 19 and see 2.2.12).

2.3.4   *Exemptions from licence requirements*

The licensing provisions do not apply to local authorities (s21(2)) or companies set up by parliament, eg, the Commission for New Towns, The White Fish Authority, the recently privatised utility companies in relation to metering equipment, and the London Docklands Development Board (s21(3)).

Also exempt are businesses which only provide credit in excess of £15,000 or provide credit only to companies (outside the provisions of the Act altogether), businesses which only provide credit under agreements exempt under s16, and those lending only under non-commercial agreements, ie, those who are not treated as 'carrying on' a business (s21(1) and see 2.2.12).

2.3.5   *Types of licences*

There are two types of consumer credit licence (s22):

- *Standard licence,* which is applied for and granted to a named individual for specific activities. Standard licences can also be issued to partnerships or unincorporated businesses covering all partners or members, and to limited companies. Except in the case of partnerships, a standard licence must not be issued in more than one name but will cover all agents and employees of the licensee.
- *Group licence,* which is applied for and granted to an identifiable group, where the DG of FT considers it to be in the public interest,

eg, Age Concern, NACAB, FIAC, the Institute of Chartered Accountants, the Law Society.

2.3.6   *Categories of licences*

A licence will be needed for each category of activity covered by a business:

Category A	Consumer credit business
Category B	Consumer hire business
Category C	Credit brokerage
Category D	Debt adjusting and debt counselling
Category E	Debt collecting
Category F	Operating a credit reference agency
Category Z	An endorsement of licence categories A–C to permit the canvassing of D–C–S agreements.[15]

2.3.7 *Duration of licences*

From June 1991 standard licences will last for five years (Consumer Credit (Period of Licenses) (Amendment) Regulations 1991 SI No 817). Group licences last for 15 years (General Notices Nos 1021–1029).[16]

Licences terminate on the death or bankruptcy of a licensee, where a licensee becomes a patient under the Mental Health Act 1983 Part VII, or on their voluntary surrender. On termination in these circumstances, a period of deferment is permitted allowing a trustee in bankruptcy or an executor to continue the licensee's business for 12 months. In the case of a voluntary surrender, the deferment period is one month.

The regulations also provide for five other 'terminating events', all relating to insolvency, compositions or deeds of arrangement.

15 The canvassing of D–C agreements (ie, cash loans) is prohibited (s49). It is proposed that in the future credit licences should normally be issued to cover all categories of credit and hire trading rather than leaving it to applicants to decide which categories are applicable to their business, although the OFT will retain the power to exclude particular types of activity in relation to particular traders ('OFT Contributes to Deregulation Initiative' (OFT press release, 27 January 1994) and 'Deregulating Consumer Credit' (OFT, April 1994), and 6.1.3).

16 General Notices are notices of acts and decisions of the DG of FT, which may be quasi-judicial or purely administrative. They are published by the OFT for the information of those affected. Some notices will have a regulatory effect, so that the decisions that they announce only become operative on publication of the notice. Others do not have a regulatory effect and are simply the prescribed manner for making known the decisions of the DG.

2.3.8 Criteria for licences

The DG of FT must grant a licence if an applicant meets the criteria; there is no discretion to refuse. There is thus a theoretical 'right' to a licence although in practice this apparent 'right' is blurred by the fact that the DG has an adjudication and judicial role in the exercise of a wide discretion to examine all circumstances relevant to the criteria laid down (see *North Wales Motor Auctions v Secretary of State* [1981] CCLR 1 and 2.3.13). The DG will be bound by general legal principles, eg, natural justice, and can be judicially reviewed if s/he is seen to misdirect him/herself as to the law or makes a manifestly unreasonable or *ultra vires* decision.

Licence applicants must satisfy the DG on certain matters:

– *Fitness*: Applicants must be fit to engage in a licensed activity (s25(1)(a)). In deciding this the DG can consider such relevant circumstances as:

  – convictions for fraud, theft, assault, etc;
  – criminal offences under consumer law, eg, Trade Descriptions Act offences;
  – breaches of the CCA 1974, eg, extortionate credit;
  – any other deceitful, oppressive, unfair or improper business practices, eg, harassment, discrimination, taking benefit books as security, failing to disclose an APR properly.

  In general, the DG can take account of lawful and unlawful activity. Misconduct need not necessarily relate to consumer credit business.

– *Trade name*: Applicants must not apply to trade under a name which is misleading (s25(1)(b)). The DG can reject any name which may be:

  – too like the name of an existing licensee;
  – misleading as to the size, scope or resources of the business;
  – suggesting a royal connection or patronage;
  – suggesting a government connection;
  – likely to give a false impression of the cost, type and/or ease of borrowing, or of the nature of the organisation, eg, Bank, International, etc.

2.3.9   Licence decisions

A licence application may be granted as applied for, granted on varied terms or may be refused. Where the DG of FT intends not to grant a licence as applied for, a 'mindful to refuse' notice must be issued to the applicant, who can make written representations within 21 days, or longer if an oral hearing is requested (s34 and see OFT leaflet 'Licensing – your right to make representations').

There are no specific provisions for third parties to make objections to licence applications and it is not clear if a third party has the standing to be able to challenge a licensing decision of the DG. It is important to note, however, that as a result of reports made to the OFT by money advisers, CABx and others of the activities of some lenders and debt collectors, a number have lost their licences, had conditions put on them or received 'mindful to revoke' notices. These include AVCO, Richard Murtagh (brokers), Credit Default Register (debt collectors) and the Mortgage Corporation.

Compulsory variation, suspension and revocation

The DG's power to vary licences arises at any time during the currency of the licence if the DG is of the opinion that if the licence had expired and had been reapplied for, s/he 'would have been minded' to grant the licence on different terms. A licence can be revoked or suspended if in the same circumstances the DG 'would have been minded' not to renew it (s32).

Appeals

A person aggrieved by a determination of the DG can challenge the decision in two ways: by appeal to the Secretary of State and thence, on a point of law and case stated, to the High Court (s41), or by application to the High Court for judicial review under the court's inherent jurisdiction over tribunals (s42 and RSC Order 53; see the Consumer Credit Licensing (Appeals) Regulations 1976 SI No 837 and the OFT booklet 'Guide on appeals for licensing determinations of the DGFT').

2.3.10 The register

A register is kept of all licence applications, licences granted, licences suspended, revoked, etc, together with details of other determinations made by the DG of FT (s35(1)). Entries on the register may be inspected and copies obtained on payment of a fee (s35(3)). Informal enquiries can be made by telephone on 0171 242 2858 although written confirmation should always be sought where it is intended to rely on the information, eg, the fact that a creditor is unlicensed.

2.3.11   *Licensing offences*

Various criminal offences relating to licensing are contained in s39. These include:

- *trading without a licence* (s39(1)) – up to a £5,000 fine and/or two years' imprisonment (s167 and Sch I);
- *trading under a different name to that on a licence* (s39(2)) – up to a £5,000 fine and/or two years' imprisonment (s167 and Sch I).

2.3.12   *Unlicensed trading*

Under s40(1) agreements with an unlicensed trader are unenforceable unless permitted by order of the DG of FT (s40(2)). Matters that the DG must consider in determining whether to make such an order include, under s40(3):

- whether and to what extent the debtor has been prejudiced by the creditor's conduct;
- whether a licence would have been granted if applied for;
- the degree and culpability shown in failing to obtain a licence.

An unlicensed trader may also enforce an agreement with the consent of the debtor (s173(3)), although there can be no contracting out of the requirement to be licensed (s173(1)).

There are similar provisions in relation to agreements with unlicensed ancillary traders, eg, credit-brokers (s148) and in relation to agreements where the debtor was introduced to the creditor by an unlicensed credit-broker (s149).

It should be noted that the provisions in s40 relating to unlicensed trading apply only to traders who have no licence at all, or a licence which does not cover the category of business carried on. It is thought, however, that they do not apply where a trader has failed to get the endorsement permitting the canvassing of D–C–S agreements away from trade premises, yet has concluded such an agreement. It is also thought that trading under a name different to that on a licence, prohibited under s24 and an offence under s39(2), will not result in the agreement being unenforceable under s40(1) (Goode III (40)).

Unlicensed agreements are neither void *ab initio* (from the outset) nor automatically unenforceable due to illegality. On attempted enforcement of a regulated agreement through the county court, a debtor can put a creditor on proof of a valid licence although the court cannot do this of its own motion. On finding that a creditor is not correctly licensed, a court can dismiss the action or adjourn it pending an application to the DG for leave to enforce. Where such an application is granted it operates as a form of retrospective valid-ation. The application for enforcement will, however, of necessity, disclose an offence, and unlicensed traders should be reminded of this.

2.3.13 Licensing case-law

North Wales Motor Auctions v Secretary of State [1981] CCLR 1
The fact that a person has completed a prison term (for tax fraud) did not make him 'fit'. The refusal of a licence is not a second punishment or a denial of natural justice.

Quinn v Williams Furniture [1981] ICR 328
Sex discrimination can lead to the revocation of a licence. A form required a husband's guarantee for his wife's loan but not vice versa.

Hunter-Jaap v Hampshire Credit Consultants Ltd [1986] CLR 73
A trader may be prevented from using a name (even where it is his/her own name) which, with intent to deceive, might mislead the public into thinking that it is someone else's business. The fact that a trader has a valid licence in that name is no defence to an action in damages for passing-off.

Pieze v Lefkowitz [1912] 2 KB 235
Slight discrepancies in a name on a licence and a trading name can be overlooked. Whether a discrepancy is material or not is a matter of law not fact.

Kirkwood v Gadd [1910] AC 422
Using the wrong name or address in negotiations or in trans-actions is not necessarily important. It is necessary to distinguish between the conduct of a business and the transactions that make up that business. If the business as a whole is carried on in the correct name and this is on the letterheads, an offence will not have been committed.

Hicks v Walker [1984] Crim LR 495

A dealer refused a licence provided credit using a licensed firm as a 'front' and was found guilty of three offences under s39.

Cohen v Lester (J) Ltd [1939] 1 KB 504; *Barclay v Prospect Mortgages* [1974] 1 WLR 837

Unenforceability due to lack of a licence entitles the debtor to rescission and delivery up of any security provided without having to repay any sums outstanding.

2.4   Seeking business (ss43–54)

2.4.1   Advertising

Prior to the CCA 1974, legislation dealt with 'pre-contract activity' in a fragmentary manner. While there was strict control under the Moneylenders Act 1927, many lenders were exempt from its provisions, banks in particular. Various controls were later imposed by the Hire-Purchase Act 1965 requiring pre-contract disclosure of the cash price of goods offered on hire-purchase or instalment credit, and by the Advertisements (Hire-Purchase) Act 1967, which put further controls on the content of credit advertising.

Following the Crowther Committee's emphasis on 'truth in lending' and its concerns about the vulnerability of consumers to insufficient, inaccurate and misleading information, the CCA 1974 provided for the first time a comprehensive and coherent pattern for control of the methods and techniques of those seeking consumer credit business.

Coverage

All forms of advertising are covered. To come under the Act's provisions advertisements must be published, ie, displayed to an individual member of the public or to the public at large, must be for business purposes and indicate that credit is available, even where the granting of credit is not the main business of the advertiser (s43(1)).

Exemptions

Three categories of advertising are exempt from the provisions of Part IV of the Act (s43(2)–(4)). These include:

– where only unsecured credit of over £15,000 is advertised;

– where credit is advertised as available only to companies;
– where it is indicated that the advertiser is not willing to enter consumer credit or hire agreements.

In addition, the Consumer Credit (Exempt Advertisements) Order 1985 SI No 621, made under s43(5), excludes:

– advertisements for credit which require not more than four payments;
– advertisements for credit where the APR does not exceed the highest of 13% or 1% over the highest base rate;
– advertisements for credit which is exempt from regulation as having a non-UK connection;
– advertisements for hire with statutory gas, electric or water companies relating to metering equipment;
– advertisements for credit that exceeds £15,000.

Categories

The Consumer Credit (Advertisement) Regulations 1989 SI No 1125, made under s44, create four categories of credit advertising: simple credit advertisements, intermediate credit advertisements, full credit advertisements and full credit variation advertisements, and specify a particular form and content for each category.

Interest-free credit advertisements are subject to certain restrictions. Goods offered on interest-free credit must be available for cash and the total payable must not exceed the cash price, eg, a trader must not offer general cash discounts.

Offences

It is a criminal offence to be in breach of any of the advertising regulations (s167(2)) and further offences are created by s45 (advertising restricted-use credit where goods are not available for cash) and s46 (false or misleading advertising). A misleading advertisment may also be prosecuted under the Trade Descriptions Act 1968.

Liability for offences is extended to other parties involved in certain circumstances, eg, newspapers, but there are defences available where there was no intentional or negligent conduct (s47).

Enforceability

An offence against the advertising provisions does not itself affect the validity or enforceability of an agreement (s170(1)), although advisers may wish to remind creditors of their potential criminal liability, where appropriate. A misrepresentation in an advertisment may, however, lead to civil liability (see 7.2.1).[17]

2.4.2   Canvassing

Definition

'Canvassing' is defined as soliciting entry into regulated agreements, off trade premises, during a visit 'carried out for the purpose of making oral representations' and not previously requested by the consumer (s48).

Off trade premises includes consumers' homes but not their places of business. It should also be noted that a 'supplier's' premises will not be 'off trade' premises, nor will the premises of a creditor, owner or canvasser (s48(2)).

Offences

Section 49 creates two offences:

- canvassing a D–C agreement 'off trade premises';
- soliciting an individual's entry into a D–C agreement during a visit carried out in response to a prior request where that request was not in writing and signed.

No offence is committed by the soliciting of a D–C agreement in response to a prior written request, by the canvassing of a D–C–S agreement or a consumer hire agreement.

An offence will be committed, however, if a person canvasses a D–C agreement during a visit to solicit a D–C–S agreement, unless a prior written request has been made. D–C loans should also not be canvassed on a visit to collect repayments under previous loans. Although it is claimed that both these happen more than infrequently, offences are difficult to prove.

Effect of unlawful canvassing

Unlawful canvassing or soliciting will not in itself affect the validity or unenforceability of an agreement (s170(1)).

---

17 Where such a misrepresentation is made by, eg, a broker or supplier, the liability of the creditor under s56 should be considered (see 2.5.1). See also s75 (a creditor's liability for breach of contract by a supplier) (at 2.6.1). It is intended to replace the current regulations relating to credit and hire advertisements by new, much simpler regulations (see 'Consumer Credit Deregulation' (OFT, June 1994) and 6.1.5).

Circulars to minors

Section 50 prohibits sending minors circulars which offer credit or hire facilities or invite applications for information on borrowing money or hiring goods. Personally delivered documents are not covered but the provisions cover all forms of credit, not only regulated agreements.

An offence of strict liability is created, but it is a defence to prove that the accused did not know or have reasonable cause to know that the person was a minor, except where a circular is sent to a school.

It would appear that a breach of s50 will not make a subsequent agreement invalid or unenforceable (s170(1)), but any such agreement may be unenforceable under the Minors' Contracts Act 1987 (see 'A Minor Irritation' (1992) 34 *Adviser* 39).

2.4.3   Unsolicited credit-tokens

Section 51(1) makes it an offence to provide a person with credit-tokens without a prior written request. Any request for credit-tokens must be in writing and signed, unless the credit-token agreement is a small D–C–S agreement (s51(2)). See also s14 and 2.2.8 ('Credit-token agreements'), s11 and 2.2.5 ('Restricted- and unrestricted-use credit') and s17 and 2.2.11 ('Small agreements').

It is not an offence to provide an unsolicited credit-token under an already existing agreement, or to replace a credit-token under an existing agreement (s51(3)). Breach of the unsolicited credit-token provisions will not lead to a voidable or unenforceable agreement (s170(1)) but any such agreement may be unenforceable for lack of proper execution (ss60–64 and see 2.5.8/10).

2.4.4   Quotations

To implement the principle of 'truth in lending' and to give prospective customers full and accurate information about what facilities are available, s52 makes provision for the provision of quotations. Full details are to be found in the Consumer Credit (Quotations) Regulations 1989 SI No 1126.

It is an offence to be in breach of the Quotations Regulations (s167(2)), but the validity and enforceability of any agreement based on the quotation will be unaffected (s170(1)).[18] A misrepresentation

---

18 It is intended to revoke the Quotations Regulations and not to replace them. A new offence of providing a materially false or misleading quotation will be considered in due course, but this is unlikely to be contemporaneous with the revocation of the current regulations.

may lead to civil liability (see 7.2.1). Also, the liability for a supplier's misrepresentations under s56 should be considered (see 2.5.1).

2.4.5 Further regulation of the seeking of business

Regulations may be made under s53 relating to the display of information and under s54 to regulate further the seeking of business. This allows 'unforeseen difficulties and abuses' to be dealt with without resort to legislation. No regulations have yet been made under either of these sections.

2.5 Entry into credit and hire agreements (ss55–74)

Part V of the Act is primarily concerned with consumer protection matters. It deals specifically with the disclosure of information required before agreements are signed, withdrawal from prospective agreements, the form and content of agreements, the requirements to provide copies, cancellation rights, and the effect of defective agreements and breaches of statutory provisions.

2.5.1 Preliminary matters (ss55–59)

No regulations have been made under s55 requiring the disclosure of information additional to the provisions of the advertising regulations.

Pre-contract or 'antecedent' negotiations, ie, any representation, oral or in writing, involving a prospective debtor and made by a creditor, are covered by s56.

Antecendent negotiations cover:

– Any negotiations between a creditor or owner and a debtor in relation to the making of a regulated agreement (s56(1)(a)).
– Any negotiations conducted by a credit-broker in relation to goods sold or proposed to be sold by the credit-broker to a creditor before forming part of a D–C–S agreement under s12(a), eg, where a dealer negotiates with a customer in relation to goods which are later sold to a finance house before becoming subject to an agreement between the creditor and the debtor – a common 'tripartite' agreement, eg, HP (s56(1)(c)).
– Any negotiations conducted by a supplier in relation to a transaction financed or proposed to be financed by a D–C–S agreement

within s12(b) or (c), ie, under a pre-existing arrangement, such as purchase of goods with a credit card (s56(1)(a)).

Any antecedent negotiations conducted with a debtor falling within s56(1)(b) or (c) will be deemed to have been conducted by the broker, supplier, etc, as agent of the creditor as well as in his/her own capacity (s56(2)). A creditor will, therefore, be vicariously liable for a supplier's representation and may be held liable in civil and/or criminal law, eg, under the Trade Description Acts 1968 and 1972 and/or under the Misrepresentation Act 1967.

While there is no remedy for a debtor in the case of an illegal advertisement (s170(1) and see 2.4.1), if statements made in advertisements are misleading, a remedy may be available to the debtor under the 'antecedent negotiations' provisions of s56. Advertisments are specifically included as 'representations' under s56(4).[19]

2.5.2   Agreements exempt from Part V of the Act

Certain agreements are exempt from the provisions of Part V of the Act, other than those of ss55 and 56.

– *Non-commercial agreements* (s74(1)(a)), ie, an arrangement made which is not 'in the course of a business carried on by the creditor'. For this exemption to apply it is necessary that credit is not granted in the course of *any* business. For example, loans made by an employer to employees *will* be made in the course of a business, even though they are not made in the course of a consumer credit business. Such a loan would not, therefore, be exempt (see 2.2.10).
– *Current account overdrafts* from specified organisations, eg, banks or building societies (s74(1)(b)).
– *Agreements to finance payments on death* (s74(1)(c) and see the Consumer Credit (Payments Arising on Death) Regulations 1983 SI No 1554).

---

19 The Act makes no provision for specific remedies for aggrieved debtors. Once a creditor' s liability is established, the debtor's recourse will be to the general law, eg, rescission or damages for misrepresentation (see 7.2.1). For a detailed discussion of possible remedies see Goode III (57). See 2.6.1 (s75) for a creditor's liability for breaches of contract by a supplier.

– *'Small' D–C–S agreements* for restricted-use credit (see s17 and 2.2.11).[20]

2.5.3   Withdrawal from prospective agreements

Withdrawal from a prospective agreement is equated with cancelling an agreement under s69. Linked transactions are similarly affected and the cancellation provisions on the return of credit paid, advances, etc, apply (ss70–73 and see 2.5.11), even where the prospective agreement was not itself a cancellable agreement (s57(1)).

A credit-broker or supplier who is the 'negotiator' in antecedent negotiations under s56 is deemed to be the agent of the creditor for the receiving of the notice of withdrawal, as is any person who, in the course of a business carried on, acts on behalf of the debtor in any negotiations (s57(3)).

Notice of withdrawal may be oral or written (s57(2)).

2.5.4   Withdrawal from prospective land mortgages

Because it was considered too difficult to apply the cancellation and cooling-off provisions to regulated secured agreements, s58 instead requires that an advance copy of a prospective regulated secured agreement be sent to a consumer, including details of the right to withdraw, in the prescribed form, at least seven days before an agreement is sent for signature. An agreement is not properly executed if these provisions are not complied with (s61(2)). This in effect gives a prospective debtor a period of isolation from unsolicited contact from a creditor to reconsider before signing; in other words, for the period of seven days the creditor may not contact the prospective debtor in relation to the signing of the agreement. No contracting out is permitted (s173(1)). The debtor may, however, voluntarily return the signed agreement within the seven-day period (s62(3)(b)).

This section was aimed primarily at 'second' mortgage lending, an

---

20 If any part of a small agreement is in writing, then the s60 regulations on form and content will apply to those parts (s74(4)). Small D–C agreements or unrestricted-use credit agreements are not exempt. It is proposed by the DG of FT that the discretionary powers under s74(3), which have already been used to exempt current account overdrafts under s74(1)(b), be extended to permit the exemption, on application by named businesses, of specified types of agreement from some or all of Part V, subject to the DG being satisfied that the exemption would be consistent with the interest of debtors or hirers ('Consumer Credit Deregulation' (OFT, June 1994)).

area where abuses have been seen in the past. Certain agreements were therefore excluded from the provisions by s58(2):

– purchase money mortgages;
– bridging loans in connection with the purchase of land.

Failure by a creditor to abide by these provisions will render an agreement unexecuted and enforceable only with the leave of the court (see *National Guardian Mortgage Corp v Wilkes* [1993] CCLR1; (1991) October *Legal Action* 16 and see 2.5.10). On dismissal of an application for enforcement, other than on technical grounds, the security is rendered void *ab initio*, ie, deemed void from the outset (ss113(3)(b) and 106 (ineffective security)).[21]

2.5.5   Agreements to enter future agreements

These agreements are void. Any payments made under such agreements should be recoverable. Linked transactions will be similarly affected (s59(1)). Under s59(2), however, the Secretary of State can make regulations to exclude specific agreements from the operation of s59(1) and regulations have been made exempting certain agreements relating to goods for business purposes. See the Consumer Credit (Agreements to Enter Prospective Agreements) (Exemptions) Regulations 1983 SI No 1552.

2.5.6   Formalities of agreements (ss60–66)

To ensure that consumers are fully informed as to the nature and detail of the transactions they are entering, the Secretary of State has a duty under s60(1) to make regulations as to the form and content of the documents embodying regulated agreements.

2.5.7   The form and content of agreements

The regulations under s60(1) are contained in the:

– Consumer Credit (Agreements) Regulations 1983 SI No 1553, as amended (the 'Agreement Regs').
– Consumer Credit (Cancellation Notices and Copies of Documents) Regulations 1983 SI No 1557, as amended (the 'CNC Regs').

---

21 It is proposed to amend the requirements as to copies of secured agreements so as to limit the maximum number that may be required to two ('Consumer Credit Deregulation' (OFT, June 1994) and see 2.5.9 and 6.1.7).

- Consumer Credit (Guarantees & Indemnities) Regulations 1983 SI No 1556 (s61(1)(a)).

Agreements which do not meet the form and content requirements will be improperly executed.

2.5.8 *Improperly executed agreements*

Improperly executed agreements fall into two categories: those which are totally unenforceable and those which are enforceable only with the leave of the court.

Totally unenforceable agreements

Prescribed terms: An agreement cannot be enforced unless it is in the prescribed form and contains all of the appropriate 'prescribed terms' specified by the Agreement Regs Sch 6 (s61(1)(a)) unless permitted under s127(3) – see below at 'Consequences of improper execution' at 2.5.10. The prescribed terms are as follows:

- *Restricted-use D–C–S agreements for fixed-sum credit,* where there is no credit charge and no advance payable, must state the amount of credit (which may be expressed as a total cash price).
- *In other fixed-sum credit agreements,* the amount of credit must be stated.
- *Running-account credit agreements* must state the credit limit or the manner in which it is to be determined, eg, by reference to an agreed monthly repayment, or the fact that there is no credit limit, and the rate of interest.
- *Running-account or fixed-sum credit* where instalments are not fixed or where the amount payable might vary, eg, a credit card or personal loan at a variable rate, must state the rate of interest.
- *All types of consumer credit agreements* must state how the obligations to make repayments are to be discharged by reference to the number, amount, frequency, timing and dates of repayments, or the manner in which any of these may be determined.
- *All types of consumer credit agreements* must contain details of any powers to vary what is payable.
- *Consumer hire agreements* must contain similar provisions relating to the making of and the variation of payments.

Essentially, any consumer credit agreement which fails to disclose the amount of credit, the credit limit or information as to how debtors are to discharge their obligations will be unenforceable (ss61(1)(a), 65(1) and 127(3)) – see below 'Consequences of improper execution' at 2.5.10.

Signature.   A regulated agreement is not properly executed unless it is in writing, legible and has been signed in the prescribed manner by both parties (s61(1)(a)). If this is not the case it will be enforceable only where s127(3) applies, ie, where a document, whether or not in the prescribed form, does contain all the prescribed terms and has been signed by the debtor (see 2.5.10).

- *Definition:* 'Signature' is widely defined as any writing placed on a document with the intention of authenticating it, including a mere cross or other mark or impression (*Hill v Hill* [1947] CL 231), and may be made by pencil, facsimile, stamp or any other form of marking (*Goodman v J Eban Ltd* [1965] All ER 763, CA).
- *Forgery:* A person signing a false name will be 'estopped' (prevented) from disputing the validity of the signature.

  The lack of a creditor's signature on a *debtor's copy* of an agreement will not necessarily make the agreement unenforceable but may be evidence that no written contract has yet been made (as required by the CCA 1974) because an agreement only becomes executed when a creditor's acceptance has been notified to a debtor.
- *Prescribed manner of signature:* See CCA 1974 Sch 5 for details of the prescribed manner for signature, the required signature box, etc.
- *Blank agreements:* It is sometimes claimed by debtors that they have signed blank agreements. If this can be proved the agreement will be unenforceable.[22]

Representations.   The agreement must embody all the terms of the agreement, other than implied terms (s61(1)(b). This may cause problems where, for example, statements are made by a dealer who is the agent of a creditor under s56. Such statements will usually not have been included in the agreement as the creditor is unlikely to be aware of them. Legally, it will depend on whether the agent's statements are

---

22 An agreement will be totally unenforceable if unsigned, but will be enforceable with the leave of the court if the agreement is defective only because of the lack of a prescribed signature or other non-compliance unless it involves the complete omission of a prescribed term or signature (ss61(1)(a), 127(3) and see 2.5.10).

'mere' representations or collateral promises, or promises which become terms of the agreement.

Where an agent's representations are deemed to be terms of an agreement and they are not embodied in the agreement, the agreement will be improperly executed and enforceable only with the leave of the court under s65(1).

Goode questions whether this was the intention of the Act 'having regard to the terms of s127(1)', and that it seems unlikely that an enforcement order would be refused, at least where the debtor has made no complaint under s56 (see Goode III (62) and 2.5.10).

Cancellable agreements.   In the case of a cancellable agreement, failure to include notice of cancellation rights in any copies provided, or failure to provide a seperate notice of cancellation rights where required, will render an agreement unexecuted (s64(5)) and totally unenforceable (127(4)(b) and see 2.5.10).

Failure to supply a copy agreement under ss62 and 63 can be rectified by the creditor although the court will be unable to make an enforcement order until this has been done (s127(4)(a)), but a failure to supply notice of cancellation rights under s64(1), whether it be by way of failure to include them in statutory copies (s64(1)(a)) or by failing to send a further notice when required (s64(1)(b)), will not be rectifiable and the court has no power to make an enforcement order (s127(4)(b)) – see below 'Consequences of improper execution' at 2.5.10.

Agreements unenforceable without the leave of the court

In addition to prescribed terms, the Agreement Regs require other information to be included and disclosed in regulated consumer credit agreements (Schs 1–4). Failure to include this information in the correct prescribed form will result in the agreement being unexecuted (s61(1)(a)) enforceable only with the leave of the court (s65(1)).

These *'non-prescribed'* terms include, where appropriate:

– a *heading* specifying type of agreement and a statement that it is regulated under the CCA 1974.
– the *names and postal addresses* of the parties;
– *description* of any goods, services or land involved;
– the *cash price*;
– details of any *advance payments*, eg, any deposit;
– the *total charge for credit* (where calculable and not variable);
– the *APR*;

- the *rate of interest* and the total amount of other charges (where the total charge for credit is not calculable);
- *details of any security* required;
- *statement of consumer rights*, in the form prescribed in Sch 4 covering, eg, cancellation rights, termination rights, liability on termination and repossession, and protection from repossession;
- *signature boxes*;
- details of *default charges*;
- the *duration* of hire agreements;
- *statements of consumer rights* under hire agreements.

Information about financial and related particulars must be shown 'as a whole' and agreements must, generally, both reflect the terms agreed and be legible.

2.5.9   *The duty to supply copy agreements*

Sections 62 and 63 contain the requirements relating to the provision of copies of regulated agreements. Great weight is attached to the statutory right of consumers to receive copies, and failure to provide the required copies will mean that agreements are improperly executed and unenforceable without the leave of the court and may mean, in some circumstances, that agreements are totally unenforceable (see 'Consequences of improper execution' at 2.5.10).

The provisions apply to all regulated agreements except those specified in s74 (see 2.5.2), agreements exempt from the majority of Part V of the Act.

The rationale behind the provisions is to ensure that debtors are given a chance to consider the terms and conditions of proposed agreements at the 'offer' or 'negotiation' stage, are informed of their rights to withdraw from or cancel agreements (s64) and are, in any event, supplied with copies of concluded agreements so as to be fully aware of the extent of their liabilities, rights and obligations.

The copies required depend largely on whether an agreement is executed by a debtor's signature or remains unexecuted. Agreements remain unexecuted until they have been signed by all parties.

- Where an unexecuted agreement is *presented personally* to a debtor for signature and the creditor has not already signed the agreement and does not sign it on the spot, ie, the agreement remains unexecuted after the debtor's signature, *a copy of the unexecuted agreement must be supplied 'there and then'* (s62(1)) and a *copy of the fully signed executed agreement* must be given within seven days of the contract being concluded by the creditor's signature (s63(2)).

– Where an unexecuted agreement is *sent* to a debtor for signature and the creditor has not signed the agreement, ie, it remains unexecuted after the debtor's signature, *a copy of the unexecuted agreement* must be sent at the same time (s62(2)) and a *copy of the fully signed executed agreement* must be given to the debtor within seven days of the contract being concluded by the creditor's signature (s63(2)).

'Given' is defined by s189(1) as 'delivered or sent'.

– Where an unexecuted agreement is *presented personally* to a debtor and it has either been signed by the creditor or is signed on the spot, ie, the agreement becomes executed on the debtor's signature, *a copy of the executed agreement* must be delivered to the debtor 'there and then' (s63(1)). *No further copy* is required (s63(2)(a)).

– Where an unexecuted agreement is *sent* to a debtor for signature and the creditor has already signed the agreement, ie, the agreement becomes executed on the debtor's signature, *a copy of the agreement* must be sent at the same time (s62(2)). No *further copy* is required (s63(2)(b)).

In the last two situations, because the agreement becomes binding on the debtor's signature, there is no separation between the 'offer stage' and the 'contract stage' at which separate second copies could be provided.[23]

Cancellable agreements

Copies of cancellable agreements provided under ss62 and 63 must contain a notice in the prescribed form detailing the debtor's right to cancel (s64(1)(a)) and must be sent by post (s63(3)).

Where only one initial copy agreement is required, ie, where the agreement becomes executed on the debtor's signature and there is no requirement for a second copy (s63(2)(a)(b)), *a separate notice of cancellation rights* must be posted to the debtor within seven days of the agreement being made (s64(1)(b)). It should be noted, however, that where s63(2) does require a second copy agreement to be supplied, no such seperate notice of cancellation rights is required

---

23 See Flowchart 3 in Appendix 1. If the form of agreement was neither presented personally nor sent to the debtor, eg, was cut out of a newspaper or collected from a dispenser, the only requirement is under s63(2) for a copy of the executed agreement to be supplied within seven days of the agreement being made.

(s64(1)(b)).[24] Failure to include notice of the right to cancel in any copy, or failure to send a separate notice of cancellation rights, where required, will result in the agreement being completely unenforceable (s127(4)(b)). Failure to send a copy of a cancellable agreement is, however, rectifiable (s127(4)(a)and see 2.5.10).

For the prescribed wording of notices of the right to cancel see the Consumer Credit (Cancellation Notices and Copies of Documents) Regs 1983 SI No 1557 Sch.[25]

Regulated secured agreements

Under s58(1), a copy of a secured loan agreement must be provided to allow a prospective debtor seven days for pre-signature consideration (see 2.5.4). Sections 62 and 63 must also be complied with. Thus, three copies may be necessary:[26]

- the advance copy under s58(1);
- a second copy of the agreement required when an agreement is presented or sent to the debtor for signature (ss62(1), 62(2), 63(1));
- a third copy of the executed agreement under s63(2) where the agreement is not executed on the debtor's signature, ie, still requires the creditor's signature, within seven days of that signature.

---

24 Catalogue and other mail order credit organisations are exempt from the requirement of s64(1)(b) to send a separate notice of cancellation rights.

25 Section 64(3) provides for regulations to be introduced requiring copy agreements to be sent with any further notices of cancellation rights but no such regulations have been made.

26 It is proposed to reduce the number of copies necessary in relation to secured agreements. The abolition of the 'pre-signature' copy under s58 was considered, but rejected on the grounds that it 'provides an important safeguard for this most sensitive category of loan'. Instead, an alternative way of achieving a reduction in the number of copies has been proposed by making secured agreements falling within s58 exempt from the provisions of s62(2) requiring a copy of an unexecuted agreement (where an unexecuted agreement is sent to the debtor for signature), and presumably also exempt from the provision of s62(1) where an unexecuted agreement is presented personally (rather than sent) to the debtor for signature.

A consumer's entitlement to copies of a secured regulated agreement covered by s58 would then comprise the pre-signature copy under s58 and a later copy of the executed agreement showing the signatures of both parties.

This proposed change would require a consequential amendment to s63(2)(b) to preserve the obligation to supply a copy of an executed agreement when the agreement becomes executed on the debtor's signature, as this section currently waives the obligation to supply such a copy if the agreement is sent to the debtor for signature and becomes executed on that signature ('Deregulating Consumer Credit' (OFT, June 1994), paras 6.23–6.30).

Where the agreement *does* become executed on the debtor's signature, no third copy is necessary (s63(2)(a) and (b)).

2.5.10   *Consequences of improper execution*

Enforcement orders

Where a regulated agreement is unexecuted as a consequence of non-compliance with certain provisions of the Act, including the provisions as to withdrawal from prospective secured agreements (s58), the form and content requirements of the Agreement Regs (s60(1)), the provisions as to copies (ss62 and 63) and notification of cancellation rights (s64), the creditor must apply to the court for an enforcement order under s127 (s65(1)). Obvious forms of 'self-help', eg, the repossession of goods or land, are prohibited under s65(2) but a debtor may consent to any enforcement action (s173(3)).

In certain circumstances, however, the court is precluded from making an enforcement order under s65(1). In these situations the agreement will be completely unenforceable.

Prescribed terms and signature.   The court cannot make an enforcement order under s65(1) unless the provisions of s61(1) have been complied with, ie, 'a document in the prescribed terms and conforming to the regulations under s60(1) is signed in the prescribed manner' (s60(1)(a)), *unless* 'a document (whether or not in the prescribed form and complying with the regulations under s60(1)) itself containing all the prescribed terms of the agreement was signed by the debtor or hirer (whether or not in the prescribed manner)' (s127(3)).

The effect of s127(3) is to make an agreement unenforceable where it is not properly signed or does not contain the appropriate prescribed terms *unless* the document actually *does* contain the prescribed terms in some form (although not necessarily in the correct prescribed form) and has been signed in some way by the debtor (although not necessarily in the correct prescribed way).

This means that a regulated agreement cannot be enforced unless it contains the appropriate prescribed terms in some form and is signed in some way. It is not necessary that the required prescribed terms be included in the correct form or that the agreement complies in other respects to the Agreement Regs. Mere lack of compliance with the Agreement Regs will not necessarily be fatal to enforcement of an agreement unless it involves the complete omission of an appropriate prescribed term or total lack of a debtor's signature.

Agreements which do contain the required information and are signed, although not in the prescribed way, will be enforceable only on the order of the court (see 'Court's powers', below).

Cancellable agreements.   Where there has been non-compliance with the 'supply of copies' provisions of ss62 and 63, and the creditor did not give the debtor a copy of the executed agreement before commencing proceedings (s127(4)(a)), the agreement remains unexecuted and unenforceable.

Section 127(4)(a) allows a creditor to rectify non-compliance with ss62 and 63 if a 'late' copy is given before proceedings, but if such a copy is given, the debtor will still of course have the right to cancel as the cooling-off period will start when the 'late' copy is received.

However, although it appears from s127(4)(a) that non-compliance with the supply of copy provisions can be rectified, it could be argued that if a statutory copy in the correct form has not been supplied within the statutory time limits, a creditor would be powerless to start the cooling-off period running by the service of a 'late copy' as this would not be, by virtue of being outside the time limits, a statutory copy, ie, would not be a copy under ss62 or 63, and receipt by the debtor of a statutory copy is necessary to start the cooling-off period running. If this is correct the debtor would have an indefinite right to cancel in these circumstances, although this right would be lost where a creditor enters judgment against the debtor.

Where a creditor takes action against a debtor in relation to an agreement which is still cancellable it is hoped that the court would point out to the debtor the on-going right to cancel. If this is done and the debtor does not cancel, the right to cancel will probably be deemed to have been waived and the court would probably exercise its discretion under s127(1) to allow the agreement to be enforced (see Goode I (1452), III (69) and 2.5.11).

In either case, the debtor will have a right to cancel. If the 'late' copy 'before proceedings' allowed by s127(4)(a) is valid in starting the cooling-off period, as appears to be the case, the time limits for cancellation under s68 will apply. If the 'late' copy does not start the cooling-off period, there will be an on-going and indefinite right of cancellation.

It should be remembered, however, that failure to include *notice of cancellation rights* in any copy under ss62 and 63 (s64(1)(a)) or failure to send *a separate notice of cancellation* rights where appropriate (s64(1)(b)) is not 'rectifiable' and the agreement will remain totally unenforceable (s127(4)(b)).

This results in the anomalous position that where a creditor fails to provide any copy of a cancellable agreement, the failure can be rectified under s127(4)(a), but the sending of a defective copy, without notice of the right to cancel in the prescribed form, cannot, nor can the failure to send a seperate notice of cancellation rights, where required under s64(1)(b)(s127(4)(b)).

See s68 and 2.5.11 for the position where the required copy or notice is sent but not received.[27]

Court's powers.   Where the court is empowered to order enforcement of an unexecuted agreement, it can refuse the order if it is just to do so, having regard to the prejudice caused by the contravention and the culpability involved (s127(1)). The court must also have regard to its power under s135 to impose any conditions on any order and under s136 to vary agreements. The intention is, however, that orders will not generally be refused unless prejudice can be shown to have been caused.

The court should look to remedy any prejudice (s127(2)) and can reduce or discharge any sums owing by a debtor as part of any enforcement order.

In *National Guardian Mortgage Corp v Wilkes* [1993] CCLR 1; (1991) October *Legal Action* 16, the plaintiff had failed to send an advance copy of a prospective regulated secured agreement to a customer and had, therefore, failed to give the defendant the required period of seven days under s58 before requesting signature of the agreement. This led to the defendant signing an agreement at a high APR. The court allowed the agreement to be enforced but only on the condition that the defendant be compensated under s127(2) for the prejudice caused by the non-compliance. Had the defendant had the period of uninterrupted consideration provided for by s58, she might have obtained a loan elsewhere at a lower rate of interest. Compensation was set at £3,200, 40% of the interest, to reflect this. A time order was also made reducing the debtor's monthly repayments to an

---

27   It should be noted that a creditor may be in breach of the statutory requirements of ss62, 63 and 64 not only by failing to supply a required copy or notice within the time limits but also by failing to supply a copy or notice in the form prescribed by the Consumer Credit (Cancellation Notices and Copies of Documents) Regulations 1983 SI No 1557.

affordable level (s129) and reducing the rate of accruing interest (s136).[28]

The effects of unenforceability.   Where there is an unenforceable *HP or conditional sale agreement,* ownership of the goods remains with the creditor and if the debtor disposes of them to a third party, title in the goods will not pass and the creditor will be able to sue the debtor in conversion. The debtor's action in disposing of the goods destroys any right to possession and it reverts immediately to the creditor (*United Transport Finance v British Car Auctions Ltd* [1978] 2 All ER 385). Note, however, the provisions in relation to the passing of title to motor vehicles on HP under Hire-Purchase Act 1964 Pt III (see 3.4.1).

If a debtor disposes of goods subject to an HP or conditional sale agreement without the consent of the creditor the fact that the agreement is unenforceable due to improper execution will not provide a defence to a charge of theft (*R v Modupe* [1991] Crim LR 530, CA and see 3.4.2).

Where a debtor remains in possession of the goods without complying with obligations to repay the creditor, the creditor's action would lie in breach of contract and an enforcement order would be required. Thus, where an agreement is unenforceable, eg, due to lack of a prescribed term or other 'fatal' flaw, the creditor will be unable to obtain leave to enforce the agreement under s127 and the debtor can retain any goods or money obtained under the agreement without having to make any repayments. If the debtor, however, states an intention both to retain the goods and to refuse payment, this may constitute conversion which could be sued for by the creditor, notwithstanding the refusal of an enforcement order, as the claim would rely not on an action to enforce a regulated agreement, ie, be in contract, but be in tort (*Bowmakers Ltd v Barnet Instruments* [1945] KB 65). However, in *Eastern Distributors v Goldring* [1957] 2 All ER

---

28 Creditors are unlikely to accept that their agreements have been improperly executed and upon default will normally issue a default notice and summons in the usual way. It will, therefore, be necessary for the adviser to assist in the submission of the appropriate defence in order to bring the issue before the court. The debtor may, however, before the issue of a summons apply to the court under s145 for a declaration that the agreement is unenforceable.

It should be noted that under CCR Ord 49 r4(9) a creditor may make application for an enforcement order by way of an originating application prior to the issue of a default summons or as part of the claim under the agreement, in which case it must be by way of fixed date rather than default action.

525, CA, under the Hire-Purchase Act 1965 s5, repealed and replaced by the CCA 1974, it was held that 'not entitled to enforce the agreement' meant that the debtor could 'enjoy the possession of the property without having to pay for it', apparently regardless of any stated intention.

The debtor may possibly be guilty of theft by refusing to surrender goods subject to an HP or conditional sale agreement as it amounts to dealing with the goods as owner although this has not been fully explored by the criminal courts (see 3.4.3).

Under a regulated *credit sale agreement* or similar, ie, where title in the goods passes to the debtor, it would appear that the debtor can retain the goods and dispose of them without the creditor being able to enforce payment. The position would be the same with a cash loan. The debtor could retain the cash without having to make any repayments.

An unenforceable agreement is not void, however, and may be enforced by a debtor or a hirer who will be able to sue the creditor if, for example, goods have been misrepresented or are not of satisfactory quality, etc.

Death of hirer/debtor.   Certain restrictions are placed on creditors' rights to enforce agreements following the death of a debtor (see 2.6.10)

2.5.11   *Cancellation of regulated agreements (ss67 and 68)*

The right to cancel, ie, to rescind, a concluded agreement was first introduced by the Hire-Purchase Act 1964 (HPA). It was primarily intended to give protection against unscrupulous high pressure door-to-door sales techniques which often relied on oral misrepresentations which could be later denied.

The provisions under the HPA 1964 were, however, both too wide, in that they applied even where there had been no personal contact between creditor and debtor (as in the case of mail order transactions), and too narrow, in that they were confined to hire-purchase and instalment credit and did not cover other forms of credit.

Cancellation rights are now covered by s67 and provide for regulated agreements to be cancellable where:

– antecedent negotiations, including oral representations, are made in the presence of a debtor (ie, in face-to-face negotiations) by an individual acting as or on behalf of a 'negotiator';
– the agreement was signed by the debtor away from the business

premises of the creditor, any creditor in a linked transaction or any party involved as an antecedent negotiator.

'*Negotiators*' include agents and employees of the creditor. Dealers involved in tripartite D-C-S arrangements would, at common law, normally be acting on their own behalf but are deemed 'negotiators', ie, agents, by s56(1) (see 2.5.1). Dealers acting in tripartite hire or leasing arrangements, however, are not covered by the definition of 'negotiators' with the result that many leasing agreements are not cancellable.

'*Business premises*' do not include a debtor's place of business, contrary to the provisions of s48 prohibiting door-to-door canvassing. An agreement signed on the debtor's premises would, therefore, be cancellable.

The definition of '*representations*' given in s189 has been considered by the Court of Appeal with reference to s67. It was held that it should be interpreted to mean a statement capable of inducing the borrower to enter an agreement. It is not necessary to show that the representation did in fact induce or had been intended to induce the borrower to enter the agreement (*Moorgage Services v Kabir* (1995) *Times*, 25 April, CA). Following the court holding that representations were made and that the agreement was, therefore, cancellable, it was unenforceable as no notice of cancellation rights had been included in the agreement (see 2.5.9 at 'Cancellable agreements').

It is not relevant where negotiations take place. What is important is where a debtor *signs*. If negotiations take place on business premises (eg, in a showroom) and a debtor takes the unexecuted agreement away to sign at home, subject to the other conditions being met, the agreement will be cancellable. This is an illustration of how the cancellation provisions go far beyond actual door-to-door selling.[29]

---

29 However, the DG of FT has recommended that s67 be amended so as to remove from the cancellation provisions all agreements where antecedent or face-to-face negotiations take place on trade premises but the agreement is signed away from trade premises (eg, is taken home for further consideration and then signed). The rationale for such a change is that it is inappropriate for there to be a right to cancel where the consumer voluntarily visits trade premises as s/he is unlikely to have been subject to high pressure doorstep selling. It should be noted, however, that there will be no change where there are antecedent negotiations away from trade premises but the agreement is then signed on trade premises – the agreement will remain outside of the cancellation provisions ('Consumer Credit Deregulation' (OFT, June 1994)).

Scope

The cancellation provisions only apply to regulated agreements. All agreements exempt from regulation, either because they fall outside the scope of s8(1) and (2) or because they are exempt under s16, are not covered.

Also excluded from the cancellation provisions are loans secured on land (but note the 'pre-consideration' provisions of s58 (see 2.5.4)), restricted-use credit agreements for the purchase of land or bridging loans (s67(a)), agreements exempt under s74 (see 2.5.2) including non-commercial agreements (s74(1)(a)), agreements permitting a current account overdraft (s74(1)(b)), agreements to finance payments on death (s74(1)(c)) and small D–C–S agreements for restricted-use credit (s74(2)).

Any provision purporting to exclude a debtor's right to cancel is void (s173(1)), although it should be noted that catalogue and mail order sales are specifically exempt from the requirement to send a separate notice of cancellation rights under s64(1)(b).

General right to cancel

A general right to cancel exists under the Consumer Protection (Cancellation of Contracts Concluded away from Business Premises) Regulations 1987 SI No 2117 (Consumer Protection Regs), made under the European Communities Act 1972, implementing a European Union directive on doorstep selling. These provisions give additional protection to 'consumers', ie, people buying 'for purposes which can be regarded as outside their business', against the unsolicited doorstep selling of goods and services (including loans) by traders, and gives a right to cancel a contract within seven days of its execution. Unsolicited visits to consumers' homes, the homes of others or consumers' places of business are covered. Information regarding the right to cancel must be provided in documentation, and in the case of cancellation, both goods and payments are recoverable.

It is important to note that the Consumer Protection Regs and the right to cancel under s67 are mutually exclusive. Agreements cancellable under the Act are not cancellable under the Regulations (reg 4(2)) but agreements not cancellable under the Act will be covered by the Regulations if otherwise within their scope.

Where there is no right to cancel under s67 of the Act it may be useful, therefore, to check whether there is an alternative right to cancel under the Regulations. This may arise in situations where creditors enjoy immunity from the cancellation provisions because they are exempt from Part V of the Act or because the amounts involved exceed £15,000. This could also apply in a D–C–S hire or lease arrangement where negotiations are undertaken by a dealer. As the dealer is not a 'negotiator' within s56 with regard to such agreements, the dealer's representations could not be relied on as the 'oral representations' required by s67. If the agreement fell outside the cancellation provisions of s67 because of this, there would be a right to cancel under the Regulations if all other requirements were met.

Various agreements are exempt from the provisions of the Regulations. These include loans related to land purchase, contracts for building work, food and drink provided on the doorstep on weekly credit, insurance contracts, investment agreements under the Financial Services Act 1986, small contracts (those involving no more than £35 or £35 of credit) and catalogue and similar sales where the terms of the arrangement are clearly set out prior to the contract.

The cooling-off period.   Where there is an agreement cancellable under the Act, a debtor may serve a notice of cancellation by the end of the fifth day following receipt of the statutory copy under s63(2) or notice under s64(1) (s68).[30]

Notice may be served on the creditor or the creditor's employee or agent. For the purposes of service of notices, a dealer in a tripartite arrangement is deemed to be an agent of the creditor (s56(1)(b) or (c)).

While the provisions relating to copy agreements and notice of cancellation rights under ss62, 63 and 64 require that creditors give or send copies and notices within seven days, the crucial date in determining the duration and expiry of the cooling-off period is the date of *receipt* by the debtor.

A delay in the receipt of a copy or notice will, therefore, prolong the cooling-off period and likewise, the non-receipt of a copy or notice will result in the agreement remaining cancellable indefinitely. Where a copy or notice is, eg, lost in the post or misdirected, the creditor will not be able to rectify this and start the cooling-off period running unless a replacement can be sent within the seven-day periods under ss62, 63 and 64. A copy or notice sent outside the statutory period would not be a statutory copy or notice and a statutory copy

30 Proposals to change the five-day cooling-off period to one of seven days in order to harmonise cooling-off periods in general have been postponed for further discussion. Advisers should also be aware of the provisions of the Timeshare Act 1992 which gives a 14-day cooling-off period (see 'Timeshare Act 1992' (1992) 32 *Adviser* 40).

or notice is required to start the cooling-off period (see Goode I (1452) and 2.5.10 at 'Cancellable agreements' for further discussion).

Where no copy or notice has been sent by the creditor, as opposed to one being delayed or lost in the post, the agreement will be unexecuted, and it is important to differentiate between the copy requirements under ss62 and 63, the requirement to include notice of cancellation rights in all copies of cancellable agreements (s64(1)(a)) and the requirement of a separate notice of cancellation rights required under s64(1)(b).

Where there is a cancellable agreement, failure to give or send a copy agreement under ss62 and 63 is rectifiable under s127(4)(a) where a copy is provided before proceedings are commenced, but failure to include notice of cancellation rights in a copy or failure to send a separate notice is not rectifiable (s127(4)(b)) (see 'Consequences of improper execution' at 2.5.10). A creditor will, therefore, be in a worse position if a copy is supplied which does not comply with s64 than if a copy is not supplied at all.[31]

Where failure to send a copy is rectified under s127(4)(a), it is not clear whether, as discussed above, this late copy is capable of starting the cooling-off period running (see above and 'Cancellable agreements' at 2.5.10). In any event, there will be a right to cancel for at least five days following the receipt of any 'late' copy.

Thus, to summarise, where a copy or notice *is sent* within the time limits but *not received*, the agreement will be properly executed and enforceable but will remain cancellable until the copy or notice has been received and the cooling-off period has expired. Non-receipt means that the agreement remains cancellable indefinitely. Where a copy is *not sent* within the time limits, this failure is rectifiable and the agreement will be enforceable under s127(4)(a), although it is not clear whether the late copy starts the cooling-off period running or whether the agreement remains cancellable indefinitely, subject to the debtor having been deemed to have waived the right to cancel, eg, where the court has drawn the debtor's attention to the right to cancel and this has not been exercised (see Goode I (1452), III (69) and 2.5.10). In any event, the debtor's right to cancel would be lost where the creditor obtains judgment.

---

31 It should be noted that to comply with the provisions of ss62, 63 and 64 a copy or notice of cancellation rights must not only be supplied within the specified time limits but also in the form prescribed by the Consumer Credit (Cancellation Notices and Copies of Documents) Regulations 1983 SI No 1557).

Notices of cancellation must be in writing (s189(1)) and can be in any form that indicates an intention to withdraw from the agreement, however expressed (s69(1)). This could include any written indication or statement by a debtor that his/her obligations under the agreement have been repudiated.

Notice can be served on the creditor or the creditor's agent, defined to include a credit-broker or supplier who participated in antecedent negotiations (s69(6)(a) and see s56(1)(b) and (c) at 2.5.1), or on anyone who in the course of business has acted as agent for the debtor (s69(6)(b)).[32]

Generally, notice is effective on receipt by the creditor or agent, although in case of notice sent through the post, cancellation will be effective at the time of posting, regardless of whether it is received or not (s69(7)). Also, under s176(3), a notice sent or delivered to the last known address of the creditor or agent shall be treated as having been sent or delivered to the correct address.

The effects of cancellation include:

- Cancellation of most actual and prospective linked transactions (s69(1)). Exceptions include D–C–S restricted-use credit agreements where finance is provided for work or the supply of goods to meet an emergency, and the supply of goods which have become incorporated into land before the service of the cancellation notice (s69(2)). Although the debtor will remain liable to pay the cash price for such goods and/or services, there will be no liability in relation to any credit or other charges (s69(2)(i)).
- The repayment to the debtor of any sums paid in contemplation of the agreement, including any item included in the charge for credit (s70(1)(a)) and release from liability to pay any sums that would have become due but for cancellation (s70(1)(b)).

Where the debtor is in possession of any goods under a cancelled agreement, s/he will retain a lien on goods in relation to any sums repayable (s70(2)).

Where there is a D–C–S agreement for restricted-use credit made under s12(b) (see 2.2.5/6), ie, a D–C–S agreement made under a pre-existing arrangement, both the creditor and the supplier are joint and severally liable to repay the debtor (s70(3)).

Where the total charge for credit includes a fee or commission

---

32 To be able to receive notice of cancellation, a supplier must have been involved in antecedent negotiations. This will not always be the case, eg, a supplier in a check-trading agreement.

charged by a credit-broker, this will be returnable subject to a retention of £3 (s70(b)).[33]
- Other than a D-C-S agreement for restricted-use credit, the agreement shall continue in force in so far as it relates to the repayment by the debtor of any credit and the payment of interest (s71(1)).

However, where the debtor repays part or all of the credit within one month of the service of the cancellation notice or, where the agreement was for instalment credit, before the due date of the first instalment, no interest is payable on the amount repaid (s71(2)) and the debtor will have use of the money interest-free for the relevant period. If the whole of the credit repayable by instalment is not repaid before the date of the first instalment, the debtor will not be liable to repay any of the credit unless and until the creditor makes a written request in the prescribed form stating the amounts of the remaining instalments, excluding all sums other than interest and principal (s71(3)).

These provisions are designed to deal with a situation where, before a regulated consumer credit agreement is cancelled or withdrawn from, the debtor has already received part or all of the credit, eg, the loan has already been paid over. The effect of the section is to discourage creditors from advancing credit in anticipation of the execution of an agreement or before the expiry of the cooling-off period.
- There is a general duty under s72 to take reasonable care of goods subject to a cancelled agreement. There is also a duty to return them, but there is no obligation to do so unless requested in writing and no obligation to 'deliver the goods except at his own premises', ie, have them collected (s72(5)).

Where no written request is made within 21 days, the duty of care ceases although there is still an obligation to retain possession. Where a written request from the creditor is not complied with the duty of care continues until the goods are delivered up (s72(8)).

The s72 provisions do not apply to perishable goods, goods which have been consumed, goods which have been supplied to meet an emergency or which have been incorporated into land (s72(9)).
- Where goods have been given in part-exchange, the debtor is entitled to the return of those goods within ten days of cancellation and, if such goods are not returned, is entitled to a cash sum equal to the part-exchange allowance (s73(2)).

---

33 It is proposed to increase the 'retention' from £3 to £5 (see 6.1.2).

In tripartite agreements, the creditor and supplier will be joint and severally liable under s73(2) (s73(3)), and the debtor will have a lien on any goods retained in possession until the part-exchange goods or an equal sum is returned (s73(5)).
– Any attempt to exclude those provisions which protect the debtor in relation to the return of money, the repayment of credit, the return of part-exchanged goods, etc, is void (s173(1)).

2.6   Matters arising during the currency of agreements (ss75–86)

The provisions in Part VI of the Act most important to money advisers are those concerning a creditor's liability for breaches by a supplier in a three-party arrangement. Other relevant matters covered include the duty to give notice before taking action, provisions relating to the duty to give information to debtors, the appropriation of payments, the variation of agreements, various provisions relating to credit-tokens and the position on the death of a debtor.

2.6.1   Liability of a creditor for breaches by a supplier ('connected lender liability') (s75)

Where there are three-party arrangements, ie, where the supplier of goods and the supplier of credit are different businesses, the supplier and the creditor are to a certain extent engaged in a joint venture. A finance company relies on a dealer or supplier as a medium for promoting its business and usually pays a commission for the introduction of business (often up to 20% of the credit charge) and 'cannot be equated with a wholly independent lender such as a bank approached independently by the debtor' (*Crowther Committee Report 1971*, Cmnd 4596, HMSO, paras 6.6.22–25).

Statutory provision was recommended, therefore, to give the debtor the right to take action against a creditor in these circumstances for any misrepresentation or breach of contract by a supplier; it was considered insufficient to leave a debtor only with a remedy against the supplier.

Section 75, therefore, extends the creditor's liability for a supplier's breach where:

– there is a restricted-use D–C–S agreement;

- it is made under pre-existing arrangements (or in contemplation of future arrangements);
- the agreement is regulated under the Act.

It provides that 'in relation to any transaction financed by the agreement', where the debtor has a claim against the supplier for misrepresentation or breach of contract, there shall also be a 'like claim' against the creditor who shall be joint and severally liable (s75(1)).

Section 75 liability does not apply to:

- non-commercial agreements (s75(3)(a)), ie, agreements not made by creditors in the course of their business (s189(1));
- claims relating to 'single items' where the cash price is £100 or less or over £30,000 (s75(3)(b));[34]
- individual users of company credit cards;
- non-regulated agreements (eg, charge cards);
- debit cards (s187(3)(a)).

It is not clear what 'single items' covers. The OFT is of the opinion that the courts will look for guidance at how goods are marketed and gives the example of a set of golf clubs sold at £200, stating that the sale would be covered although the constituent parts of the set of clubs individually are worth less than £100. Each case will depend on its individual facts.

It should also be noted that where a deposit of £100 or less is paid towards an item which has a cash price of over £100, the agreement will be covered (s189(1) – a 'transaction' includes a transaction financed wholly or in part by the agreement).

Section 75 only applies where the creditor and the supplier are different businesses. It is common in three-party arrangements for the creditor to purchase the goods from the dealer and then sell them on, on credit, to the debtor. This situation is not covered by s75 as the

34 While s75(3)(b) applies a cash limit of £30,000, to be regulated the *credit* advanced must not exceed £15,000. Thus a purchase at below £30,000 may not be covered if it involves credit of more than £15,000. The DG of FT has recommended changing the monetary limits under s75 by relating them to the amount of credit involved rather than the cash price of an item. The recommendations provide for a reduced upper limit of £25,000 while retaining the current lower limit of £100 ('Connected Lender Liability – a further report' (OFT, May 1995)). While these proposed changes in the monetary limit of s75 are included in the DTI consultation document's list of proposed new monetary limits, it is stated that the DTI is not currently consulting on connected lender liability and changes are, therefore, unlikely in this area during the current deregulation round (see 6.1.2 and 6.1.9).

creditor will be directly liable as 'supplier' with no liability attached to the 'dealer'. The creditor may also be liable in these circumstances where the debtor has relied on antecedent representations from the dealer (s56 and see 2.5.1).

The effect of the section is to give the debtor a right of action against the creditor where there is a complaint of misrepresentation or breach of contract against the supplier/dealer. The debtor may sue the creditor for damages.

In such circumstances, the level of damages is not limited to the amount of the transaction or of the credit involved. Creditors will also be liable for consequential lossess ('contingent liability') and responsible for any damages resulting from the supplier's breach; see *Hadley v Baxendale* [1854] 9 Exch 341 for guidance as to the level of damages – they should be quantified on the basis of 'the estimated loss directly and naturally resulting' or on the basis of what could be reasonably foreseen as 'flowing naturally from the breach' (*Koufos v C Czarnikow, the Heron II* [1969] 1 AC 350).

Set-off and counterclaims

The connection between the creditor's right to be paid under the agreement and the debtor's statutory s75 claim is close enough to entitle the debtor to assert a set-off against a creditor or plead a set-off and counterclaim if sued under the agreement for default in payment.

Linked transactions

The Scottish case *UDT v Taylor* [1980] SLT 28, SC, appeared to hold that as the credit agreement and the supply contract are linked transactions, they stand or fall together and that rescission of the supply contract entitles a debtor to rescission of the credit contract. However, Goode and all other commentators consider this case to be wrongly decided, and that the linked transaction argument is 'misconceived' as it is the linked transaction (the supply contract) that depends on (or stands or falls on) the regulated credit agreement and not vice versa (see Goode I (1581)).[35]

Exclusion of liability

Liability under s75 cannot be excluded by a creditor (s173(1)) but

---

35 Note that a creditor's liability for a negotiator's antecedent misrepresentations under s56 is on the basis of deemed agency and not on the basis of joint and several liability.

where a supplier successfully excludes liability, the creditor can take advantage of that exclusion. In cases where suppliers have attempted to exclude liability, expert legal advice will be necessary as the position with regard to exclusion clauses is complex. Apart from the Unfair Contract Terms Act 1977 (see 7.2.4), the Unfair Contract Terms Regulations 1995 SI No 3159 (see 7.2.5) and the provisions of the various Sale and Supply of Goods and Services Acts, etc, the common law holds that there is no rule of law invalidating exclusion clauses because they are unfair or unreasonable, or because they exclude liability for a fundamental breach of contract. Any exclusion clause construed to cover the breach complained of will be effective, however widely drawn (*Suisse Atlantique v Rotterdamsche KCNW* [1967] 1 AC 361 and *Photo Productions v Securicor Transport* [1980] AC 827). The court will be reluctant, however, to sanction any exclusion clause purporting to exclude liability for a breach of contract of a fundamental nature unless a true construction leaves no alternative.

Problem areas

A number of problem areas have arisen where creditors have denied liability under s75.

Foreign supply contracts.   Both the OFT and Goode are of the opinion that where a regulated consumer credit agreement is used to finance the purchase of goods or services abroad, the liability of the creditor is not affected and that s75 applies. The basis for the debtor's claim against the supplier, and therefore the liability of the creditor, would of course be under a foreign system of law.[36]

36 The application of s75 has been spelt out by the DG of FT, who stated 'although only the higher courts can provide a definitive rule on s75, I have reached the firm view that, as it currently stands, the law is neither unclear nor ambiguous . . . I therefore look to card issuers, in dealing with claims, to treat consumers on the basis that s75 does indeed apply equally to all credit card transactions regardless of where they take place or the particular merchant-acquirer involved' ('Connected Lender Liability' (OFT, March 1994)).
   In OFT press release 21/95, 15 May 1995, the DG of FT announced that following consultation and a further report 'Connected Lender Liability – A further report by the DG of FT on section 75 of the Consumer Credit Act 1974' (OFT, May 1995), major credit card issuers had agreed to meet foreign transaction claims. The OFT's report proposes that:
   – Claims against credit card issuers be limited to the amount of credit involved.
   – The financial limits of s75 should be defined in terms of the amount of credit involved rather than the cash price of the items, and that while the lower limit should remain at £100, the higher limit should be the same as the upper monetary limit for regulated consumer credit agreements, currently £15,000 but pro-

The Banking Ombudsman has ruled, however, that s75 does not apply when credit cards are used abroad. This decision is probably incorrect but is yet to be ruled on by the courts.

Payments to agents.   There is some doubt concerning the liability of the creditor when payment is processed through an agent and not made directly to the supplier. In the recent International Leisure Group/Air Europe collapse, Barclaycard refused to make refunds unless payment had been made directly to the airline; 'where the card holder paid a travel agent, we believe we are not legally liable' (Barclaycard, *Guardian*, 16 March 1991). Whether a creditor is liable in these circumstances will depend on whether the (travel) agent is acting as agent of the tour operator/holiday company or of the consumer, with the former more likely to be the case.

Credit cards where there is no 'merchant-acquirer' agreement between the creditor and the supplier.   In the Lowndes Queensway collapse, Barclaycard denied liability under s75 because the supplier, Lowndes Queensway, had been recruited into the Visa network by another bank. The OFT is of the opinion that Barclaycard was liable (see Graham Winton & Brian Stewart, 'Equal liability and credit cards' (1991) 26 *Adviser* 34).

Second card users.   Many card issuers allow a second card to be issued on a single account, eg, to a spouse of a card holder. The second card holder then becomes an authorised user of the account. In such cases it is the view of the OFT that the second card holder is acting as agent for the principal card holder. Any s75 claims that arise in respect of a purchase by the second card holder should be made by the principal card holder

---

posed to be increased to £25,000. Consumers who pay a deposit by card and then pay the balance in cash would, therefore, lose their right to claim the full amount from the card issuers.

Pending any legislative change (see 6.1.9), the major card issuers agreed to meet foreign transaction claims, up to the amount of the credit granted, until 31 December 1996, when the matter was due to be reviewed. No review has taken place, however, and from 1 January it is for creditors to decide on their individual policy.

In spite of this agreement, aggrieved consumers should still be entitled to enforce their rights to compensation over and above the amount of the credit granted as the agreement between the OFT and the card issuers was purely of a voluntary nature and did not change the law.

Further information is available from the OFT, PO Box 2, Central Way, Feltham, Middlesex TW14 0GT (tel: 0181 398 3405) and the Credit Card Research Group (tel: 0171 436 9937).

Non-family members.   A number of cases arose, also as a result of the Air Europe collapse, where card issuers refused to accept liability where tickets were purchased directly from an airline for a non-family member. There is nothing in the Act specifically restricting liability in this way and it is unclear why it should be relevant for whose benefit a credit card holder makes a purchase. The card holder would, of course, have to make the claim.

Where creditors do attempt to deny liability, they will sometimes settle on an *ex gratia* basis where claims are strongly pressed and proceedings threatened or issued.

2.6.2   Duty to give notice before taking certain action

Provision is made in s87 for the service of a default notice in the event of the breach of a regulated agreement by a debtor (see 2.7.1) and in s98 for notice of termination in non-default cases (see 2.7.2).

Section 76 deals with cases where a creditor wishes to take action to enforce any term of an agreement, such as demanding early payment, recovering possession of goods or land, or treating any right conferred on a debtor by the agreement as terminated, restricted or deferred (s76(1)), but which does not involve default under the agreement by the debtor or actual termination of the agreement itself by the creditor.

Under s76 a creditor cannot enforce a term of a fixed-term agreement, as above, unless and until seven days' notice has been given. Such notice must be in the prescribed form laid out in the Consumer Credit (Enforcement, Default and Termination Notices) Regulations 1983 SI No 1561, and must state what enforcement action is intended, when it will occur, what payment is required (if any) and that a time order can be applied for. A creditor can, however, withdraw credit facilities or restrict them without serving a s76 notice thus preventing the debtor using further credit (s76(4)).

Section 76 only applies to fixed-sum agreements which a creditor is entitled to enforce at any time before the expiry of the agreement. Such a power may be reserved for specific events, eg, the bankruptcy of the debtor or the levy of distress on a debtor's goods, or may be 'at large', when a creditor would have complete discretion whether and when to enforce an agreement, but will not apply where a loan is repayable on demand – the agreement must be for a fixed period subject to a creditor's right to enforce, as above, before the expiry of the period.

The service of a s76 notice entitles a debtor to apply for a time order (s129(1)(b)(ii) and see 4.1).

If an agreement is enforced without the issue or before the expiry of the requisite notice, various remedies arise. These are the same as those available when no default notice is served (see 2.7.1 at 'Effects of breaches of s87' at p94).

2.6.3   *The duty of creditors to give information and provide copies of agreements*

Section 77 applies to fixed-sum credit agreements and requires a creditor, following a request by a debtor, to provide copies of agreements and statements of account. A fee of 50p is required for each agreement requested.

Under Consumer Credit (Cancellation Notices and Copies of Documents) Regs 1983 SI No 1557 reg 3(1)(the CNC Regs) every copy required by the Act must be a 'true copy'. This does not mean that an *exact* copy must be supplied.

The meaning of 'true copy' has been established by cases under the Bills of Sale Acts which have held that 'true copy' does not mean an exact reproduction of an original agreement (*Burchell v Thompson* [1920] 2 KB 80 and *Re Hewer ex parte Kahen* (1882) 21 Ch D 871). Errors and omissions in copies which are not material and which cannot mislead or cause misunderstanding will not prevent a copy being a 'true copy'.

However, under the CNC Regs copies must not deviate significantly from the requirements on prescribed information or presentation, eg, in the form of cancellation notices, and any such deviation cannot be dismissed as immaterial.

Reg 3(2) allows certain information to be omitted from copies, and in relation to copies under s77 permits the exclusion of:

– any information included for the use of the creditor and not required by the Act;
– any signature box, signature or date of signature.

The CNC Regs also contain special provisions that relate to agreements executed before 19 May 1985 which 'have been lost etc'. Where 'due to an accident or some other cause beyond his control, the creditor . . . does not have in his possession the executed agreement . . . or any copy thereof', the provision allows a copy to comprise an 'easily legible statement of the current terms of the agreement insofar as they are known to the creditor' (reg 9).

Thus it can be seen that it is not necessary for an exact copy of the actual agreement which was executed with the debtor to be supplied under s77. A copy of a pro forma agreement, for example, of the type of which the debtor signed would appear to suffice although the details relevant to the debtor would have to be included.

Any copy or statement of account should be provided within 12 working days, the period prescribed by the Consumer Credit (Prescribed Periods for Giving Information) Regulations 1983 SI No 1569. If a creditor fails to comply with a debtor's request, the agreement cannot be enforced while the default continues (s74(4)(a)), and an offence is commited if the default continues for one month (s74(4)(b)). Where a creditor is prevented from enforcing due to ongoing default, action may nevertheless be taken in some circumstances by the creditor outside the terms of the agreement, eg, in tort for conversion if a debtor disposes of goods subject to an HP agreement. For further discussion of this, see 2.5.10 at 'The effects of unenforceability', p69, and 3.4.3. Non-commercial agreements are not covered (s74(5)).

Section 78 applies to running-account credit agreements and contains similar provisions relating to account information and copy agreements and, in addition, requires the creditor in any event to provide periodic account details, at least annually (s78(4)). Non-commercial agreements are excluded from these provisions, and small running-account agreements (s17 and see 2.2.11) are excluded from the requirement to give regular account details (s78(7)).

Section 79 applies to regulated consumer hire agreements and contains similar provisions to ss77 and 78 in relation to account details and copy agreements. Non-commercial agreements are excluded.

Where account details are provided following a request under ss77, 78 or 79, the creditor will generally be bound by the figures provided (s172 and see 2.6.4).

Due to the effects of non-compliance with ss77–79, ie, unenforceability/criminal offence, advisers should always follow up requests for account details and copy agreements. It should be remembered, however, that a formal request must be made and a fee of 50p per request paid.[37] Although there is no prescribed way in which such a request should be made, advisers should make it clear that the request is being made under the Consumer Credit Act.

Where a creditor does not provide a photocopy of a debtor's agreement it may be evidence that no agreement has been properly executed. In practice it appears that this happens with some catalogue

---

37 It is proposed to raise the fee for ss77–79 requests to £1 ('Consumer Credit Deregulation' (OFT, June 1994)).

companies. If this is the case the agreement will be unexecuted due to lack of proper documentation and unenforceable (see 2.5.10) unless the agreement is exempt from regulation (s16 and 2.2.10) or exempt from the provisions of Part V of the Act (s74 and see 2.5.2).

2.6.4   Termination statements

Under s103 a debtor may serve on a creditor a notice stating that indebtedness under a regulated agreement has been discharged, that the agreement has ceased to have any operation and requiring that the creditor confirm those statements or serve a notice disputing them. The creditor must then confirm or dispute the statements within 12 days (Consumer Credit (Prescribed Periods for Giving Information) Regulations 1983 SI No 1569) and commits a criminal offence if non-compliance continues for one month (s103(5)). These provisions do not apply to non-commercial agreements or if a previous request has been complied with (s103(3)).

Any incorrect statement or notice stating that the debtor is not indebted to the creditor under an agreement will be binding on the creditor (s172(2)), although in any proceedings the court may grant such relief to the creditor as appears just (s172(3)). It would appear, however, that on a literal reading of the section a creditor will only be bound under s172(2) by an incorrect statement or notice where that statement or notice has been sent within the prescribed period of 12 days. Goode postulates that a 'late' statement is not a statement 'under' or 'in compliance' with s103 and that, therefore, the section will not apply and a debtor who wishes to rely on such an incorrect statement must attempt to invoke equitable estoppel or the common law (Goode III (173)).

In deciding whether to grant relief to a creditor following an incorrect statement, the court is likely to consider:

- Whether the mistake should reasonably have been noticed by the debtor.
- Whether the mistake is an obvious result of human, typographical or similar error.
- The extent to which the debtor has been prejudiced, eg, by altering his/her position to his/her disadvantage by reliance on the statement.
- Whether the debtor's reliance on the mistake was honest. In *Lombard North Central v Stobart* [1990] CCLR 53, CA; (1990) *Times*, 2 March, the court held that the debtor's reliance on a figure quoted

need not be reasonable providing it was honest, and that equitable estoppel could be relied on to bind the creditor to the erroneous statement. The creditor mistakenly quoted a settlement figure of £1,044 for a vehicle held on conditional sale. The actual sum due was £5,814 out of a total price of £10,946. The debtor paid the quoted settlement figure and sold the vehicle for £5,100. The Court of Appeal held that the debtor's act of conversion did not prevent him relying on equitable estoppel and upheld the decision at first instance that it was not inequitable to deny the creditor the right to insist on his strict legal rights. Goode states, however, that the decision appears 'very generous to the debtor' as the mistake 'might be expected to be discovered on the back of an envelope', ie, a settlement figure five-and-a-half times smaller than the sum due. An early settlement statement under s97 (see 2.7.6), also binding on a creditor under s172, was not relevant, either because the figure was given orally or because the agreement was made prior to April 1985, the date the early settlement provisions came into force (see Goode III (173)).

2.6.5   *Appropriation of payments.*

Section 81 provides that where a debtor is liable to make payments to the same creditor under two or more regulated agreements, s/he shall be entitled, where a payment is insufficient to meet what is due under all the agreements, to appropriate what is paid to one single agreement or specify how it is to be divided between more than one agreement (s81(1)). The debtor cannot, however, appropriate a payment between agreements so as to pay more than is due to one and leave a deficit on another.

Where a debtor makes no appropriation, where one of the agreements is an HP, conditional sale, hire or secured agreement, a payment must be appropriated on a 'pro-rata outstanding balance' basis.

Section 81 will not apply where a debtor is liable under two agreements, only one of which is regulated, and probably not where a debtor is liable under three agreements, two of which are regulated. The creditor could probably rely on a power of appropriation contained in the unregulated agreement to appropriate the whole of the payment.

Any attempt to exclude a debtor's rights under s81 in relation to regulated agreements is void (s173(1)), although there are no sanctions specified in the Act for non-observance. Non-compliance is neither actionable nor an offence (s170(1)). It is possible, however, that in any proceedings relating to regulated agreements, a court would be free to re-open an appropriation made by a creditor in breach of s81, and may also be able to require a creditor to rescind or amend an appropriation made in contravention of s81 where it considers it just to do so, using its powers to impose conditions when making an order in relation to a regulated agreement (s135(1)) (see Goode III (82)).

These provisions may be particularly relevant where debtors owe money to banks under more than one agreement. They enable debtors to stipulate how payments should be divided between various liabilities and will prevent a bank choosing where a debtor's payment will be allocated, as any contractual provisions allowing a creditor to appropriate contrary to the provisions of s81 will be void.

2.6.6 Variation of agreement

Where the terms of a regulated agreement permit the creditor to vary the agreement, no variation shall take effect before notice of it is given to the debtor in the form prescribed by the Consumer Credit (Notice of Variation of Agreements) Regulations 1977 SI No 328, as amended (s82(1)).

The section does not apply to variations which occur automatically under the agreement and without action on behalf of the creditor, eg, variations in interest rates due to a link to bank base rates.

Where an agreement (a 'modifying agreement') varies or supplements an earlier agreement, it will revoke the earlier agreement and will be treated as combining the effects of the two agreements (s82(2)). Modifying agreements are generally not cancellable (s82(6)) unless the earlier agreement was cancellable and the cancellation period for that earlier agreement had not expired when the modifying agreement was signed, an unlikely situation.

There is no sanction for failure to serve a notice under s82(1) (s173(1)). The variation will not take effect although the creditor will be able to enforce the original terms of the agreement.

2.6.7 Liability for misuse of credit facilities

Under s83(1) a debtor under a regulated consumer credit agreement shall not be liable to a creditor for any loss arising from the use of the credit facility by another person not acting, or treated as acting, as the debtor's agent.

Excluded from this provision are non-commercial agreements and any loss arising from a misuse of an instrument to which Cheques Act 1957 s4 applies, eg, the misuse of cheques, dividend and interest warrants, and bankers' demand drafts (s83(2)).

The provisions apply to all forms of credit, although are more likely to arise in relation to running-account credit, and will cover claims by a creditor or a creditor's assignee, but will not apply to losses incurred by third parties, eg, a supplier. There will be no protection from the misuse of credit facilities unless the misuse results in the debtor incurring a debit balance or an increased debit balance. A reduction in a credit balance following misuse will not be covered. This is because the section is aimed at giving immunity from liability to a creditor and not an indemnity against loss. The protection given by s83 cannot be varied or excluded by the terms of an agreement (s173(1)).

2.6.8   *Liability for misuse of credit-tokens*

Under s84, s83 does not prevent the debtor under a credit-token agreement, eg, a credit card agreement, from being made liable to the extent of £50 or the credit limit if this is a lower figure (s84(1)), providing the agreement permits this. There will be no protection where a third party acquired the credit-token, eg, a credit card, with the debtor's consent (s84(2), for example, the issue of a second card to an authorised user at the debtor's request.[38]

There will be no liability, however, in relation to the misuse of a credit-token following notification to the creditor (orally or in writing) that it has been lost, stolen or is for any other reason liable to misuse (s84(3)), or where the agreement itself fails to provide particulars of the person(s) to whom notice of loss, etc, should be given (s84(4)).

Oral notice under s84(3) of loss, etc, will not take effect unless it is confirmed in writing within seven days where the agreement so provides (s84(4)).

The protection given by s83 cannot be limited or varied by the terms of an agreement (s173(1)).

As under s83 protection will only apply to the extent that misuse of the credit-token incurs or increases a debit balance (as above at 2.6.7).

---

38   If a claim is made by a creditor for use of a credit-token which the debtor states was unauthorised, it is for the creditor to prove that the use was authorised or that the use occurred before the creditor had been given notice under s84(3) (s171(4)).

2.6.9   Duties on issue of new credit-tokens

Section 85 requires that whenever, in connection with a regulated agreement, a credit-token (other than the initial one provided) is given by the creditor to the debtor, the creditor shall give the debtor a copy of the executed agreement (if any) and of any other documentation referred to in it (s85(1)).

Failure by the creditor to comply with s85(1) will mean that the agreement cannot be enforced while default continues (s85(2)(a)) and a criminal offence is committed if default continues for one month (s85(2)(b)).

These provisions do not apply to small agreements (s17 and see 2.2.11).

The obligation to provide a copy of the executed agreement will arise, for example, on the issue of replacements for expired or lost tokens (eg, credit cards) and on the issue of any additional tokens (eg, where the debtor is entitled to and applies for an additional card to be issued to an authorised user).

The section does not apply to the first token(s) issued under a new credit-token agreement as Part V of the Act, ss60–66, will apply in these circumstances, as will be the case where the issue of a new token (eg, to an additional authorised user) requires amendment to the original agreement.

It is not required that a copy under s85 is given contemporaneously with the giving of the new token(s), but it should be given at 'substantially the same time'. Where this has not happened the default can be rectified by the provision of a 'late' copy under s85(2)(a).

2.6.10   Death of debtor or hirer

Section 86 is designed to prevent, inhibit and control the enforcement of a regulated agreement by any of the steps mentioned in s87(1), eg, terminating the agreement, demanding early payment, etc (see 2.7.1), by reason of the death of the debtor or hirer. If at the date of death, the agreement was 'fully secured' no such steps may be taken (s86(1)). If the agreement was 'only partly secured or unsecured' the creditor or owner is prevented from enforcing, as above, other than on the basis of a court order (s86(2)). Under s128, where such an order is sought, the court is required to make the order only if the creditor or owner can prove that s/he has been unable to satisfy him/herself that the present and future obligations of the debtor or hirer 'are likely to be discharged'.

'*Secured*' is not specifically defined in this section but is presumed to take the meaning in s189(1), thus covering real security (eg, a mortgage or pledge) and personal security (eg, a guarantee or indemnity). It is less clear what '*partly secured*' covers. It may be that it will depend on whether the security, when originally taken, was expressed to secure the whole debt, even where its actual value is now insufficient to cover what is outstanding. It is more likely, however, that the actual value of the security must be assessed in relation to the outstanding balance owed at the date of death in order to ascertain whether the agreement is then actually fully secured or not. This may be problematic, especially in the case of personal rather than real security.

In relation to the court granting an order under s128, it appears that a creditor or owner will have to show not only that the debtor (defined by s189(1) to include 'the person to whom the debtor's rights and duties under the agreement have passed by assignment or operation of law') is not likely to meet the obligations under the agreement but that any security will also be unable to do so. As Goode puts it, 'ironically, therefore, in order to enforce the security the creditor must show that he is not satisfied that the security is good for the money' (Goode III (87)). Where the creditor can meet the required standard of proof, the court must ('shall') make an order permitting enforcement but may impose any conditions or suspend any order under its general powers under s135, and could make a time order under 129(1)(c) and consequently amend the agreement (s136) (see 'Time Orders', Chapter 4).

The section does not, however, prevent the termination of an agreement where the agreement was for an undetermined period or of a fixed-term agreement where the term has expired s86(3), nor does it prevent a creditor from restricting the right to draw further credit and taking such steps as necessary to effect this (s86(4)). It also does not affect the operation of any agreement for the payment of any sums due on the death of the debtor from the proceeds of a policy of insurance on the debtor's life, eg, under a mortgage protection or credit insurance policy (s86(5)).

The provisions of s86 cannot be varied or excluded (s173(1)) and any attempt to do so will be void (s173(1)) but the debtor, ie, the personal representative(s), may consent to enforcement (s173(3)).

2.7   Default and termination (ss87–104)

Part VII of the Act covers default and termination. The areas of most importance to money advisers are those covering default notices (ss87–89), those dealing with protection from repossession of goods on hire-purchase (ss90–93) and those allowing for early settlement by debtors (ss94–97)

2.7.1   Default notices

Section 87 controls the exercise of the remedies that can be used by a creditor against a debtor defaulting under a regulated agreement. It requires the service of a default notice complying with s88, in the form prescribed by the Consumer Credit (Enforcement, Default and Termination Notices) Regulations 1983 SI No 1561, before the creditor can take any action specified in s87(1), that is:

– terminate the agreement;
– demand earlier payment of any sum;
– recover possession of any goods or land;
– treat any right conferred on the debtor as terminated, restricted or deferred;
– enforce any security.

Section 87 applies to all kinds of breach and restricts both the remedies expressly included in an agreement and those conferred by general law in so far as they are covered by s87(1).

A default notice is not necessary:

– Where there is a non-commercial agreement (Consumer Credit (Enforcement, Default and Termination Notices) Regs 1983 SI No 1561 reg 2(9)), ie, not made in the course of business (s189(1)).
– To allow a creditor to restrict or prevent a debtor from drawing further credit (s87(2)), eg, stopping cheques, demanding a return of credit cards, notifying retailers, etc.
– Where a breach by the debtor crystallises a floating charge (s87(3)). This will very rarely apply.
– Where a breach by a debtor triggers another provision of an agreement, eg, accelerated payment. A default notice is only necessary for the original breach and not for non-compliance with the 'triggered' term (s88(3)).
– Where the creditor is only suing for arrears; this is not demanding early payment and is not covered by s87(1) unless the demand also involves the recovery of goods or land.

FIGURE 1: DEFAULT NOTICE

Our Ref:

Mr Thomas Telford
10 Ironbridge Road
Dawlish
West Midlands

Flexi Bank plc
Central Collections
Westhampton
ZZ3 1XY

IMPORTANT – YOU SHOULD READ THIS CAREFULLY

DEFAULT NOTICE Served Under Section 87(1) of the Consumer Credit Act 1974

Personal Loan Account No: 1234567
Current Balance: £5357.42
Arrears: £172.82

1. Provisions of Agreement Breached:- Under Condition 1 of the Agreement described above you are required to repay the total amount payable by monthly instalments of £172.82.
2. Nature of Breach:- You have breached the Agreement by failing to pay instalments, resulting in arrears of £172.82 which includes Personal Loan Payments Insurance.
3. Action Required to Remedy:- In order to remedy this breach you must make a Payment of £172.82, directly to your Flexi Bank Branch, on or before 29 December 1995.

IF THE ACTION REQUIRED BY THIS NOTICE IS TAKEN BEFORE THE DATE SHOWN NO FURTHER ENFORCEMENT ACTION WILL BE TAKEN IN RESPECT OF THIS BREACH. IF YOU DO NOT TAKE THE ACTION REQUIRED BY THIS NOTICE BEFORE THE DATE SHOWN THEN THE FURTHER ACTION SET OUT BELOW MAY BE TAKEN AGAINST YOU.

4. Intended Action:- Your account will be referred to our Solicitors with instructions to commence proceedings against you. This will involve additional costs which will be added to the amount outstanding. In addition, information relating to your failure to pay will be lodged with the following credit reference agencies:- CCN Systems Ltd, Infolink Ltd and Equifax Europe Ltd. You may be able to avoid this action by telephoning us immediately to discuss repayment proposals.

IF YOU HAVE DIFFICULTY IN PAYING ANY SUM OWING UNDER THE AGREEMENT OR TAKING ANY OTHER ACTION REQUIRED BY THIS NOTICE, YOU CAN APPLY TO THE COURT WHICH MAY MAKE AN ORDER ALLOWING YOU OR ANY SURETY MORE TIME.

IF YOU ARE NOT SURE WHAT TO DO, YOU SHOULD GET HELP AS SOON AS POSSIBLE, FOR EXAMPLE, YOU SHOULD CONTACT A SOLICITOR, YOUR LOCAL TRADING STANDARDS DEPARTMENT OR YOUR NEAREST CITIZENS ADVICE BUREAU.

The Bank makes a standard charge to cover the additional costs involved in these circumstances and your cheque account will be debited accordingly. Details of charges are available from Branches upon request.

If statements are issued on your account (excluding Flexible Savings and 60 Day Notice Accounts) the charge will be notified to you, by statement, at least 14 days before it is applied to your account.

Dated this day:- 19 December 1995

- Where goods on HP, conditional sale or hire have been wrongfully disposed of. In these circumstances, as s87(1) limits only rights exercisable 'by reason of any breach by a debtor of a regulated agreement', the creditor has a distinct non-contractual cause of action, ie, an action in tort for conversion or breach of bailment.
- Where a regulated agreement has been rescinded, eg, for fraud or misrepresentation, unless it is intended to proceed against a guarantor, as this will be deemed to be enforcing a security under s87(1)(e).[39]

Form of default notices

Notices must be in the form prescribed by Consumer Credit (Enforcement, Default and Termination) Regulations 1983 SI No 1561 reg 2(2) (see Figure 1), and must include, under s88(1):

- the nature of the breach complained of;
- if the breach is capable of remedy, the action necessary to remedy it and the date by which it is to be taken;
- if the breach is not capable of remedy, the sum required as compensation and the date by which it is to be paid;
- information about the consequences of failure to comply with the default notice (s88(4)).

Any date specified in a default notice must be not less than seven full days after the service of the notice (s88(2)). This excludes the day upon which the notice is given to the debtor (*Re Railway Sleepers Supply Co Ltd* (1885) 29 ChD 204).[40]

39 The difference between rescission and termination is important. Rescission cancels the contract from the beginning so it is treated as never having existed. Parties must, therefore, be returned as nearly as possible to their original positions. Where restitution is not possible, eg, where goods have been wrongly disposed of, the right to rescission is lost and the remedy is damages (see 7.3.1 and 7.3.2). Termination puts an end to future obligations without disturbing the accrued rights and liabilities, with damages as the remedy for innocent parties.

See Misrepresentation Act 1967 s2 for how the court may substitute damages in lieu of rescission (see 7.3).

Where a creditor is demanding early payment (s87(1)(b)), sole reliance cannot be placed on a default notice – a further separate demand must be made following the expiry of the default notice. This further demand is a 'condition precedent' at common law (*Esso Petroleum Co Ltd v Alstonbridge Properties Ltd* [1975] 2 All ER 385). This does not apply to the other default remedies in s87(1).

40 The date of service of a default notice is the date on which it is delivered or sent by post to the debtor. Service by post will be effective even where it is not received by the debtor (*Lombard North Central v Power-Hines* [1995] CCLR 24; [1994] CLY 501; (1994) December *Legal Action* 26).

Effects of breaches of s87
Breaches of the s87 requirements can come about in three ways:

- failure to serve a default notice at all;
- service of a default notice defective under s88 of the regulations;
- taking enforcement action before the expiry of a valid notice.

The remedies for an aggrieved debtor will be the same in each of these cases:

- Where the debtor is evicted from land or premises, damages can be awarded for trespass and possession can be regained, either peaceably or by court action.
- Where goods are wrongfully seized, the debtor may sue the creditor for conversion which can include a claim for damages and/or an application for return of the goods (*Eshun v Moorgate Mercantile Co Ltd* [1971] 2 All ER 402, CA). Debtors may also peaceably recover goods ('peaceable recapture').
- A debtor may also be able to apply for an injunction to prevent unlawful enforcement and the debtor will in any event, where appropriate, be able to apply for a time order (s129(1)(a)(i)) (see Chapter 4).

Advisers should always check that where default notices are required that they have been served, are in the correct form and that action is not being or has not been taken before the expiry of the time limit.

Compliance
When a default notice results in the breach being 'remedied', the creditor will not be able to enforce the agreement. As the breach is treated as not having occurred, the creditor will be prevented from relying on it as a default for any other purpose, eg, to demonstrate at a later date the continuing incapacity or unwillingness of the debtor to perform the contract (s89).

2.7.2   Notice of termination of agreements

While s76 (see 2.6.2) deals with the enforcement in non-default cases without terminating an agreement and s87 deals with all default cases, s98 deals with the termination of agreements in non-default cases. Section 98 provides that a creditor is not entitled to terminate a regulated agreement except where a notice of termination has been served on the debtor in the form prescribed by Enforcement, Default and Termination Regs (p93 above) reg 2(3), giving at least seven clear days' notice (s98(1)).

The section only applies where there is a fixed-term agreement which has not run its term (s98(2)), but does not prevent a creditor from treating the right to draw on any credit as restricted or deferred, and taking steps to effect this (s98(4)).

The service of a termination notice entitles the debtor to apply for a time order (s129(1)(a)(i)) (see Chapter 4).

2.7.3   Termination of hire-purchase and conditional sale agreements

Hire-purchase and conditional sale agreements, including details of goods protected from repossession without a court order, a debtor's right to terminate an agreement, liability on such a termination and termination by a creditor, are dealt with in Chapter 3.

2.7.4   Termination of hire agreement

Section 101 gives a hirer under a regulated consumer hire agreement a right of termination on the giving of notice. Exercise of the right does not affect already accrued liabilities, eg, arrears of rental or liability for loss or damage to hired goods (s101(2)).

Various *minimum periods of notice* are specified:

– subject to minimum periods of notice below, unless the agreement provides for a shorter period, notice of termination must not expire earlier than 18 months after the making of the agreement (s101(3));
– where an agreement provides for payments to be made at equal intervals, the minimum notice period is the lesser of one interval or three months (s101(4));
– where an agreement provides for payment at unequal intervals, the minimum notice period is the lesser of the shortest interval or three months (s101(5));
– in any other case, the minimum notice period is three months (s101(6)).

There are three exceptions to the statutory rights to terminate regulated hire agreements:

- agreements which provide for the making of payments in excess of £900 (Consumer Credit (Increase of Monetary Amounts) Order 1983 SI No 1571) in any one year (s101(7)(a));[41]
- three-party leases, ie, agreements under which goods are hired for business purposes and were acquired by the owner at the hirer's request from 'any person other than the owner's associate', ie, from an independent third party (s101(7)(b));[42]
- sub-leases, ie, agreements under which the hirer requires the goods for the purpose of hiring them to other persons in the course of business (s101(7)(c)).

No contracting out is permitted (s173) and any penalties and/or additional charges payable on termination will, therefore, be void.

2.7.5   Default interest

Section 93 permits agreements to provide for interest to be charged on arrears provided that it does not exceed the contractual rate of interest that is included in the total charge for credit. Where there is no interest specifically itemised, default interest is limited to the rate of the total charge for credit, excluding any charges in respect of linked transactions. Any clauses in an agreement permitting higher rates to be charged are void (s173(1)).

The provision permits compound interest, ie, interest on accumulated arrears of interest, but if credit is provided on an 'interest-free' basis, no default interest may be charged at all during the 'interest-free' period.

Default interest does not form part of the total charge for credit calculation.[43]

Some creditors, particularly those specialising in second mortgages, include two rates of interest in their agreements: a 'standard rate', and a lower 'discount' rate which applies while payments are

---

41 It is proposed to remove all business lending and hiring from regulation under the Act and to increase the monetary figure in relation to exempt agreements under s101(7)(a) from £900 to £1,500 ('Consumer Credit Deregulation' (OFT, June 1994) and see 6.1.1 and 6.1.2).

42 An associate is a partner, a spouse or relative of the hirer, or the spouse or relative of a partner (s184).

43 The restriction on default interest does not effect the operation of 'accelerated payment' clauses, although if the application of such a clause does not allow for an early settlement rebate (in the case of early settlement) it may be challengeable as a penalty at common law (see also 2.2.4 at p16 et seq for methods of charging interest).

up-to-date and which sometimes requires that payments are made by standing order. When one payment is overdue, usually by seven days, the lender is entitled to raise the interest rate to the 'standard rate', sometimes resulting in as much as a 10% increase.

2.7.6   Early settlement

Under s94 debtors have the right to settle regulated fixed-sum consumer credit agreements ahead of time by giving notice to the creditor and paying all amounts owing, less any rebate due under s95. There is no entitlement to rebates for the early settlement of hire agreements, running-account credit agreements or where debtors have terminated HP or conditional sale agreements.

Notice need not be in any prescribed form but must be in writing. In three-party arrangements notice can be given to creditors, their agents or employees.[44]

The right to early settlement arises when a debtor pays the amount owing, or when all or part of the sum becomes payable before the time fixed by the agreement. Specifically covered are debtors refinancing to pay existing liabilities early (s95(1)).

The issue of early settlement rebates and consumer credit agreements subject to county court judgments was dealt with by the Court of Appeal in *Forward Trust v Whymark* [1990] 2 QB 670; [1989] 3 All ER 915; [1989] 3 WLR 1229, which held that judgment should be given for the full amount claimed without provision for an early settlement rebate. This was subject to the proviso, however, that a judgment debtor can claim a rebate to be calculated at the date the judgment debt is discharged. In most cases this will be after the date originally fixed in the agreement, when there will, therefore, be no rebate entitlement.

It has also been decided that when a time order (see Chapter 4) is made rescheduling repayment of the whole outstanding balance owing under a regulated agreement, any entitlement to an early settlement rebate should be disregarded. Following *Foward Trust v Whymark*, the court stated 'the amount of rebate allowable is ascertained by reference to the settlement date, the date on which the debtor pays the sum by which early settlement is actually effected and total indebtedness actually discharged' (*Southern & District Finance v Barnes* [1995] CCLR 62; (1995) *Times* 19 April, CA).

---

44   Giving notice to a dealer or supplier in a three-party arrangement will not be sufficient.

There will be no rebate entitlement where a debtor makes a voluntary partial settlement, eg, by paying instalments in advance before going on holiday. To attract a rebate a debtor must pay the whole amount due.

The details of the early settlement provisions are contained in the Consumer Credit (Rebate on Early Settlement) Regulations 1983 SI No 1562, as amended by SI 1989 No 596, and the Consumer Credit (Settlement Information) Regulations 1983 SI No 1564.

The settlement date, ie, the date at which the rebate is calculated, will be:

- Where the debtor requests a settlement statement:

  - *Where credit repaid at monthly or shorter intervals:* The date of the next instalment following the expiry of 28 days after the receipt of the request.
  - *In any other case:* 28 days after the receipt of the request (or later if so requested by the debtor).

- Where settlement is to take place on an instalment date: the date at which the settlement is made.
- Where settlement is to take place between two instalment dates and credit is repaid at monthly or shorter intervals and:

  - *The debtor gives notice of early settlement:* The date of the next instalment due after the date of the service of the notice if accompanied by full payment or, where payment does not accompany the notice, the date of actual payment.
  - *Where debtor defaults:* The date of the next instalment after the date specified in the default notice, provided the debtor pays.
  - *Where the creditor terminates the agreement:* The date of the next instalment after the date specified in the termination notice, provided the debtor pays.
  - *In any other case:*The date of the next instalment after the debtor pays.

- Where settlement is to take place between two instalments and credit is repaid by instalments at intervals longer than one month and:

  - *The debtor gives notice of early settlement:* 14 days after the date of either the service of the notice if accompanied by payment or, where not accompanied by payment, the actual date of payment.

- *Where the debtor defaults:* 14 days after the date specified in the default notice, provided the debtor pays.
- *Where the creditor terminates the agreement:* 14 days after the date specified in the termination notice, provided the debtor pays.
- *In any other case:* 14 days after the date when payment is made.

Under Consumer Credit (Rebate on Early Settlement) Regulations 1983 SI No 1562 reg 5, a creditor can defer the settlement date to provide a loading factor to cover the initial cost of setting up the transaction which would not be adequately covered by the application of a straight mathematical formula. Once the settlement date has been determined the creditor can treat the settlement date as deferred by:

- *two months* where the credit is to be spread over five years or less;
- *one month* where the credit is to be repaid over a period of more than five years.

Contracting out

No contracting out of the early settlement provisions is permitted (s173 (1)), although creditors can allow a debtor a rebate greater than that provided for by the regulations. Debtors cannot be deprived of their right to settle early or be subject to conditions for the exercise of such right more stringent than those provided for by the regulations. This would preclude, for example, the term sometimes seen in secured regulated agreements which stipulates that a debtor wishing to redeem must give six months' prior notice or pay six months' interest in lieu of notice. However, debtors will often find it to their advantage to give notice or pay interest in lieu, as the result is likely to be more favourable than relying on the statutory rebate.

Rebates

Rebates are calculated according to the five formulae contained in the Early Settlement Regs (p98 above) which allow for different repayment arrangements. The most commonly used formula is known as the 'Rule of 78 (Part I)' which covers rebate calculations where credit is paid in equal instalments at equal intervals. The formula is as follows:

$$\frac{M(M+1)}{N(N+1)} \times K = \text{Rebate due under the agreement}$$

M = total number of instalments not yet due
N = total number of instalments
K = total charge for credit

EXAMPLE 2

A loan of £1,000 is agreed to be repaid by 36 monthly instalments of £48 starting one month after the date of the loan and the debtor decides to settle the loan at the end of the thirtieth month, ie, with six monthly instalments outstanding.

1) Calculate settlement date; in this case it is the date on which the customer settles. This date is then deferred by two months.

   M is therefore $6 - 2 = 4$
   K is $36 \times £48 - £1,000 = £728$
   N is 36

2) Calculate rebate

   $$\frac{4(4 + 1)}{36(36 + 1)} \times £728 = £10.93$$

Linked transactions

Linked transactions are also affected by early settlement of principal agreements. Where a debtor makes early settlement of a regulated agreement, obligations under a linked transaction are automatically discharged except where:

- A debt has already become payable (s96(1).
- Where the linked transaction is 'itself an agreement . . . providing the debtor . . . with credit' (s96(2)).
- The linked transaction is a contract of insurance (Consumer Credit (Linked Transactions) (Exemptions) Regulations 1983 SI No 1560). Third party motor insurance will be covered, ie, will not be automatically discharged or terminated.

Under s97(1) a creditor is obliged to provide an early settlement statement within 12 days (Consumer Credit (Settlement Information) Regulations 1983 SI No 1564) of a debtor's written request and such a statement is binding on the creditor subject to the power of the court to grant relief (s172(1) and (3) and see 2.6.4). An offence is committed if a statement is not provided within one month and the agreement is not enforceable while the default continues (s97(3)). Having paid the amount stated by a creditor in an early settlement statement the debtor is entitled on request to a termination statement under s103 (see 2.6.4).[45]

2.8 Judicial control (ss127–144)

This section deals with the various powers exercisable by courts in respect of regulated agreements. Those dealing with extortionate credit (ss137–140 and see Chapter 5), HP agreements (ss129–136 and see 3.3 and 4.3), time orders (ss129–136 and Chapter 4) and the enforcement of agreements where the creditor is in breach of CCA 1974 requirements (s127 and see 2.5.10) are dealt with elsewhere. Here county court jurisdiction is considered.

2.8.1 Jurisdiction

Section 141 explicitly states that sole jurisdiction over consumer credit agreements lies with the county court, and that any case brought in the High Court should be transferred immediately and automatically to the county court. There is, however, widespread abuse of this provision, many actions for the recovery of money under regulated consumer credit agreements being started each year in district registries of the High Court.

Section 141 states:

(1) In England and Wales the county court shall have jurisdiction to hear and determine –

    (a) any action by the creditor or owner to enforce a regulated agreement or any security relating to it;

    (b) any action to enforce any linked transaction against the debtor or hirer or his relative,

and such an action shall not be brought in any other court.

(2) Where an action or application is brought in the High Court which, by virtue of this Act, ought to have been brought in the county court it shall not be treated as improperly brought, but shall be transferred to the county court.

---

45 It is proposed by the OFT to revise the calculation of early settlement rebates to make them more equitable to borrowers. The 'Rule of 78' formula is likely to be replaced by an 'actual reducing balance' formula, the provisions permitting the deferment of settlement dates are likely to be revoked with lenders permitted instead to charge an appropriate early settlement fee, perhaps subject to a monetary ceiling of approximately £100, any such fee to be disclosed at the start of an agreement ('Consumer Credit Deregulation' (OFT, June 1994) and see 6.1.4).

However, from 1 July 1991, the Courts and Legal Services Act 1990(CLSA) came into effect. CLSA 1990 s2(1) amended County Courts Act 1984 (CCA 1984) s40 in relation to the transfer of proceedings to the High Court and provides that:

> (1) Where the High Court is satisfied that any proceedings before it are required by any provision of a kind mentioned in subsection (8) to be in a county court it shall –
>
>> (a) order a transfer of the proceedings to a county court; or
>> (b) if the court is satisfied that the person bringing the proceedings knew, or ought to have known of that requirement, order that they be struck out.

The provisions referred to above in subsection (1) are any made under CLSA 1990 s1 or by or under any enactment (CCA 1984 s40(8)).

At the time CLSA 1990 came into force, there was much discussion about whether the amended s40(1) superseded CCA 1974 s141(2), and whether consumer credit actions wrongly brought should be transferred under CCA 1974 s141(2) or struck out under CCA 1984 s40(1)(see 'Courts and Legal Services' (1991) 28 *Adviser* 33).

There have subsequently been a number of decisions on the apparent conflict between CCA 1974 s141(1) and CCA 1984 s40, as amended by CLSA 1990 s2(1).

In *Barclays Bank v Brookes* (1992) unreported, Quarterly Account No 23, in which Barclays sued under a regulated agreement in the High Court, it was decided on appeal to a High Court judge in chambers that the provisions of the amended County Courts Act 1984 took precedence and the action was struck out. The case also appeared to decide, however, that in spite of the mandatory nature of 'shall' in s40(1), the court had discretion whether to strike out or transfer to the county court, and that the plaintiff had to offer some reason or justification for wrongly issuing in the High Court to avoid the exercise of the court's discretion to strike out the proceedings.

It had been previously thought that this decision was wrong in allowing discretion where there should have been none, but the Court of Appeal has since taken a similar view in *Restrick v Crickmore* [1994] 1 WLR 420; [1994] 2 All ER 112. This case involved a personal injuries claim for less than £50,000 which was incorrectly brought in the High Court. In considering the provisions of CCA 1984 s40(1), following the case being struck out at first instance, it was held that striking out was a draconian sanction and, as no injustice was involved to the defendant in transferring the case to the county court, as it was otherwise a properly constituted action, the appeal against the striking out was allowed. Certain guidance was given as to the circumstances in which the discretion to strike out should be exercised, that is where the action should plainly have been started in the county court and failure to do so was not due to a bona fide mistake but could be seen as an attempt to harass the defendant or to deliberately run up unnecessary costs, where the case was wrongly brought in the High Court following a warning from the defendant as to the correct venue, or where a party persistently commenced actions in the wrong court.

It is still difficult to see how the word 'shall' allows the court discretion in these circumstances. The court clearly has a decision to make in deciding whether CCA 1984 s40(1)(b) has been satisfied, ie, in deciding whether the plaintiff knew, or ought to have known the correct court in which to commence proceedings, but having come to a decision that this is the case, it is still submitted that the striking out should be mandatory and not discretionary. Nevertheless, the Court of Appeal's decision must be considered as a binding precedent, although it could possibly be distinguished on the grounds that the case did not relate to a regulated consumer credit agreement.

Advisers must be careful to check that regulated consumer credit proceedings are not wrongly issued in the High Court and must be familiar with the necessary High Court procedure to be able to prepare applications to strike out or transfer. In brief, the acknowledgement of service should be returned within the 14-day time limit indicating that it is the debtor's intention to contest the proceedings. A summons must then be prepared asking for the case to be struck out or, in the alternative, transferred to the county court, and an affidavit sworn setting out the grounds for the application, ie, lack of jurisdiction. These must be sent to the court for a hearing date to be fixed and for sealing, and are returned to the debtor for service on the plaintiff.

If a default judgment is entered following proceedings wrongly brought in the High Court, once the irregularity is brought to the court's attention it should be set aside of the court's own motion and transferred to the county court (*Automobile Association Financial Services Ltd v Doherty* (1987) unreported, 10 November, but noted in *Supreme Court Practice 1995* (Sweet & Maxwell, 1994), vol 1, para 6/2/22).[46]

---

46 It should be remembered that Diners Club and American Express are not regulated agreements and can be sued for in the High Court.

2.8.2 Parties

Under s141(5) it is a requirement that all parties to a regulated agreement, including any surety, shall be made parties to any proceedings relating to that agreement. This requirement can be dispensed with under CCR 1981 Ord 49 r4(3) on an ex parte application by the creditor. It is not unusual, however, for a creditor to pursue only one of two joint debtors and/or not make a guarantor party to proceedings, but it does provide a way for an aggrieved debtor to ensure that action is also taken against a joint debtor.

An exception to this 'all parties' requirement exempts an assignee of a debt, eg, a debt collector who has purchased the debt, from joining the original creditor to an action unless the court so directs (CCR 1981 Ord 49 r4(4)).

2.8.3 Enforcement of judgments

Following the insertion of art 8(1A) into the High Court and County Court Jurisdiction Order 1994 SI No 724, all judgments arising out of consumer credit agreements can only be enforced in the county court. No enforcement of any kind can take place in the High Court.

CHAPTER 3

Hire-purchase and conditional sale agreements

Hire-purchase (HP) agreements are defined by s189 and are agreements, other than conditional sale agreements, under which:

(a) goods are hired[1] in return for periodical payments by the person to whom they are hired (the debtor); and

(b) ownership of the goods will pass to the debtor if the terms of the agreement are complied with and one or more of the following occur:

   (i) the exercise of an option to purchase by the debtor;

  (ii) the doing of any other specified act by any party to the agreement;

 (iii) the happening of any other specified event.

Conditional sale agreements are agreements for the sale of goods or land under which the purchase price or part thereof is payable by instalments and ownership of the goods or land is retained by the seller (the creditor), notwithstanding that the buyer is to be in possession of them, until such conditions as to the payment of instalments or otherwise as specified in the agreement are fulfilled (s189).

A conditional sale agreement does not create a security interest and should not be seen as a 'secured' agreement. The parties are merely exercising their right under Sale of Goods Act 1979 s17 to decide at what time and on what conditions ownership passes to the buyer (the debtor).

The distinction between HP and conditional sale agreements was established in *Helby v Matthews* [1985] AC 471. A conditional sale agreement commits a buyer to purchase. An HP agreement must be drafted so as to avoid such a commitment to purchase, even if the event causing ownership to pass to the debtor is not a voluntary act of

---

1 Although s189 actually uses the term 'bail' rather than 'hire', hire is in fact the correct term under English law in relation to HP agreements.

the debtor but the happening of some other specified event (see (b)(ii) and (iii) above).

The fact that a debtor under a conditional sale agreement regulated by CCA 1974 is given a statutory right to terminate the agreement does not make it a HP agreement.

The Act contains provisions which apply exclusively to HP and conditional sale agreements:

- they are excluded from the definition of 'small agreements' (s17 and see 2.2.11);
- only goods relating to HP and conditional sale agreements are subject to the 'protected goods' provisions of s90 (see 3.2.2);
- only such goods are subject to the provisions restricting entry into premises for the purpose of repossession under s92 (see 3.2.3);
- special provisions give debtors a statutory right to terminate agreements under s99 and to limit liability on such termination under s100 (see 3.1.1);
- special powers are given to the courts in relation to return and transfer orders under s133 (see 3.3).

There are two types of HP and conditional sale agreements:

- *Direct collection* where the retailer or dealer sells the goods to a finance company which then lets them on HP or sells them on conditional sale to the debtor.
- *Block discounting* where the retailer or dealer enters directly into an agreement with the debtor and thereafter sells the contract to the finance company, often continuing to collect the instalments as they fall due on behalf of the creditor. With these agreements, the retailer or dealer will usually sell a batch or block of agreements to the finance company at a discount.

3.1   Termination rights

Termination rights are governed by common law, contract law and statute. The Hire-Purchase Act 1965 is now fully repealed other than Part III (see 3.4.1) and most of the statutory provision is contained in CCA 1974. Agreements can be terminated by either the debtor or the creditor. Calculation of the debtor's liability to the creditor is different on each occasion.

3.1.1   *Termination by debtor*

A debtor under a HP or conditional sale agreement (other than a conditional sale agreement relating to land where the title has passed to the debtor (s99(3))), has a statutory right to terminate the agreement at any time before the final payment (s99(1)). Whilst this right cannot be excluded by the terms of an agreement (s173(1)), where the agreement contains an accelerated payment clause, on the invoking of such a clause, the amount payable under it becomes the 'final payment' and the debtor's right to terminate will have been lost. However, since the service of a default (s87) or termination (s76) notice is required before an accelerated payment clause can be invoked, the debtor will still retain the right to terminate before an early payment demand is made (or where such a demand is not necessary, before the notice expires). The right to terminate will also be lost where the debtor is deemed to have repudiated the agreement, eg, following default, either under the terms of the agreement or on the facts of the case (see 3.1.2).

The exercise of a right to terminate will not affect any 'already accrued' liabilities, eg, arrears and/or liability for damage to goods (ss99(2) and 100(4)), and liability on termination is not affected by the early settlement provisions (Consumer Credit (Rebate on Early Settlement) Regulations 1983 SI No 1562 reg 2(3)) (see 2.7.6).

Under s100, unless the agreement provides for a lower payment or no payment at all, on termination the debtor must pay any arrears and then the amount (if any) necessary to make up the total amount paid to one-half of the total HP price (s100(1)). In addition to any amount payable under s100(1) the debtor will also be liable to compensate the creditor for any failure to take reasonable care of the goods (or land under a conditional sale agreement). If there has been a charge for any installation, this will have to be paid in addition (s100(2)). Liability may also be expressed by the following formula

$$\text{Liability} = \text{Arrears} + \left(\frac{\text{Total HP price}}{2}\right) - \text{Payments made} + \text{Compensation}$$

It should be noted that any deposit or part-exchange allowance counts as payment towards the half of the total purchase price, with the effect that the half may already have been paid at the time of entry into the agreement, and similarly the one-third making the goods 'protected' immediately under s90 (see 3.2.2). Agreements themselves are required to show the one-half and one-third figures in boxes and advisers need to check liability against these and not think in terms of the half as half of the instalments.

In spite of the debtor's right being clearly stated in the Act and required to be shown on agreements, when debtors terminate, it is not unknown for creditors to send demands for the whole balance owing following the sale of a vehicle and a discount of unaccrued interest. This should only be done where the figure demanded is less than the half figure which it invariably is not. Advisers should look out for this.

If the court feels that a sum less than that calculated as above is equal to the loss sustained by the owner, it can make an order for this lower sum (s100(3)). Goode feels the loss can be calculated on the basis of the fact that the hirer would receive the full amount if the debtor had not terminated the agreement (Goode III (101)).[2] Thus the formula would be the total price less:

– payments made;
– the value of the goods returned on termination;
– the option to purchase fee (in the case of an HP agreement);
– a discount for early receipt by the creditor, although there is no statutory rebate (*Overstone v Shipway* [1962] 1 All ER 52 and Early Settlement Regulations (above) reg 2(3)).

As stated above, under s100(4) the owner can be recompensed if the debtor has breached any other contractual obligation, eg, failing to take reasonable care of the goods. Reasonable care excludes wear and tear but not negligence. These damages are recovered in addition to any payments due under the 50% formula. Care must be taken, however, not to duplicate damages. If the sum the debtor pays is based on 'the loss sustained by the creditor', the sum realised on the sale of the goods, which is set against the hire-purchase price, reflects the debtor's lack of care and the creditor is not entitled to damages for this as well.

3.1.2   Termination by creditor

Termination by the creditor can happen in two ways:

– Under the terms of the agreement.
– When the debtor commits any serious breach equal to repudiation. The general rule is that any dealing with goods by the debtor

---

2 Professor Guest takes a different view, arguing that any alternative calculation of 'loss' under s100(3) should not make allowance for the creditor's 'lost profit' under an agreement.

inconsistent with their hire, eg, disposing of goods to which the debtor does not have title, amounts to repudiation and entitles the owner to recover possession. Repossession does not release the debtor from the consequences of default. However, accepting a tender or offer by the debtor may amount to the creditor waiving the right to terminate the agreement. Default in payment may also amount to repudiation (see below).

Any repossession or seizure must not be by force, but peaceable and orderly, and is subject to a default notice under s87 (see 2.7.1), and ss90 (see 3.2.2) and 92 (see 3.2.3). The creditor can recover the outstanding sums due following repossession or seizure by county court action.

In most money advice cases, the most typical cause of termination will be repudiation by the debtor. Serious and persistent default will have led to breach and repudiation of the agreement. The creditor's remedies in this instance depend partly on common law, partly on the terms of the agreement and partly on the CCA 1974.

The creditor's remedies vary according to the nature of the transaction. The creditor is entitled to repayment with interest and can call-up the whole loan in default. Any such accelerated payment clause must allow for an early settlement rebate but only on payment (*Forward Trust Ltd v Whymark* [1990] 2 QB 670; [1989] 3 WLR 1229 and *Southern & District Finance v Barnes* [1995] CCLR 62, *Times*, 19 April, CA, and see 4.5 and 4.9). These cases held, in relation to a default judgment and a time order, that entitlement to an early settlement rebate only arises on actual payment of an accelerated sum (whether accelerated by a term of the agreement or a court judgment). An accelerated demand must, however, make allowance for a rebate, eg, in a default, calling-in or termination notice, but the debtor will only be entitled to the rebate on payment. The owner can also enforce any security. As far as hire-purchase agreements are concerned, the owner can recover the debt, ie, arrears outstanding at the date of termination, plus damages for breach of contract. Serious breach amounts to repudiation of the agreement and the owner can repossess, subject to the goods being protected against seizure without a court order (see 3.2.2) and the restrictions on entry onto premises (see 3.2.3).

Repudiation needs to be defined. Any breach of an agreement entitles the creditor to sue for damages, but not every breach brings the agreement to an end. The breach must go to the 'root of the contract' to amount to repudiation by the debtor. Even so, such a breach does not automatically terminate the agreement until it is 'accepted' by the owner. A non-repudiatory breach will only entitle the creditor to sue for arrears and interest but not damages in respect of future instalments (*Financings Ltd v Baldock* [1963] 2 QB 104; [1963] 1 All ER 443), although in practice creditors sidestep this by providing in agreements that making prompt payment is of the essence of the contract, so that any default will amount to repudiation (*Lombard North Central v Butterworth* [1987] QB 527; [1987] 1 All ER 267, CA). Repudiation will normally occur, therefore, on any failure by the debtor to make full and prompt payment and the creditor will then be entitled to sue for recovery and for damages in respect of future instalments.

Yeoman Credit Ltd v Wagarowski [1961] 1 WLR 1124, CA, determined the sums the owner is liable to receive. Wagarowski repudiated the agreement by six months' default. Yeoman Credit therefore terminated, repossessed and sold. It then claimed damages and arrears. Wagarowski claimed it had not shown any damage at all and that the damages claim was misconceived as it was really a claim for damages for non-payment of money. The Court of Appeal rejected this argument and held that the creditor's claim for damages was proper in respect of the debtor's failure to carry through the agreement to its conclusion. Damages are thus to be calculated on the basis that the debtor is bound by the contract to pay instalments up to the end of the agreement. The owner, therefore, has a prima facie claim for the loss of future payments since the debtor has refused to carry the contract to its conclusion, and this includes loss of any future interest.

The damages claimed will, as a result, be the full hire-purchase price less:

- the sums already paid including the deposit;
- the sums realised on sale (see below);
- the option to purchase fee (in the case of an HP agreement);
- a discount to allow for early receipt by the creditor (*Overstone v Shipway* [1962] 1 WLR 117).[3]

The debtor must be given credit for the value of the goods repossessed or the proceeds of sale thereof. The creditor cannot also claim damages for failure to take reasonable care as this is reflected in the

---

3   The discount for early receipt would be, in the case of a regulated agreement, an early settlement rebate under s95 and Early Settlement Regs reg 2(1) as the statutory rebate is only excluded under reg 2(3) where the debtor terminates under s99 (see 3.1.1). Any entitlement to a rebate will only occur, of course, at the date of actual settlement (see *Forward Trust v Whymark*, p109 above).

reduced sale price obtained. The creditor must obtain the best price reasonably possible, and any delay in selling goods and subsequent depreciation should not be visited on the debtor (*Financings Ltd v Baldock* [1963] 2 QB 104). There is some doubt about what should be regarded as the true value of the goods: the retail price or the price on sale to the trade. Finance houses are not equipped to sell at retail and, therefore, often auction repossessed goods. This will usually be acceptable but it is for the court to decide if creditors have been reasonable in their actions and the price subsequently achieved.

In *Wagarowski* (see p110 above), however, the court was dealing with a pre-CCA 1974 case and, therefore, an unregulated agreement. In relation to regulated agreements Goode argues that:

> it seems clear that an award of substantial damages . . . *must* in the case of a regulated agreement take s100 into account, even if the debtor has expressly undertaken by the terms of the agreement to pay the whole or substantially the whole of the purchase price, this is not an enforceable promise in the sense that ss99 and 100 enable him to escape a substantial part of that liability. It seems accordingly that the sum set out in s100(1) represents the absolute maximum which may be recovered by the creditor in respect of a repudiatory breach (and from that sum there must, of course, be deducted the debtor's payments). It may also follow, if this is correct, that a minimum agreements clause which provides for any greater sum will be held to be penal in so far as it is relied upon by the creditor in the event of a breach by the debtor. (Goode III (101))

Presumably, the creditor would also be entitled to recover damages under s100(4) for a debtor's failure to take reasonable care of goods or land subject to the agreement. This view on the effect of s100 on liability following a creditor's termination and repossession has not been tested in court.

The owner's rights are also expressed in the hire-purchase or conditional sale contract. The agreement will usually contain express provisions conferring a range of remedies on the creditor in the case of debtor's default, such as:

– Default interest.
– Acceleration of the balance.
– Termination of the agreement on breach.
– Repossession and sale.
– Fixing damages in advance if they are a reasonable pre-estimate of the likely loss, ie, a 'minimum payment clause' giving compensation for early termination. This will be a fixed amount or fixed

percentage of the hire-purchase price, but can only be enforced if it covers actual loss and does not require payments so high as to act as a 'penalty clause' to secure performance of the contract. A minimum payment clause would replace the damages described above.

CCA 1974 adopts and strengthens the rights of debtors that were contained in the Hire-Purchase Act, imposing certain restrictions on creditors including:

- The requirement that a default notice must be issued before any action can be taken by the creditor. The notice must detail the default, state how it can be remedied, give the debtor at least seven days to take the necessary action (eg, pay arrears) and specify the consequence of the debtor not doing so (s87 and see 2.7.1).
- Similar provisions in relation to calling-in (s76 and see 2.6.2) and termination notices (s98 and see 2.7.2).
- The right of the debtor to apply for a time order (ss129 and 130 and see Chapter 4).
- The requirement that a court order is needed to repossess goods in certain circumstances (see ss90 and 92 and see 3.2.2/3).
- A limit on default interest (see s93 and see 2.7.5).
- The extortionate credit provisions (see Chapter 5).

3.2   Repossession

3.2.1   Pre-action notice

A default, termination and/or calling-in notice must be served prior to repossession (ss87, 76 and 98, and see 2.7.1, 2.6.2 and 2.7.2). Although no sanction for non-compliance is given in the Act, repossession without a default notice may give rise to an action under the Torts (Interference with Goods) Act 1977, as the creditor will be liable in conversion. The remedy is return of the goods and/or damages. The debtor could also 'recapture' the goods from the owner. The debtor could resist the creditor's attempt to repossess or seek an injunction under s170(3), use non-compliance as a defence where the creditor takes court action and/or apply for a time order (Chapter 4). Damages could also be sought for trespass.

3.2.2   Protected goods

These are goods where over one-third of the total price has been paid (s90).[4] They cannot be repossessed without a court order. This does not apply if the debtor has terminated the agreement. A debtor can consent to repossession of 'protected' goods (s173(3)), although such consent must be genuine and voluntary, albeit reluctant. A term in the agreement providing for such consent will be void under the contracting out provisons of s173(1).

The creditor can also repossess protected goods where they have been abandoned, as repossession will not be from the debtor, but cannot repossess where the goods are with an authorised third party, eg, a garage where a vehicle is under repair.

If goods are repossessed in contravention of s90, then under s91:

- The agreement is terminated (s91(a)). The debtor can apply to court for a declaration to this effect under s142(2).
- The debtor is released from all liability and entitled to recover from the creditor all sums previously paid (s91(b)).

These are the only sanctions available under the Act (s170(1)). The debtor could not, for example, claim damages for interference with goods.

3.2.3   Entry of premises to repossess

Under s92 a court order is needed for a creditor to enter any premises to repossess goods. This applies whether or not the goods are protected under s90. The debtor can consent to entry and repossession without a court order (s173(3)). 'Premises' are not defined. It may mean privately owned real property of any kind but is likely to have a narrower meaning, ie, buildings, enclosures and their curtilages. Certainly, a vehicle parked on the debtor's drive or in the debtor's garage would be covered, although s92 refers to 'any' premises, which could include those of a third party.

Entry without an order is a breach of statutory duty and the remedy would seem to be a county court action for damages for trespass. The damages will be assessed as a natural consequence of the breach. No specific remedies for non-compliance are included in the Act. Wrongful recovery under s92 might also attract other penalties, eg, under Theft Act 1968 s5(1) – recovery must be both wrongful and dishonest. It would be a defence for creditors to say they believed they had a right in law to deprive the debtor of the property. The penalty is

---

4 Any deposit, as well as instalments that have been paid, must be taken into account in relation to the one-third figure.

a fine, imprisonment, compensation and/or restitution. Also, under Criminal Law Act 1977 s6(1), it is an offence to use and threaten violence to gain entry to any premises. The penalty is up to six months' imprisonment.

3.2.4   Form of proceedings

Where a creditor wishes to take court proceedings to repossess HP or conditional sale goods it will be by way of fixed date action. For examples of the relevant forms see Figures 2 and 3 (pages 115–117). Where an action is only for arrears or the balance owing following termination and repossession, it will be by way of default action.

In relation to land under a conditional sale agreement, a creditor can only recover possession on an order of the court. The form of proceedings would be by fixed date summons for the possession of land.

3.3   Powers of the court in HP and conditional sale cases

The court has broad powers under s133 of the Act in respect of hire-purchase and conditional sale agreements. Where just, it may make:

- a return order;
- a transfer order.

These powers may be exercised either on application for enforcement or a time order (s133(1)(a)), or during recovery proceedings after termination (s133(1)(b)). The court may impose conditions or suspend or postpone an order under s135, and amend the agreement in 'consequence' of an order (s136), eg, freeze interest.

If goods are not returned to the owner in contravention of any transfer or return order, the court may, on application from the creditor:

- revoke so much of the order as relates to the goods (s133(6)(a));
- order the debtor to pay the creditor the unpaid portion of so much of the total price as is referable to the goods (s133(6)(b) (see 3.3.2). Thus the creditor receives some compensation in lieu of recovery.

FIGURE 2: FIXED DATE SUMMONS

N. 4
Fixed Date Summons
Order 3, Rule 3(2)(b)
(Royal Arms)

Seal

To the defendant

● The plaintiff claims _____ (see particulars enclosed)

Court fee

Solicitor's costs

Total amount

Summons issued on

● The claim will be heard

on   at   am/pm

at

when you are summoned to attend. Failure to attend may result in judgment being entered against you.

Important–you must read the information on the back of this form. It will tell you more about what to do

Please read this page: it will help you deal with the summons

You have **21 days from the date of the postmark** to reply to this summons. (*A limited company served at its registered office has 16 days to reply.*) **If this summons was delivered by hand, you have 14 days from the date it was delivered to reply.**

General information
Court staff cannot give you advice on points of law, but you can get help to complete the reply forms and information about court procedures at **any** county court office or citizens' advice bureau. The address and telephone number of your local court is listed under 'Courts' in the phone book.

When corresponding with the court, please address forms or letters to the Chief Clerk. Always quote the whole of the case number which appears at the top right corner on the front of this form; the court is unable to trace your case without it.

If you do nothing
● **Judgment may be entered against you without further notice. This may make it difficult for you to get credit.**

Registration of Judgments
If the summons results in a judgment against you for money, your name and address may be entered in the Register of County Court Judgments. **This will make it difficult for you to get credit.** A leaflet giving further information can be obtained from the court.

Interest on judgments
If judgment is entered against you and is for £5000 or more, the plaintiff may be entitled to interest on the full amount.

FIGURE 3: FIXED DATE SUMMONS REPLY FORM

N. 10(HP/CCA)
Form of Admission, Defence and Counterclaim to Accompany Forms N3 and N4
Order 3, Rule 3(2)(c)

Form for Replying to a Summons (return of goods)

- *Read the notes on the summons before completing this form*
- *Tick the correct boxes and give the other details asked for*
- *Send or take this completed and signed form immediately to the court office shown on the summons*
- *You should keep your copy of the summons*
- *For details of where and how to pay see the summons*

What is your full name? (BLOCK CAPITALS)
Surname . . . .
Forenames . . . .
Mr ☐ Mrs ☐ Miss ☐ Ms ☐

How much of the claim do you admit?
☐ **All of it** *(complete only sections 1 and 2)*
☐ **Part of it** *(sections 1, 2, 3, 4, 5)* **Amount**
£   :
☐ **None of it** *(complete sections 3, 4 and 5 overleaf)*
Are the goods in your possession?
Yes ☐   No ☐
If the claim is under an Hire Purchase or Conditional Sale agreement: I understand that if the plaintiff accepts my offer of payment by instalments the court will make an order for the return of the goods but the plaintiff will not be able to enforce this order so long as I pay the instalments punctually.

Section 1   Offer of payment

I offer to pay the amount admitted on (date)
. . . . **or for the reasons set out below**
I cannot pay the amount admitted in one instalment
but I can pay by monthly instalments of £   :
Fill in the next section as fully as possible. Your answers will help the plaintiff decide whether your offer is realistic and ought to be accepted. Your answers will also help the court, if necessary, to fix a rate of payment that you can afford.

Section 2   Income and outgoings

a. Employment I am
☐ Unemployed
☐ A pensioner
☐ Self employed as . . . .
☐ Employed as a . . . .
My employer is . . . .
Employer's address:

continue on a separate sheet if necessary–put the case number in the top right hand corner

In the		County Court
	Always quote this	
Case Number		
Plaintiff (including reference)		
Defendant		

b. Income *specify period: weekly, fortnightly, monthly etc.*
My usual take home pay . . . . £   :
Child benefit(s) total. . . . . £   :
Other state benefit(s) total. . . . .£   :
My pension(s) total . . . .£   :
Other people living in my
home give me . . . .
. . . .£   :
Other income *(give details)*   £   :

c. Bank account and savings
☐ I do not have a bank account
☐ I have a bank account
The account is   in credit ☐
overdrawn ☐ by   £   :
☐ I do not have a savings account
☐ I have a savings account
The amount in the account is   £   :

d. Dependants *(people you look after financially)*
Number of dependants
(give ages of children) . . . .

e. Outgoings

	weekly	monthly		
Mortgage		☐	£	:
Rent	☐	☐	£	:
Mail order	☐	☐	£	:
TV rental/licence	☐	☐	£	:
HP repayments	☐	☐	£	:
Court orders	☐	☐	£	:

specify period: yearly, quarterly etc.
Gas . . . .   £   :
Electricity . . . .   £   :
Council tax . . . .   £   :
Water charges . . . .   £   :

Other regular payments *(give details below)*
£   :
Credit card and other debts *(please list)*
£   :
Of payments above, I am behind with payments to
£   :

Give an address to which notices about this case should be sent to you	I declare that the details I have given above are true to the best of my knowledge
	Signed *(to be signed by you or by your solicitor)*
Post code	**Position** *(if signing on behalf of firm or company)*
	Dated

FIGURE 3 (CONT)

Case No. ....

Section 3	Defending the claim: defence

Fill in this part of the form if you wish to defend the claim or part of the claim

a. How much of the plaintiff's claim do you dispute?
 All of it ☐
 Part of it ☐ *give amount*   £. . . . . . .

If you dispute only part of the claim, you must complete sections 1 and 2 overleaf and part b. below

b. What are your reasons for disputing the claim?

Section 4	Making a claim against the plaintiff: counterclaim

Fill in this part of the form only if you wish to make a claim against the plaintiff

If your claim against the plaintiff is more than his claim against you, you may have to pay a fee. Ask at the court office whether a fee is payable.

a. What is the nature of the claim you wish to make against the plaintiff?

b. If your claim is for a specific sum of money, how much are you claiming?
                                   £...........................

c. What are your reasons for making the claim?

Continue on a separate sheet if necessary–put the case number in the top right hand corner

Section 5 Arbitration under the small claims procedure

How the claim will be dealt with if defended

If the total the plaintiff is claiming is £3,000 or less, it will be dealt with by arbitration (small claims procedure) unless the court decides the case is too difficult to be dealt with in this informal way. Costs and the grounds for setting aside an arbitration award are strictly limited. If the claim is not dealt with by arbitration, costs, including the costs of help from a legal representative, may be allowed.

If the total the plaintiff is claiming is more than £3,000, it can still be dealt with by arbitration if you or the plaintiff ask for it and the court approves. If your claim is dealt with by arbitration in these circumstances, costs may be allowed.

Please tick this box if you would like the claim dealt with by arbitration. ☐

Give an address to which notices about this case can be sent to you	**Signed** *(to be signed by you or by your solicitor)*
	Position *(if signing on behalf of firm or company)*
Post code ☐	**Dated**

3.3.1 *Return orders*

These can be either:

- *Absolute:* the item is repossessed and the debtor is ordered to return it to the creditor.
- *Conditional*, eg, on payment of the value of the goods or on payment of the contractual instalments plus arrears. Most commonly this will be done by the court making a return order under s133(1), which is either:

  - conditional under s135(1)(a), or suspended under s135(1)(b), eg, on terms of payment, as above, with the possibility of interest being reduced or frozen under s136; or
  - a time order under ss129 and 130 (and s136) where the debtor cannot afford the current instalment (see Chapter 4).

As noted above, the terms of a conditional or suspended return order will usually be the payment of the equivalent of contractual instalments together with an amount, determined by the court, towards arrears. Advisers should always be prepared to argue for an 'affordable' amount based upon the debtor's financial statement and enter this figure on the reply to the creditor's summons (see Figure 3). The debtor's financial statement should be presented at the hearing.

If default interest is accruing on arrears at the time of the making of the suspended or conditional order, advisers should consider an application under s136 for that interest to be reduced or frozen (see 4.7).

Where the whole balance under the agreement has become payable, eg, following termination of the agreement and a demand for accelerated payment, that whole balance will be owed and in 'arrears', and the problem of accruing default interest will be particularly acute.

Where an agreement upon which interest is accruing on the whole outstanding balance is made subject to a suspended or conditional order, the issue of accruing interest should be addressed by advisers and drawn to the court's attention. If the court is to permit interest to accrue following the making of an order the district judge should be requested to limit the order to interest on the arrears of instalments at the date of termination. The difficulties of allowing interest on the whole balance payable should be pointed out to the court. On what balance and at what time should such interest be calculated, as each payment under the order reduces the 'principal' outstanding? It should also be drawn to the court's attention that where the whole balance is payable this will already include the full interest payable under the agreement, and that to allow accruing interest on the full balance would be unjust as it would be interest on interest. In any event, as noted above, an application to reduce or freeze all accruing interest under s136 should be considered. This will be particularly necessary where the amount of any accruing interest exceeds, equals or substantially absorbs the repayment ordered, and in these circumstances could be argued to be 'just' and 'in consequence' of the order as it will be necessary to give effect to it (see 4.7).

In any event, an application for a time order under s129 together with an order under s136 may be considered more appropriate. This will certainly be the case where the debtor cannot afford contractual payments or the equivalent. It should be noted that a time order application can be made as an originating application following the issue of a default notice before a creditor issues proceedings (see Chapter 4).

A debtor under an unregulated HP (and probably a conditional sale agreement) has a right to equitable relief against forfeiture or repossession (*Trading Haulage v Leyland Daf plc* (1994) *Times*, 15 January), and there is no obvious reason why this should not be the case with a regulated agreement. However, a history of default will weigh heavily against the grant of such relief (*Croker v NWS Bank plc* (1990) *Times*, 23 May, CA). Money advisers will normally be dealing with debtors in default but have found on many occasions that courts will exercise a discretion to suspend return orders in cases of default. It will help in these situations to be able to show that debtors have been in difficulty through no fault of their own, that the goods subject to the agreement are essential, eg, a vehicle necessary for employment or business, that substantial payment has already been made under the agreement and/or (where possible) the equivalent of contractual payments can now be met or are likely to be able to be met in the future. This will be the case whether a suspended or conditional return order, or a time order, is being sought.

On completion of payments under a suspended order, title vests in the debtor under s133(5). If the debtor defaults, the creditor's position depends on the form of the order, ie, whether the court provided for suspension to end automatically on default or required the creditor to make a further application to court. A return order, whether absolute, or where the terms of any suspension have been breached, is enforceable by a warrant of delivery. This can be suspended on terms or a time order can be made, on the debtor's application on form N244, at the discretion of the court.

3.3.2   *Transfer orders*

Such orders transfer title of certain goods to the debtor while the creditor retains title to the remainder. They are made as follows:

– designate the transferable goods as the court thinks fit;
– calculate the paid-up sum, ie, the total so far paid;
– ascertain the 'referable value'. Is the difference between the paid-up sum and the referable value equal to at least one-third of the unpaid balance of the total price?;
– make the transfer order where the one-third rule is satisfied.

The court is not obliged to transfer goods to the maximum value following this computation as it must have regard to what it thinks just. Transfer orders are only likely if transferring a small amount or value of goods or, if a large amount, most of the agreement has been paid. They are obviously only applicable where the goods can be split or divided and are rarely encountered by advisers. An example is shown at Figure 4.

FIGURE 4: EXAMPLE OF TRANSFER ORDER

Agreement for 2-piece suite –
Total price	£900.00
Paid-up sum	£680.00
Unpaid balance	£220.00

Transfer order stages (transfer of sofa)

1) *designate goods* – transfer sofa
2) *paid-up sum* – £680
3) *referable value* – split total price £600/£300
    therefore value of sofa = £600
4) *check*
    (a)   1/3 of unpaid balance = £73
    (b)   difference between 2 and 3 = £80
5) *transfer order* made as (b) exceeds (a)

OR if armchair to be transferred

1) armchair
2) as above
3) *referable value* = £300
4) *check*
    (a)   1/3 of unpaid balance = £73
    (b)   difference between 2 and 3 = £380
5) *transfer order* made as (b) exceeds (a)

3.4   Wrongful disposal

As stated at the beginning of the chapter, ownership of HP or conditional sale goods does not pass to the debtor until the last payment has been made. Until then, any dealings with the goods are unlawful, being both a criminal offence and a civil wrong. This naturally has implications for the debtor, but also for the purchaser, to whom ownership of (or title to) the goods cannot be passed. There is, however, an exception.

3.4.1   Motor vehicles

The Hire-Purchase Act 1964 (HPA) was repealed in full in 1985 apart from Part III thereof. This remains in force and relates to title to vehicles on HP or conditional sale. Under HPA 1964 s27, when the debtor disposes of a vehicle to another before title has vested in him/her, if the purchaser buys in good faith without notice of the agreement, the disposition takes effect as if the creditor's title vested in the debtor immediately before disposition. The purchaser thus obtains good title. Where the disposition is to a trader or finance house, then the first private buyer thereafter who purchases in good faith without notice of any outstanding agreement again receives good title.

These provisions do not exonerate the debtor from any criminal or civil liability, nor do they exonerate any trader. However, they protect the innocent buyer, particularly as HPA 1964 s28 states that in all such situations there is a presumption that the purchaser acted at all times in good faith and without notice of any outstanding agreement. The creditor should, therefore, not attempt to repossess wrongly disposed of goods from an innocent purchaser, but see Police (Property) Act 1887 s1(1), below at 3.4.2.

3.4.2   Offences

Wrongful disposal can be theft under Theft Act 1968 s1. Disposal of HP or conditional sale goods is classified as 'appropriation' under Theft Act 1968 s3. This is 'any assumption by a person of rights of an owner . . . and this includes, where he has come by property (innocently or not) without stealing it, any later assumption of a right to it by keeping or dealing with it as owner'. Over and above this, if the debtor does not disclose his/her lack of ownership, criminal deception in relation to the purchaser is also involved (Theft Act 1968 s15).

If the debtor honestly intends to remit the proceeds of sale to the creditor it could be argued that there is no offence of theft as the debtor's conduct would be unlikely to be seen as dishonest, although there could still be a criminal deception in relation to the purchaser. If the debtor both declared an intention to remit the proceeds and declares lack of title to the goods, it may be neither theft nor deception. If, however, the debtor is guilty of theft in these circumstances, the buyer may be guilty of handling stolen goods (*R v Staton* [1993] Crim LR 190, CA). Both debtor and purchaser would be liable in tort for conversion (see 3.4.3).

It may also be an offence for a debtor under a HP or conditional sale agreement to refuse to surrender the goods to the creditor. It may amount to an appropriation as it amounts to dealing with the goods as owner. It was assumed (without dispute or argument) in *R v Falconer-Atlee* (1973) 58 Cr App Rep 348, CA, that such a refusal was dishonest. However, under a regulated agreement where the creditor has no right to repossess, eg, due to the agreement being unenforceable due to improper execution or because the goods are protected, any refusal is unlikely to be seen as dishonest as the debtor would be doing no more than allowed by the law. According to *R v Morris* [1984] AC 320; [1983] All ER 288, HL, an appropriation requires an act which is inconsistent with the rights of the owner, and if under civil law a creditor has no right to repossess, the debtor's refusal to return goods could not be seen as dishonest (see also 2.5.10). In any event it is likely that the police would treat such a matter as a civil one.[5]

Criminal liability may also arise in relation to the insurance proceeds of goods subject to HP or conditional sale. If a vehicle is 'written-off' and the proceeds of comprehensive insurance are used by the debtor, eg, to purchase a new vehicle, it will amount to an appropriation of those proceeds and, therefore, theft.

Although money advisers have encountered situations where debtors have disposed of vehicles on HP on numerous occasions, it is comparatively rare for criminal prosecutions to result, especially where it is admitted what has happened and arrangements negotiated to repay the debt.

---

5   The fact that a regulated agreement is unenforceable will provide no defence to a charge of theft (*R v Modupe* [1991] Crim LR 530, CA). Where a debtor is dishonest from the outset and never intended to pay for goods under an HP or conditional sale agreement there will be an offence of obtaining goods by deception. In *R v Hirock* (1978) 67 Cr App Rep 278, a debtor purchased a car on HP, made no payments and sold it immediately. He was convicted of both theft and obtaining by deception. A threat by a creditor to invoke criminal sanctions may be harassment under Administration of Justice Act 1970 s40.

Under Theft Act 1968 s3(2) a bona fide purchaser has a defence against accusations of theft where the purchase is made in the belief that the seller has good title. Nevertheless, there may be problems. If an innocent purchaser is contacted by the hire-purchase company, a reply should be sent stating that the purchase was in good faith and including any available documentation. However, the creditor may notify the police that the vehicle has been stolen, in which case it may be impounded under Police (Property) Act 1887 s1(1) pending the court's decision as to title. The lender will also notify Hire-Purchase Information Ltd (HPI), which maintains records of title transactions relating to vehicles bought on HP. This is consulted by dealers and as it will be shown as still subject to an HP agreement, it is unlikely that any third-party purchaser would then be able to sell or part-exchange the vehicle to a dealer or garage. Disposal by private sale would be the only option, though a declaration of title by the court could overcome these difficulties.

3.4.3   Conversion

Besides being in breach of the agreement and liable for damages to the owner, the debtor may also be sued for conversion under Torts (Interference with Goods) Act 1977 s2(2). Conversion is the loss of goods which the debtor has allowed to happen in breach of his/her duty to the owner. To succeed in the claim the creditor would need to prove to the court that the debtor was guilty of a wilful act that interfered with the creditor's title and thus intended to deny that title or assert a right contrary to the creditor's. Selling to a third party is a clear example of this. An action could be commenced forthwith, the measure of damages being the value of the goods at the date of conversion plus any consequential damages. Judgment for specific restitution of the goods cannot be given where the sale passes title under Hire-Purchase Act 1964 s27(see 3.4.1).

An action in conversion may also be commenced against the purchaser. A complete defence is available for the innocent bona fide purchaser under HPA 1964 Part III. If such a defence fails the creditor can seek restitution or damages, with the latter the more likely redress. Only the lesser of the balance of the HP or conditional sale price or the value of the goods is recoverable (*Wickham Holdings Ltd v Brook House Motors* [1967] 1 All ER 117). The owner is not entitled to recover the goods by force from an innocent third party. Such an action would be trespass.[6]

6   See 2.5.10 regarding the sale of goods subject to unenforceable agreements.

CHAPTER 4

Time orders (ss129, 130 and 136)

Section 129(2)(a) permits the court, in some circumstances, to rewrite any consumer credit agreement, changing the amount of payments, their frequency and duration. Section 129 can be coupled with s136, which permits an agreement to be amended, eg, by a reduction or freeze in the rate of interest. The prime consideration will be what the debtor can afford, what is 'owed' and what is 'just'. Some courts have been reluctant to use these powers because of the controversy that has attached to secured loans (see below) and county courts have made many conflicting decisions. The Court of Appeal has now resolved some of the issues in question.

FIGURE 5: CCA 1974 ss129, 130, 135 AND 136

Time orders

129 (1) If it appears to the court just to do so –
(a) on an application for any enforcement order; or
(b) on an application made by a debtor or hirer under this paragraph after service on him of –
  (i) a default notice, or
  (ii) a notice under section 76(1) or 98(1); or
(c) in an action brought by a creditor or owner to enforce a regulated agreement or any security, or recover possession of any goods or land to which a regulated agreement relates,
the court may make an order under this section (a 'time order').
  (2) A time order shall provide for one or both of the following, as the court considers just –
(a) the payment by the debtor or hirer or any surety of any sum owed under a regulated agreement or a security by such instalments, payable at such times, as the court, having regard to the means of the debtor or hirer and any surety, considers reasonable;
(b) the remedying by the debtor or hirer of any breach of a regulated agreement (other than non-payment of money) within such period as the court may specify.

Figure 5 (cont)

Supplemental provisions about time orders

130 (1) Where in accordance with rules of court an offer to pay any sum by instalments is made by the debtor or hirer and accepted by the creditor or owner, the court may in accordance with rules of court make a time order under section 129 (2) (a) giving effect to the offer without hearing evidence of means.

(2) In the case of a hire-purchase or conditional sale agreement only, a time order under section 129 (2) (a) may deal with sums which, although not payable by the debtor at the time the order is made, would if the agreement continued in force become payable under it subsequently.

(3)–(6) [*Not reproduced.*]

Power to impose conditions, or suspend operation of order

135 (1) If it considers it just to do so, the court may in an order made by it in relation to a regulated agreement include provisions –
(a) making the operation of any term of the order conditional on the doing of specified acts by any party to the proceedings;
(b) suspending the operation of any term of the order either –
   (i) until such time as the court subsequently directs, or
   (ii) until the occurrence of a specified act or omission.

(2) The court shall not suspend the operation of a term requiring the delivery up of goods by any person unless satisfied that the goods are in his possession or control.

(3) In the case of a consumer hire agreement, the court shall not so use its powers under subsection (1) (b) as to extend the period for which, under the terms of the agreement, the hirer is entitled to possession of the goods to which the agreement relates.

(4) On the application of any person affected by a provision included under subsection (1), the court may vary the provision.

Power to vary agreements and securities

136 The court may in an order made by it under this Act include such provision as it considers just for amending any agreement or security in consequence of a term of the order.

4.1 Application

4.1.1 Applications for time orders

Time orders can be applied for by debtors in three situations:

– Following the service of a default notice under s87 (see 2.7.1), a calling-in notice under s76 (see 2.6.2) or a termination notice under s98 (see 2.7.2) (s129(1)(b)). Application is by way of originating application on court form N440 (see Figure 6 at p127) (CCR 1981 Ord 49 r4(5)) with a fee of £80. Prior to 15 January 1997 all county court fees were automatically waived for income support claimants and others could apply for waiver on the grounds of undue financial hardship due to exceptional circumstances. However, from 15 January 1997, the general provisions for the exemption and remission of county court fees have been abolished, with the only exemption remaining in respect of small claims actions and personal injury cases (below £1,000) for those in receipt of income support or other applicants where payment of the full fee would result in undue financial hardship, with a minimum fee of £10 payable in these circumstances (County Court Fees (Amendment) Order 1996 SI No 3189).

– Following the issue of proceedings by a creditor to enforce a regulated agreement, any security relating to it or to recover possession of any goods or land subject to a regulated agreement (s129(1)(c)). Application is on court form N244 (see Figure 7 at p130) with a fee of £20 payable. The court may also make a time order of its own motion in these circumstances.

– Following an application by a creditor for an enforcement order (see 2.5.10), eg, where an agreement is improperly executed (s129(1)(a)). Application will be on N244 with a fee of £20 payable and again the court has the power to make a time order of its own motion.

The terms of an order will depend primarily on the debtor's circumstances, what is 'owed' and what the court considers 'just', including consideration of the creditor's position and of the debtor's future prospects. Proposed payments should be based on the balance of essential expenditure on the financial statement after allowance for essential outgoings. Payment will also have to be negotiated with other priority creditors. If accruing interest would exceed or substantially absorb the proposed instalment, the rate will need to be varied, either by freezing it altogether, calculating a new rate that would effectively make the agreement interest only, or calculating a compromise rate, perhaps based on the bank base rate/building society rates, which allows the debtor to cover accruing interest and make some payments towards the principal owed. The court will also have to consider whether such an order is 'just', which will involve consideration of the creditor's position.

FIGURE 6: TIME ORDER ORIGINATING APPLICATION **N440**

IN THE   BIRMINGHAM   COUNTY COURT

Case no. 89/103105

IN THE MATTER OF AN APPLICATION FOR A TIME ORDER UNDER SECTION 129
OF THE CONSUMER CREDIT ACT 1974

Between _____ THOMAS TELFORD _____ Applicant
(insert your full name in block capitals)

and _____ SECURE LOANS LTD _____ Respondent
(insert the full name in block capitals of the company to whom you make your payments)

1. *I (Name)* THOMAS TELFORD

of *(Address)* 10 IRONBRIDGE ROAD

DAWLISH, WEST MIDLANDS

apply to the court for a time order under section
129 of the Consumer Credit Act 1974.

2. The following are the details of the regulated
agreement in respect of which I am asking for a
time order.

a. The agreement is dated   10 . 3. 88

and the reference number is   SL14761-WM

b. The names and addresses of the other parties
to the agreement are:

      SECURE LOANS LTD.
      HIGH STREET
      DAWLISH
      WEST MIDLANDS

c. The name and address of the person (if any)
who acted as surety

is   N/A

of

d. *(Delete if not applicable)* ~~The signed the~~
~~agreement was sent to me~~
~~at my address passed to me at specified~~
~~an XXXXXXXXXXX where the time when has XX~~
~~XXXX NONE XX XXXXXX XX XXXX XX XXXXr)~~

~~PXXXXXXXXs~~

e. I signed the agreement at *(here give the address of
the shop or other place where you signed the agreement)*

      SECURE LOANS LTD.
      HIGH STREET
      DAWLISH, WEST MIDLANDS

f. I agreed to pay instalments

of £ 165   ~~a week~~ [X]   a month [ ]

g. [ ]   The unpaid balance due under the

agreement is £ 3000

~~or XXXXXXXXXX XX XXXX XXX XXXXX XXXXXe~~

h. [ ]   I am £ 660   in arrears

with my payments

~~or XXXXXX XXXX XXX XXXX XXX XXXX XXX XXXXX~~
~~XX~~

N440. Notice of application for time order by debtor or hirer under Consumer Credit Act 1974 s. 129 before
     proceedings have been instituted by creditor. Order 49 Rule 4.

FIGURE 6 (CONT): TIME ORDER ORIGINATING APPLICATION N440

i. On   the Respondent served on
me:

- [X] a default notice

- [ ] a notice given under section 76(1)

- [ ] a notice given under section 98(1)

or I attach a copy of the notice which the
Respondent served on me on _____

j. *You should complete this section if you are applying for*
time to pay, if not cross it out.

My proposals for payment are £ 38.08 per
to clear the arrears (if any) and then by
instalments of £ _____

k. *You should complete this section if you have failed to*
comply with the agreement in any other respect.

I am in breach of the following provisions of the
agreement:

N/A

And my propsals for remedying the breach(es)
are as follows:

N/A

3. I have answered the questions about my
financial circumstances set out in the schedule to
this application.

4. The names and addresses of the persons to be
served with this application are: *(You must include*
any sureties)

SECURE LOANS LTD.
HIGH STREET
DAWLISH, WEST MIDLANDS

week and I request that under
Section 136 of the
Consumer Credit Act 1974
the court orders the
interest on the arrears to
be frozen to prevent it
accruing and increasing my
indebtedness further.

5. My address for service is:

10 IRONBRIDGE ROAD
DAWLISH
WEST MIDLANDS

6. Signed

(Solicitor for the) Applicant.

Dated

FIGURE 6 (CONT): TIME ORDER ORIGINATING APPLICATION N440

SCHEDULE

● please write in black ink

Case number	89/103105
in the BIRMINGHAM	County Court
Applicant	THOMAS TELFORD
Respondent	SECURE LOANS LTD.

1. What is your occupation?

ENGINEER

2. Your employer   Name

BRUNEL ENGINEERS

Address

COALBROOKDALE ROAD

BILSTON, WEST MIDLANDS

3. Money you receive *(give average weekly figures)*

Pay before deductions £ Please see attached financial statement

overtime, bonuses, fees, allowances, commissions

£

Usual take home pay £   pensions £

State benefits £   Other incomes £

Contributions from your household £

4. If anyone depends on you financially, give their names and ages including any children.

5. How much rent or mortgage should you pay?

£

Is this weekly ☐   or monthly ☐

6. How much do you actually pay? £

7. What rates should you pay? £

Is this weekly ☐   or monthly ☐

8. How much do you actually pay? £

9. Do you have to pay under any Court Orders? Please give details including name of court, case number, amount still owing and instalment you pay.

Please see attached schedule of debts

10. What other regular payments do you have to make (for credit, hire purchase etc?)

Please see attached financial statement and schedule of debts and proposed repayment programme

11. Give details of any other regular expenses you wish the court to take into account.

Please see attached financial statement, schedule of debts and proposed repayment programme

12. Are the goods in your possession?

Yes ☐   No ☐   N/A

I understand that if the plaintiff accepts my offer of payments by instalments the Court will make an order for the return of the goods but the plaintiff will not be able to enforce this order so long as I pay the instalments punctually.

FIGURE 7: TIME ORDER APPLICATION N244

Notice of Application

Plaintiff / defendant's address

Thomas Telford
10 Ironbridge Rd
Dawlish
West Midlands

In the	
BIRMINGHAM County Court	
Case no. 96/105103	
Warrant no. *(if applicable)*	
Plaintiff *(include Ref no.)* SECURE LOANS LTD	
Defendant THOMAS TELFORD	

State nature and grounds of application

I wish to apply for

A Time Order in respect of the above loan

When obtaining this loan on 10.03.88, I was working considerable and regular overtime, and my wife was working full time. Unfortunately, in the summer of 1993, my overtime ceased and I had periods of short time working. In addition, my wife had to reduce her hours of work considerably to look after one of our children who was (and still is) ill at home.

I have a first mortgage with the Salop Building Society, on which there are arrears of approximately £605. The Society has agreed to accept payment of these over a two year period.

My wife and I have unsecured creditors in excess of £7,000 and we hope to pay these accounts on an equitable pro-rata basis, and in order to do this, we require the Court's assistance in the matter of this application. I enclose a financial statement, a schedule of debts and a copy of the proposed re-payment programme.

I would therefore respectfully ask the court that I be allowed to continue making the monthly contractual payment of £165, and also request that, under section 136 of the Consumer Credit Act 1974, the Court considers varying the agreement between the Plaintiffs and myself to freeze the interest charges that are accruing on the outstanding arrears in order that my indebtedness is not further increased whilst I continue to make the above mentioned contractual payments under the agreement.

Signed ... *Thomas Telford* ... Plaintiff / Defendant   Dated 06.03.96

Address for   10 Ironbridge Rd, Dawlish, West Midlands

service ....

This section to be completed by the court

To the plaintiff / defendant
Take notice that this application will be heard by the District judge / Judge

at

on   **at**   **o'clock**

If you do not attend the Court will make such order that it thinks fit

The court office at
33 BULL STREET, BIRMINGHAM B4 6DS,
is open from 10am to 4pm Monday to Friday. When corresponding with the courts please address forms or letters to the Chief Clerk and quote the case number

N244 Notice of application. Order 13 Rule 1 (2)

4.1.2   Effects of time orders

During the currency of time orders, a creditor cannot, without prejudice to any action taken before the order is made, take any steps to terminate the agreement, recover possession of any land or goods, treat any right conferred on the debtor as terminated, restricted or deferred, or enforce any security (s130(5)(a)).

4.1.3   Default following a time order

Where a debtor defaults on the payment of instalments ordered under s129(2)(a) following the making of a time order, the creditor can issue execution for the sum remaining unpaid, or for part of it, as long as the sum is £50 or more, the amount of one monthly instalment or four weekly instalments, whichever is the greater. Execution can be prevented by the debtor tendering the arrears prior to the issue of the warrant, in which case the time order continues in force (see CCR 1981 Ord 25, r13(5)).

Where a time order has been combined with a conditional or suspended return order, default entitles the creditor to execute immediately if the order was suspended under s135(1)(b)(ii) and expressed to be until default in payment, but will require order of the court if made under s135(1)(b)(i), ie, until such time as the court shall direct.

4.1.4   Variation and revocation

A time order may be varied or revoked by the court on application of any party affected by it (s130(b)).[1]

4.2   Unsecured agreements

Time orders may be made for such agreements but in practice their utility will be limited, as advisers will often be able to negotiate similar terms, and any enforcement by default action should produce an order to repay the debt at an affordable rate with interest automatically frozen, ie, the same result. Time orders may, however, be useful where a creditor has issued a default notice but has not commenced court action and is meanwhile refusing to negotiate, allowing interest

---

1 It should be noted that as a time order is not a 'judgment', it may be useful for those particularly concerned about having judgments registered against them, eg, where employment may be at risk. It is likely, however, that any default will be notified to credit reference agencies.

to accrue. This has been successfully achieved on a number of occasions.

4.3   HP agreements

There is no doubt that time orders may be used to reschedule HP agreements. This will be particularly useful when applying for a conditional (eg, suspended) return order to prevent repossession of HP goods. The court may need to be satisfied that the goods in question are essential to the debtor, eg, a car is necessary for work, in order to grant this relief (see 3.3).

The reason that the court's ability to change fundamentally the terms of the agreement is not in doubt is to be found in s130(2) (see Figure 5 at p125) This permits existing arrears and future instalments to be 'rolled up' and rescheduled. Calculating this is not problematic as, being a fixed-sum agreement, at any point in time it is possible to calculate exactly how much has been paid and how much is due.

4.4   Second mortgages

The controversy and debate about time orders has focused upon secured loans. There were two schools of thought as to the effect of time orders on secured agreements.

4.4.1   *Arrears only*

One view was that time orders were only able to give a debtor more time to pay arrears due on a loan. There is no doubt that this was the minimum the court could do. The court has jurisdiction under County Courts Act 1984 s21 in possession proceedings brought by first mortgagees. It may make possession orders, suspended on terms of repayment of the arrears, using the powers granted by Administration of Justice Act 1970 s36, as amended by Administration of Justice Act 1973 s8. However, County Courts Act 1984 s21(9) states that this section does not apply to regulated agreements. Consequently, in order to make a suspended possession order, the court would have to exercise alternative powers. These are to be found at ss129 and s135 (see Figure 5 at p124). Some district judges felt this is all a time order could do. One reported case in particular was quoted to support this.

Ashbroom Facilities v Bodley [1992] CCLR 31: A registrar in Birmingham County Court suspended a possession warrant and made a time order rescheduling the debt over 15 years at an APR of 20.5%, reduced from 35.3%, which was regarded as being too high considering the security. On appeal by the plaintiffs the judge ordered that the previous judgment be set aside, the time order being dismissed and the possession warrant allowed to proceed. The judge stated that a time order must refer to sums actually owing, ie, arrears at the time the matter comes before the court. It was held that the court's only power was to make an instalment order relating to those arrears, if it considers it just to do so, and that s136 in those circumstances gave no authority for the rewriting of the agreement.

4.4.2   Re-scheduling the loan

The alternative interpretation of s129 suggested that a radical rewrite of the whole loan was permitted. The arguments for and against this reading hinged upon the interpretation of the phrase 'any sum owed' in s129(2)(a). Clearly, on the restrictive view, the phrase would be limited to the arrears due at the date of application. Advisers argued, however, that this was too narrow a view that failed to acknowledge the situation in which the application would arise. The creditor will be endeavouring to enforce the security to recover the outstanding balance. A default notice is issued for the arrears, but if these are not paid within the specified period, an action is commenced to obtain possession of the property, which is then sold to clear the whole debt. A number of decisions supported this argument.

Cedar Holdings v Jenkins [1988] CCLR 34: A time order had been made, reducing monthly payments and the rate of interest payable, so as to make the agreement, in effect, interest only. Cedar Holdings appealed on the grounds that it was wrong in law as the court did not have the power to vary the interest rate. It was held that there had been no error in law and that s129, together with s136, gave the court the necessary powers.[2]

First National Bank plc v Syed [1991] 2 All ER 250, CA: The Syeds, who were unrepresented, appealed an order made by the county court judge dismissing their appeal against a possession order made on their home in Dulwich. The defendants had a second charge with First National Bank but fell into arrears after Mr Syed was made redundant. Possession proceedings were begun for the full balance of

---

2   In this case the agreement stated that the whole loan, plus interest, would fall due on default. Cedar Holdings had issued a default notice for arrears and followed with a final demand for the whole balance.

the loan including interest, which had fallen due on default under the terms of the agreement. The original order had been suspended to allow the Syeds to reduce their arrears but they were unable to pay being in receipt of income support. Consequently, the suspension lapsed and the application for a further suspension was refused.

Giving judgment in the Court of Appeal, Dillon LJ observed 'the remedy of a time order . . . would seem to be directed at rescheduling the whole of the indebtedness under the regulated agreement, the principal which has presently become payable as a result of default as well as the arrears and current interest'. In the event he felt that the Syeds had no prospect of being able to make any payments and because the court, in deciding whether or not it is just to make an order, must give consideration to the creditor's position, a time order was refused.

National Guardian Mortgage Corp Ltd v Wilkes [1993] CCLR 1; (1991) October *Legal Action* 16: Ms Wilkes took out a loan of £12,000 at 40.28% APR, the monthly instalment being £316.67. She fell behind and a default notice was issued in July 1990, followed by possession proceedings later that year. With interest, the total balance due rose to £19,890.03. The most that Ms Wilkes could afford to pay was £250 per month. A deputy district judge made a time order under s129 and an order under s136, reducing her payments to £200 towards interest, the rate of which was reduced accordingly, and £50 towards capital. This was upheld on appeal.

4.4.3   Reducing the rate of interest

Further difficulties arose in relation to the court's powers under s136 to amend agreements by reducing (or freezing) interest following the making of a time order reducing payments under s129(2)(a).

A broad interpretation of the powers available under s136 was taken in a number of cases, including *Jenkins* and *Wilkes* (above) where the rate of interest was reduced. Other cases, however, took a narrower approach, some taking the view that it was not the 'intention' that the section should permit the writing of the agreement and that if this was the intention it would make the extortionate credit provisions of ss137–140 'otiose' or irrelevant.

Advisers should, therefore, when applying for repayments to be rescheduled and interest rates to be varied also, where appropriate, consider making an application for the agreement to be reopened under the extortionate credit provisions on an 'and/or' basis. See also 4.11.3.

4.4.4   Interim time orders

It is not infrequent at hearings of time order applications for creditors to request adjournments in order to prepare legal arguments to oppose debtors' applications or because there are procedural errors. This can have the effect of exacerbating the indebtedness of borrowers who, by applying for relief, have already admitted to financial difficulties and their inability to pay the loans which are the subject of the applications.

This was the position in *J & J Securities Ltd v Ewart & Ewart* (1993) unreported, 3 June, Blackpool CC. The defendants borrowed £6,983 over seven years at an APR of 31.5% with instalments of £190.80 per month. Arrears of £1,327.20 accrued and possession proceedings were issued even though payments of £30.00 per week had been made. The defendants applied for a time order. An application by the plaintiffs for an adjournment was opposed by the defendants on the grounds that they would be prejudiced because of the increasing arrears and high rate of interest, and in the case of the adjournment being granted, the defendants requested an interim order rescheduling payments at £30.00 per week and amending the agreement by reducing the interest rate to 10.5% APR. Granting the plaintiff's application for an adjournment, the district judge refused to make an interim time order but directed that the benefit of any future order granted would take effect from the date of the first hearing, ie, would be retrospective. Although this case was eventually dealt with by the Court of Appeal (see 4.10.2) no comment was made on the 'interim' issue.

4.5   Time orders – a definitive decision?

The application and scope of time orders was finally considered in detail by the Court of Appeal in *Southern District Finance v Barnes* [1995] CCLR 62; (1995) *Times*, 19 April, CA, heard together with appeals in the cases of *Ewart v J & J Securities* and *Equity Home Loans v Lewis* (see above).

The court ruled on the general legal position and on its application to the three individual cases with leave to appeal refused by both the Court of Appeal and the House of Lords. Four main points were under consideration:

– the meaning of 'any sum owed' in s129;
– whether there is any power under s136 to amend an agreement and

vary the rate of interest following the making of a time order under
s129;
– what is 'just';
– whether a rebate for early settlement should be taken into account
under the Consumer Credit (Rebate on Early Settlement) Regulations 1983 SI No 1562.

4.6 'Any sum owed'

It was argued that to 'be owed' a sum does not mean it has to be
immediately payable and submitted that 'any sum owed under a
security' extended to the whole outstanding balance under a
mortgage.

4.6.1   Effects of s130(2) – HP agreements

The effect of s130(2), which provides that in relation to HP and conditional sale agreements only, a time order can be made in relation to
'sum not yet payable' (see Figure 5 at p125), was considered. The
court in the *Barnes* case rejected the argument that s130(2) should be
interpreted to treat loans or credit sale agreements in the same way as
HP or conditional sale agreements. It was held that s130(2) is
expressly limited to HP and conditional sale agreements and that the
section would not be 'necessary if orders relating to sums not yet
payable could in any event be made in respect of all types of regulated
agreements'. In other words, time orders cannot be made in non-HP/
conditional sale agreement cases in relation to sums not yet payable,
ie, sums not yet owed or due.

4.6.2   Non-HP agreements

In relation to non-HP/conditional sale cases, it was held that 'any sum
owed' means any sum which the lender is entitled to recover by action.
'Any sum owed must mean a sum which is due and payable as a
matter of law in the sense that it could be sued for without further
ado. If the full loan has not been called in, nothing but the outstanding arrears is owed' (*Barnes* case).

4.6.3   Terms of the agreement and wording of default notice

In the absence of a creditor specifically calling a loan in (or taking possession proceedings, see below), the wording of a default notice and the agreement itself should be considered.

The terms of an agreement may specifically provide for the whole loan to become repayable automatically on default and, providing a default notice has been served, it can be argued that a separate calling in is not necessary and that the whole outstanding balance is now owed as it could be sued for without ado (see *Syed* above at 4.4.2): 'The remedy of a time order ... would seem to be directed at rescheduling the whole indebtedness under the regulated agreement, the principal which has become presently payable as a result of default' (*Barnes* case).

Whether or not there is an automatic accelerated payment clause in an agreement, the specific wording of a default notice should be checked. If the notice demands repayment of the whole outstanding balance and/or specifies that the whole loan becomes repayable where the default cannot be remedied, ie, the arrears paid within the specified time, then it may be possible to argue that the creditor is in a position to sue for the whole outstanding balance and, therefore, the court is in a position to treat the whole balance as owed and reschedule its repayment.

4.6.4   *Possession proceedings taken*

Where possession proceedings have been taken by a creditor, regardless of whether the loan has been specifically called in, 'any sum owed' will be the whole outstanding balance due under the agreement.

> An application for an order for possession is an exercise by the creditor of the right to realise the whole indebtedness secured by the charge on the property. As a matter of law as well as of common sense, when a creditor brings a possession action he demands payment of the whole sum outstanding under the charge. (*Barnes* case)

4.6.5   *Summary*

Thus, where a secured lender takes a possession action following default under a secured regulated agreement, the court will have the power under s129, in so far as it considers it just, to reschedule repayment of the whole outstanding balance of a loan.

Where a default notice has been served and the whole loan specifically terminated and/or called in, again the court will have the power to reschedule the whole outstanding balance under the loan.

Where, however, a default notice has been served but the loan has not been specifically terminated and called in, in the absence of possession proceedings, the court will only be able to reschedule the repayment of arrears, unless, as discussed at 4.6.1, there is an automatic accelerated payment clause in the agreement, or perhaps the default notice relates to the whole outstanding balance and states that the loan becomes due if the default is not remedied.

4.6.6 Delaying a time order application

Although the court may perhaps look more favourably and sympathetically on a debtor who makes an originating application to the court rather than waiting until a creditor starts proceedings, in circumstances of doubt, advisers may wish to wait until possession proceedings have been issued to ensure that the court will be able to reschedule payment of the whole outstanding balance owed, although where there is such a delay, there will often be problems of accruing arrears and increasing indebtedness between the service of the default notice and the issue of proceedings. However, given the clear statement of the courts' powers once possession proceedings have been issued, advisers may be in a stronger position to negotiate concessions from lenders by way of agreed reduced payments and/or reductions in rates of interest prior to the issue of possession proceedings.

4.7 Power to vary agreements under s136

It was argued before the Court of Appeal in the *Barnes* case (above) that s136 gave no power to rewrite agreements because these powers were contained in the extortionate credit provisions of ss137–140, and that these would be otiose if agreements could be rewritten in any event by the combined use of ss129 and 136. The counter-argument was that this was not the case because the extortionate credit provisions are not restricted to regulated agreements, as are the time order provisions, and that the extortionate credit provisions can be invoked at any time, whereas time orders are only operative following default. It could have also been argued that the extortionate credit provisions can operate retrospectively whereas time orders cannot.

4.7.1 In consequence

While no comment was made on these arguments, it was held that 'unless the contemplated amendment is truly a consequence of a term of the time order, and the making of it is also just, there is no power to make it' (*Barnes* case).

Thus, it appears that where the court has decided to make a time order and it is necessary, in order to make that order effective in giving relief to the indebted borrower, the court can also amend an agreement where and insofar as it considers it just. 'If a time order is made when the sum owed is the whole outstanding balance due under the loan, there will inevitably be consequences for the term of the loan or for the rate of interest, or both' (*Barnes* case). If, therefore, a reduction in contractual interest is necessary to make the relief of a time order to reduce payment of benefit to the debtor, it will be 'in consequence' of that order.

4.7.2   Accruing interest and s136 applications

Following default, interest will usually be accruing on arrears. It will often be the case that following the termination and/or calling in of a loan the whole balance will be 'in arrears' with default interest accruing on it. Where this is the case the court should be requested to permit interest to accrue only on the arrears of instalments before the matter came before the court. The difficulties of allowing interest to accrue on the whole balance should be drawn to the court's attention; on what balance and at what time should interest be calculated as the amount owed is reduced by a debtor's payments? It should also be pointed out that where the whole balance is payable it will already include the full interest due under the agreement and that to allow interest on that balance would include 'interest on interest' and be unjust.

In any event, advisers will have to assess the necessity for an application under s136. It should be argued that it will be necessary and 'in consequence' of a time order reducing payment where accruing interest exceeds, equals or substantially absorbs that payment. In these circumstances the time order will be ineffective and of little or no benefit to the debtor where the debt will increase, become in effect an interest-only loan or result in repayment of the debt being extended for an unreasonable period of time.

In appropriate circumstances, for example where substantial amounts have already been paid in interest, especially where a high rate has been charged, advisers should consider asking the court to freeze any further interest (see *Lewis* at 4.10.3). An interest freeze may also be appropriate where the debtor's circumstances justify it, ie, where the debtor cannot afford to pay it (see also 4.11.4).

4.8   Justice/judicial control

> When a time order is applied for, or a possession order is sought . . . the court must first consider whether it is just to make a time order. That will involve consideration of all the circumstances of the case, and of the position of the creditor as well as that of the debtor. (*Barnes* case)

4.8.1   *Relevant matters*

The court should, therefore, consider all relevant matters, and in considering the issues that the court may deem important it is useful to look back at previous (and often unreported) county court cases which illustrate different situations which advisers may encounter and how these have been dealt with by the courts.

Conduct of the debtor
Whether the loan application was truthful and whether the debtor was feckless or foolish in taking out the loan.   'In my judgment, it is very important to keep in perspective the merits of the case . . . I form the view that the defendants were very foolish . . . (and) . . . wrongly completed the loan application and an order which led to the arrears increasing would be unjust' (*Ashbroom Facilities v Bodeley* [1992] CCLR 31).

Whether the debtor had taken on further commitments.   'It seems to me to be an extraordinary situation that after a freely negotiated mortgage, a defendant is allowed, perhaps after taking on further obligations and increasing payments due out of the household budget, to come along to the court and say "I cannot now pay the amount I agreed to pay, but I would be able to pay something under the agreement provided that the rate of interest was reduced to a figure that fitted with my ability to pay"' (*First National Bank v Holgate* (1989) unreported, 30 October, Nelson CC).

History of default, debtor's circumstances and prospects for improvement.   'I cannot think it is just, in the circumstances of this case, and in the light in particular of the fairly long history of default and merely sporadic payments on the defendants' behalf, and of the absence of realistic, as opposed to merely speculative, prospects of improvement in the debtors' finances, to require the plaintiff to accept instalments that the defendants can afford, when those will be too little even to keep down the accruing interest on the defendants' account' (Dillion LJ, *First National Bank v Syed* [1991] 2 All ER 250, CA – see also 4.8.2).

The lack of blame attached to the debtor. 'Section 129 makes it clear that the test is subjective and in looking at the defendant's position I note that she found herself in this position as a result of the breakdown of her marriage and the tardiness of the DSS . . . this is not a case where the defendant has closed her eyes to the situation' (*Cedar Holdings v Kench* (1992) unreported, 6 July, Bow CC). 'She is a lady who has clearly made every effort to see that her obligations are covered by insurance and there is some suggestion . . . that these arrears accrued when her claim was being considered by the insurers. I consider it just in view of the fact that Mrs Thompson was made redundant, that she has not been able to obtain a job with sufficient income to repay all her outgoings including those now paid by the insurance company, to vary the rate of interest' (*Cedar Holdings v Thompson* (1991) unreported, 20 September, Croydon CC).

Balance of interest between the parties
'The court must exercise its discretion judicially and must take account of the interests of both the creditor and the debtor; the extent to which an exercise of the power does work or is capable of working an injustice to one or the other and, if necessary, balancing the relative potential injustices the one against the other' (*First National Bank v Colman* [1994] CCLR 39, CC). 'In comparison (to losing her home), the proposed order is only a small loss for the plaintiff, that is accruing interest on £1,619.25 for eight or nine years' (*Cedar Holdings v Kench* (above)). See also *Syed* (above) and *Ewart v J & J Securities Ltd* at 4.10.2, in which the Court of Appeal approved an order which 'struck a balance'.

Justice and extortionate credit
'It cannot be just to arbitrarily reduce the rate of interest to coincide with what the defendant can afford . . . the extortionate credit provisions would be completely and utterly irrelevant if a court could do what this defendant is asking me to do' (*First National Bank v Holgate* (above)). 'It would in my mind be completely unjust to a creditor if it were a correct construction of s136 that the court may vary the rate of interest without having regard to the constraints set out in s138' (*Hursthanger v Semakula* (1991) unreported, Bow CC (see also 4.10.3)).

Conduct of the lender
See the comments made on the rate of interest charged in *Equity Home Loans Ltd v Lewis* at 4.10.3).

The court should also be aware of situations where a creditor has been intransigent in negotiations, especially when initially approached by a debtor or money adviser.

The extent to which a proposed order would change the contractual position of the parties
See *Barnes v Southern & District Finance plc* at 4.10.1, *Ewart v J & J Securities Ltd* at 4.10.2 and *Equity Home Loans Ltd v Lewis* at 4.10.3.

Interest rates, payments made and timescale
The length of time that a debtor has been paying interest, the rate of interest charged (as above) and the amount that has already been paid under the agreement may also be factors. It is perhaps unlikely that a court will see it as just to make a time order under s129 and reduce the rate of interest under s136 where a debtor has defaulted shortly after entering an agreement unless it can be shown that these are exceptional circumstances. See also 4.11.3 and 4.11.5.

4.8.2   Temporary financial difficulties

> When a time order is made it should normally be for a stipulated period on account of temporary financial difficulty. If, despite the giving of time, the debtor is unlikely to be able to resume payment of the total indebtedness by at least the amount of the contractual instalments, no order should be made. In such cases it is more equitable to allow the regulated agreement to be enforced. (*Barnes* case)

The idea that orders are only appropriate in circumstances of temporary financial difficulties introduces a new problem for borrowers seeking relief which was touched upon in *Syed*, where a time order was refused, *inter alia*, because there was no realistic prospect of the debtor's circumstances improving and/or the debtors being able to make any payments (see 4.4.2). No guidance was given as to the circumstances in which orders could be made for indefinite periods, or to the meaning of 'temporary' in terms of appropriate time periods. It was also not made clear whether debtors will have to show that there is a positive and realistic expectation of their circumstances improving, whether creditors will have to show that there are no such expectations, or whether debtors may be given 'the benefit of the doubt' and allowed temporary relief in the hope that their circumstances improve. It would seem to be the case, however, that where it can be seen that there is little evidence of a possible improvement in circumstances (eg, long-term unemployment, disability or sickness) time orders are unlikely to be seen as 'just' to the creditor.

The linking of time orders to temporary stipulated periods based on temporary difficulties will mean that time orders cannot now 'normally' be seen as a long-term solution to reduced ability to make payments equivalent to contractual instalments.

It is also not clear what the scope of 'normally' is, and it is interesting to note that in two of the cases under appeal, time orders were apparently made without any indication that the borrowers' circumstances were likely to improve. In *Equity Home Loans v Lewis* (see 4.10.3), the borrower's serious illness and the excessive rate of interest charged may have led the court to decide that it was not a 'normal' case, but it is difficult to find any such circumstances in the *Ewart v J & J Securities* (see 4.10.2). In *Barnes* (see 4.10.1) the order was for a specified and limited period but there was no discussion of any likely improvement in circumstances.

It may be open to advisers, perhaps with a little imagination, to argue that the particular circumstances of their borrowers do not fall into the category of 'normal' cases.

4.9   Early settlement rebates

The issue of where a time order is made, whether the order should be in relation to the outstanding balance subject to an early settlement rebate, arose in *Equity Home Loans v Lewis* (see 4.10.3). The Consumer Credit (Rebate on Early Settlement) Regulations 1983 SI No 1562 reg 2(1) states:

> Subject to the following provisions of these Regulations, the creditor shall allow to the debtor under a regulated consumer credit agreement a rebate at least equal to that calculated in accordance with the following provisions of these Regulations whenever early settlement takes place, that is to say whenever, under section 94 of the Act, on refinancing, on breach of the agreement, or for any other reason, the indebtedness of the debtor is discharged or becomes payable before the time fixed by the agreement, or any such becomes payable by him before the time so fixed.

It was argued that under this regulation, a rebated figure should be used when determining the extent of a borrower's indebtedness when making a time order rescheduling payment of the whole outstanding balance under the loan following breach of the agreement by the debtor.

4.9.1   *Forward Trust v Whymark*

However, following *Forward Trust v Whymark* [1990] 2 QB 670; [1989] 3 All ER 915; [1989] 3 WLR 1229, CA, it was held that while the Early Settlement Regs fix entitlement to a rebate 'the amount of rebate allowable is ascertained by reference to the settlement date, the date on which the debtor pays the sum by which early settlement is actually effected and total indebtedness is actually discharged'.

4.9.2   *Conclusion*

Therefore, when making a time order, early settlement rebates should be disregarded. 'In the unlikely event of a person who has been obliged to apply for a time order proving able to pay off the debt prematurely, any rebate to which he is entitled will no doubt be automatically accorded to him by the creditor' (*Barnes* case).

4.10   The cases under appeal

Having considered the general legal position, the Court of Appeal looked at the three individual cases under appeal.

4.10.1   *Barnes v Southern & District Finance plc*

Following default, arrears of £1,300 and a default notice in respect of those arrears, possession proceedings were issued. Although dismissing the application for a time order, on the grounds that the default notice only related to arrears, the assistant recorder suspended possession for 12 months on a reduced monthly payment of £150 (as opposed to a contractual payment of £260), but declined to reduce the rate of interest on the grounds that s136 could not be used to alter obligations under the agreement. A review date was set for reconsideration of the instalment order.

The Court of Appeal held that the assistant recorder was incorrect in finding that s129 could only relate to arrears and wrongly concluded that s136 did not empower him to alter the rate of interest.

> It would have been a proper exercise of discretion, in order to mitigate the impact of interest on the unpaid instalments, to reduce the monthly rate of interest from 1.952% per month to 1% during the period of the suspension of the possession order.

4.10.2   *Ewart v J & J Securities Ltd*

Following default on monthly instalments of £190.80 under an agreement charging monthly interest of 2.31%, a default notice was served and a calling-in letter sent in relation to arrears of £572.40. Subsequently, a second default notice was served and a second calling-in letter sent in relation to arrears of £1,327.20. Possession proceedings were then taken. Following the making of a time order by a district judge reducing monthly payments from £198.80 to £150 and an order reducing monthly interest from 2.31% to 2%, an appeal was allowed and a 28-day possession order made. It appeared that the judge only considered s136, taking the view that an order varying the contractual interest rate would not be consequential to a time order but was 'on the facts of the case a prerequisite of a time order in that any time order would be nugatory if the contractual rate of interest was not reduced', also stating that it would not be just.

The Court of Appeal held that the judge's approach was incorrect. The judge should have started by asking whether it would be just to make a time order. 'The order made by the DJ would have had the effect of delaying receipt of the money by the lenders by about a year, which does not seem unreasonable'. The judge 'only considered whether it would be just to amend the rate of interest, and did not consider the amount of instalments'. It was held that the DJ's original order 'struck a balance'. The appeal was, therefore, allowed and the original order restored.[3]

4.10.3   *Equity Homes Loan Ltd v Lewis*

The borrower defaulted on a loan of £4,000, repayable over 15 years by 180 monthly instalments of £105.56, at monthly interest of 2.72% (APR 44.1%). A default notice was served and possession proceedings taken with arrears standing at £680.49. An application for a time order was rejected by a district judge, but the defendant's appeal was allowed and a time order made for the payment of the outstanding balance of £16,994.94 by six instalments of £25 and 174 instalments of £96.81. It was also ordered that no further interest should be charged.

The Court of Appeal took the view that the facts of the case were

---

3 No reference was made in this case to the need for a time order to be for only a stipulated period in relation to temporary financial difficulties. Perhaps it was considered just in any event as the repayment period was extended by only 12 months as a result of the time order, but this was not discussed.

'extreme, with the loan bordering on the extortionate, although that was not alleged'. When the judge rescheduled the instalments due under the agreement, he did so over a fresh period of 15 years. The original loan having been taken out in 1991, since when nearly three years had passed since the agreement had been made, this had the effect of extending the agreement to 18 years.

> The judge reduced the rate of interest to nil, since otherwise throughout the extended period of the loan interest would have been payable on the arrears at the exorbitant rate prescribed, and that would have defeated the purpose of giving time. In effect as a sanction for non-payment of instalments a suspended possession order was substituted for a penal rate of interest. Though the judge's methods were robust and his reasoning economical, his instincts were sound and his order just.

Here, the Court of Appeal specifically sanctioned as just an order under s136 freezing any accruing interest following the making of a time order. Clearly, the court's view of the high rate of interest charged was a major factor.[4]

Advisers should note the comments as to extortionate credit, remember the effect high interest rates may have on a court's view of the justice of an instalment reduction and of any interest rate reduction and, where interest rates may be seen to be well above average levels, plead extortionate credit in addition to and as an alternative to a request for a time order. This was done in *J & J Securities v Yeatman* (1993) 36 *Adviser* 27; (1993) January *Legal Action* 24, CC, although it is unclear on what basis the decision in that case was made.

4.11   Conclusions

4.11.1   'Any sum owed'

'Any sum owed' will be the whole outstanding balance due under a

---

4   Again, as in *Ewart v J & J Securities Ltd*, no mention was made of the need for a time order to be restricted to a stipulated period in relation to a borrower's temporary financial difficulties. Perhaps it was not considered a 'normal' case due to the 'penal' or 'exorbitant' rate of interest charged, the very large sum (£19,000) required to repay a relatively small loan (£4,000), and the borrower's personal circumstances of serious ill health.

'Obiter' comments were made in relation to the APR of 44.1% charged by Equity Homes Loan Ltd. It was stated that this 'must have bordered on the extortionate', with the borrower having to repay £19,000 over 15 years in order to borrow £4,000, and later described as both 'extortionate' and 'penal'. No ruling could be made on whether the loan was extortionate, however, as this had not been alleged by the borrower.

loan where the loan has been specifically terminated and called in or where possession proceedings have been taken.

Where the loan has not been called in and no possession proceedings have been taken, unless perhaps there is an automatic accelerated payment clause in the agreement (4.6.3), 'any sum owed' will only be arrears. In these circumstances, the court will only be able to make a time order rescheduling arrears, unless the case involves an HP agreement (s130(2) and see 4.3).

4.11.2   Debtor's means

Whether the time order application relates to the whole outstanding balance or only arrears, the court must consider what instalments would be reasonable, both as to amount and timing, having regard to the means of the debtor.

4.11.3   The justice of a time order

The court must also consider whether it is just to make a time order rescheduling payments, including giving consideration to the creditor's position. In doing this the court is likely to consider, *inter alia*:

- the extent to which an order would alter obligations entered under the agreement, eg, by how much would contractual payments be reduced and/or by how long would the period of the loan be extended;
- the conduct of the debtor(s);
- the conduct of the lender, including the rate of interest charged, whether a high rate can be justified, whether a high rate has already taken into account the risk that difficulties in repayment might occur, the length of time the debtor has been paying at a high rate of interest and the amount that has already been repaid;
- whether it is a 'normal' case, whether the debtor's financial difficulties are temporary, whether there is any prospect of circumstances improving, and/or whether there is any reason why long-term relief should be considered appropriate;
- the relative effect on the parties of making/not making the order.

See also 4.8.1.

4.11.4   Amending an agreement in consequence of a time order

Where a time order has been made reducing monthly instalments, it will be necessary for the court to consider whether it is necessary to reduce the rate of interest to give the debtor effective relief.

A reduction in the interest rate is likely to be 'in consequence' of a time order where otherwise interest would accrue at a rate faster than the rescheduled payments. It would be a minimum requirement to reduce the interest rate so that interest equalled the reduced payment, ie, to make the loan effectively 'interest only'. It would, however, be preferable for the rate to be reduced sufficiently so as to allow the new reduced instalment to cover both accruing interest and repay some of the principal, or to freeze interest completely (see also 4.7.2 and 4.11.6).

4.11.5   The justice of reducing the rate of interest

Where a time order has been made rescheduling and reducing monthly payments and a reduction in the rate of interest is seen to be necessary to make the relief effective, the court must consider whether it is just to make such an amendment, including consideration of the creditor's position. The court is likely to consider:

- the rate of interest charged by the creditor under the agreement: the more 'exorbitant' or 'penal' that it seems to be, the more likely that a reduction will be seen as just;
- the period of time that the debtor has been paying under the agreement, the amount by which the creditor will have already 'profited' from the interest chargeable and the amount the borrower has already paid;
- the length of time before the outstanding balance will be discharged, eg, is the creditor's receipt of the money only being delayed for a comparatively short period (see *Ewart v J & J Securities* at 4.10.2) and to what extent will an extended period of repayment result in an increased amount of total interest payable, albeit at a lower monthly rate over a longer period?;
- to what extent are the terms of the contract to be varied;
- the relative effect on the parties of making/not making an order;
- whether it is a 'normal' case, whether the debtor's financial difficulties are temporary and whether there is any realistic prospect of circumstances improving.

See also 4.8.1.

4.11.6   *Rescheduling of arrears*

Where it is only the repayment of arrears that is at issue, ie, the debtor is in a position to meet the amount of contractual payments and something towards arrears, it is clear that where this cannot be successfully negotiated with the lender the court can make a time order rescheduling repayment of those arrears. In these circumstances there will be no issue as to the meaning of 'any sum owed' and an originating application should be issued as soon as a default notice has been served where negotiations are proving unsuccessful.

Where this results in interest accruing on arrears faster than they can be repaid, or where interest substantially absorbs the debtor's payment, it will be necessary to apply for the interest to be reduced or frozen under s136 (see 4.7.2).

CHAPTER 5

Extortionate credit

As noted in Chapter 1, the history of credit legislation in England has featured a continued conviction that there should be a statutory limit on the rate of interest that it is permissible to charge. Although the level was usually low, the most recent ceiling was 48% under Moneylenders Act 1927 s10. Anything over this figure was prima facie 'harsh and unconscionable' under Moneylenders Act 1900 s1 and could be corrected by the court. These provisions were, however, of limited efficacy because borrowers often did not pursue their rights, the Acts were limited to money lending agreements and, although the onus lay with lenders to refute the accusation, they could usually justify the cost on the grounds of the risk, size of loan, etc.

The Crowther Committee recommended keeping the 48% cap but extending the coverage to all credit bargains (Crowther Report, Cmnd 4596, HMSO, para 6.6.9). The CCA 1974 extended applicability to all credit granted to individuals but abandoned any specific limit. The effect, as will be seen, has been to make it very difficult to determine accurately which agreements are extortionate.

5.1 Consumer Credit Act provisions

Sections 137 and 139 of the Act provide the definition of extortionate credit bargains and the court's powers in such cases (see Figure 8).

The phrase 'harsh and unconscionable' has been replaced with 'extortionate'. This is either a bargain which is 'grossly exorbitant' in respect of payments required (s138(1)(a)) or which 'otherwise grossly contravenes ordinary principles of fair dealing' (s138(1)(b)). Factors to consider to assist in reaching a conclusion are provided for the court. The provisions apply to *all* credit agreements, not just those regulated by the CCA 1974 but all others where an individual is provided by a creditor with any amount of credit. Consequently

---

FIGURE 8: CCA 1974 ss137–139

Extortionate credit bargains

137 (1) If the court finds a credit bargain extortionate it may reopen the credit agreement so as to do justice between the parties.

(2) In this section and sections 138 to 140, –

(a) 'credit agreement' means any agreement between an individual (the 'debtor') and any other person (the 'creditor') by which the creditor provides the debtor with credit of any amount, and

(b) 'credit bargain' –

  (i) where no transaction other than the credit agreement is to be taken into account in computing the total charge for credit, means the credit agreement, or

  (ii) where one or more other transactions are to be so taken into account, means the credit agreement and those other transactions, taken together.

When bargains are extortionate

138 (1) A credit bargain is extortionate if it –

(a) requires the debtor or a relative of his to make payments (whether unconditionally, or on certain contingencies) which are grossly exorbitant, or

(b) otherwise grossly contravenes ordinary principles of fair dealing.

(2) In determining whether a credit bargain is extortionate, regard shall be had to such evidence as is adduced concerning –

(a) interest rates prevailing at the time it was made,

(b) the factors mentioned in subsections (3) to (5), and

(c) any other relevant considerations.

(3) Factors applicable under subsection (2) in relation to the debtor include –

(a) his age, experience, business capacity and state of health; and

(b) the degree to which, at the time of making the credit bargain, he was under financial pressure, and the nature of that pressure.

(4) Factors applicable under subsection (2) in relation to the creditor include –

(a) the degree of risk accepted by him, having regard to the value of any security provided;

(b) his relationship to the debtor; and

(c) whether or not a colourable cash price was quoted for any goods or services included in the credit bargain.

(5) Factors applicable under subsection (2) in relation to a linked transaction include the question how far the transaction was reasonably required for the protection of debtor or creditor, or was in the interest of the debtor.

Reopening of extortionate agreements

139 (1) A credit agreement may, if the court thinks just, be reopened on the ground that the credit bargain is extortionate –

FIGURE 8 (CONT)

(a)   on an application for the purpose made by the debtor or any surety to the High Court, county court or sheriff court; or

(b)   at the instance of the debtor or a surety in any proceedings to which the debtor and creditor are parties, being proceedings to enforce the credit agreement, any security relating to it, or any linked transaction; or

(c)   at the instance of the debtor or a surety in other proceedings in any court where the amount paid or payable under the credit agreement is relevant.

(2)   In reopening the agreement, the court may, for the purpose of relieving the debtor or a surety from payment of any sum in excess of that fairly due and resonable, by order –

(a)   direct accounts to be taken, or (in Scotland) an accounting to be made, between any persons,

(b)   set aside the whole or part of any obligation imposed on the debtor or a surety by the credit bargain or any related agreement,

(c)   require the creditor to repay the whole or part of any sum paid under the credit bargain or any related agreement by the debtor or a surety, whether paid to the creditor or any other person,

(d)   direct the return to the surety of any property provided for the purposes of the security, or

(e)   alter the terms of the credit agreement of any security instrument.

(3)   An order may be made under subsection (2) notwithstanding that its effect is to place a burden on the creditor in respect of an advantage unfairly enjoyed by another person who is a party to a linked transaction.

(4)   An order under subsection (2) shall not alter the effect of any judgment.

(5)   In England and Wales, an application under subsection (1)(a) shall be brought only in the county court in the case of –

(a)   a regulated agreement, or

(b)   an agreement (not being a regulated agreement) under which the creditor provides the debtor with fixed-sum credit or running-account credit

(5A)   [*Repealed.*]

(6)   In Scotland an application under subsection (1)(a) may be brought only in the sheriff court for the district in which the debtor or surety resides or carries on business.

(7)   In Northern Ireland an application under subsection (1)(a) may be brought in the county court in the case of –

(a)   a regulated agreement, or

(b)   an agreement (not being a regulated agreement) under which the creditor provides the debtor with fixed-sum credit not exceeding £1,000 or running-account credit on which the credit limit does not exceed £1,000.

mortgages, charge cards and other forms of credit not regulated by the Act can all be examined. If a bargain is extortionate the court can reopen it, retrospectively if it so chooses, and substitute a fairer, lower rate of interest (s139).

5.2 Definitions

The problem with these provisions is that because the ceiling figure has been removed, the exact meaning of 'extortionate', and particularly 'grossly exorbitant', has become very hard to define. The court is given guidance but it tends to mean that each case focuses on its own particular facts and it is very difficult to produce general principles that can be followed. It has proved easier in cases where security has been provided, and accordingly these will be considered separately.

5.2.1 'Harsh and unconscionable'

Does 'extortionate' mean the same as 'harsh and unconscionable'? Opinion is divided as to whether the terms can be equated. Goode thinks they mean 'much the same thing' and that there is an 'obvious resemblance between the terms . . . and [that] s138 sets out criteria very similar to those developed by the courts under the old Acts' (Goode I (2913), III (138)). This view was supported expressly in *Castle Phillips v Khan* [1980] CCLR 1 where it was held that the meaning is 'precisely the same', although this is not to say that s138 should be construed solely by reference to Moneylenders Act decisions.

By way of contrast in *Davies v Directloans Ltd* [1986] 2 All ER 783; [1986] 1 WLR 823 (see 5.5) it was stated that CCA 1974 provides a comprehensive definition and it is neither 'necessary nor permissible' to look elsewhere, and in *Ketley v Scott* [1980] ICR 240; [1980] CCLR 37 (see 5.5) it was held that it was 'unwise to read s137 in general terms' with each case depending on its facts.

Thus pre-1974 decisions clearly cannot be seen as authorities and should be treated with caution. Nevertheless, Moneylenders Act cases can provide some helpful guidance on the wide range of factors that need to be considered in each case.

Levene v Greenwood (1904) 20 TLR 389. The court can reopen a transaction where, due to a term of the bargain understood by the lender but not explained to or understood by the debtor, the rate of interest is considerably increased beyond that contemplated by the borrower.

Carrington Ltd v Smith [1906] 1 KB 79.   A businessman received 12 loans to pay debts. A rate of 75% was held reasonable because of the risk, lack of security and the borrower's understanding of the bargain.

Samuel v Newbold [1906] AC 461.   A 'man of means' was loaned £2,000 on a promissory note of £3,300. The high rate of interest was held to make the bargain harsh due to the lack of risk and a reduced rate was substituted.

Blair v Buckworth (1908) 24 TLR 476.   A high rate of interest may be justified if the loan is risky. As Alverstone LCJ said, 'the rate of interest might in certain cases be of itself a fallacious test'. Nevertheless, it should be noted that in this case, because the lender took advantage of the borrower's need for cash at short notice, a rate of 44% was reduced to 10%.

Kerman v Wainewright (1916) 32 TLR 295.   A rate of 500% was held to be excessive and the bargain was reopened.

Reading Trust v Spero [1930] 1 KB 492.   Spero was an antiques dealer speculating in a very profitable business. Loans for £200 and £100 at 60% and 80% respectively were made and the court did not hold the charges to be excessive.

Dunn Trust v Asprey (1934) 78 SJ 767.   A rate of 480% on a loan of £100 was held to be excessive and reduced to 100%.

Collings v Charles Bradbury Ltd [1936] 3 All ER 369.   A woman of no business experience but some means borrowed £50, giving a promissory note to pay back instalments totalling £72. The interest rate was 81.23%. The rate was reduced to 25% because it was held not to be fair dealing to have made no enquiries about the woman's circumstances.

Parkfield Trust Ltd v Portman (1937) 81 SJ 687.   A loan of £600 under a promissory note of £1,000 plus interest at 177.7% was held to be reasonable because the borrower's position was unstable, the business highly speculative and a solicitor's advice had been taken.

Tattersall v Mason & Wood Ltd (1956) *Times*, 3 March.   A loan at 70%, to clear loans to other firms, was not excessive because of the risk involved.

Edgware Trust v Lawrence [1961] 3 All ER 141.   It was unfair dealing for a bargain to comprise a contract which referred for some of its terms to another document, a copy of which was not given to the debtor.

City Land Property (Holdings) v Dabrah [1968] Ch 166. Premiums on a loan of £2,900, which increased it to £4,500, represented a return out of all proportion to current interest rates, especially as it rendered the security offered deficient.

It is clear that extortionate and unconscionable are very similar concepts, but the court should interpret s138 on its language and the facts of the particular case alone. It is also clear that a wide range of factors have to be considered. The court must look at the whole agreement. In *Castle Philips v Williams* (see 5.5) reference was made to looking at the bargain 'in the round'.

5.3 Matters that the court must consider under s138

The general definition of extortioniate credit is contained in s138(1) with the particular factors that must be considered in s138(2)–(4).

5.3.1 Grossly exorbitant payments

Under s138(1)(a) a credit bargain will be extortionate if it requires the debtor to make payments which are grossly exorbitant. This requires the court to look at whether the financial burden placed upon the debtor is in excess of what may be fairly stipulated and go beyond what is 'fairly due and reasonable' (s139(2)).

While the most relevant factor will normally be the total credit charge and the APR (see 5.3.3 regarding rates of interest) other amounts payable will also be considered, such as:

– any penalties imposed on the debtor in default, such as minimum payment clauses;
– the debtor's obligations under ancillary or linked transactions.

5.3.2 Unfair dealing

Under s138(1)(b) a credit bargain will be extortionate if it grossly contravenes the ordinary principles of fair dealing. Issues that the court should consider include any non-monetary terms of a credit bargain and the circumstances in which the agreement was made, although these will often overlap with the factors covered in s138(2)–(4) (at 5.3.3–5).

Non-monetary terms that must be considered include:

– the effect of any default by the debtor, such as forfeiture or repossession of property, or loss of deposit;

- the nature and gravity of events which trigger the creditor's right to enforce the agreement;
- the duration of the agreement;
- the extent to which the debtor was required to enter into any ancillary transactions.

The circumstances in which the agreement was entered encompass:

- any unfair dealing by the creditor, including any abuse of the creditor's position or bargaining power;
- any 'moral culpability' will be relevant although unlawful behaviour is not necessary;
- the circumstances of the debtor (see 5.3.4).

Under the Moneylenders Act 1900 'misconduct' by the creditor was capable of making a 'hard' bargain a 'harsh and unconscionable' one although an agreement may be held to be extortionate without such behaviour. In *Davies v Directloans Ltd* (above at 5.2.1 and see 5.5), it was stated that 'the starting and ending point' must be the words of s138(1) and that the test is extortion and not morality.

Where the terms of the agreement are not themselves unfair it will require a considerable degree of 'misconduct' by the creditor to make the agreement extortionate (*Wills v Wood* [1984] CCLR 7, CA) (see 5.5). In any event, the creditor should not take advantage of the debtor's position to impose terms which go beyond what is reasonable for profit and/or protection.

In *Avon Finance Ltd v Bridger* (1979) 123 SJ 705; [1985] 2 All ER 281, CA, a son exerted undue influence over his parents to obtain their signatures on a secured loan agreement. The agreement was declared void because of the son's undue influence but Lord Denning stated (obiter) that the same result could have been achieved under s137 as the lender had appointed the son to procure the signatures (see also *Barclays Bank v O'Brien* at 5.3.5). A lender can be impugned by a third party's conduct not only where the third party is acting as the creditor's agent, as above, but also where there is no such relationship provided the creditor connived with the misconduct of the third party and perhaps where the creditor knew of the misconduct and 'adopted' it by failing to 'undo' it. This was established in *Coldunell v Gallon* [1986] QB 1184; [1986] 1 All ER 429; [1986] 2 WLR 466, CA, although on the facts of the case the creditor was held not to be responsible for or to have colluded with the actions of a son who persuaded his father to secure a loan on a failing business and then forged his signature on the loan documents.

However, the imposition of onerous terms which may in themselves appear to be extortionate may be justifiable in certain circumstances, for example where the debtor required a loan within 24 hours and failed to disclose his true financial position (*Ketley v Scott*, above, at 5.2.1 and see 5.5). The debtor's personal circumstances may also justify onerous terms (see 5.3.4 and 5.3.5).

5.3.3   Interest rates

Under s138(2)(a) the court must have regard to interest rates prevailing at the time the agreement was made. It is not enough, however, to consider the rate in isolation. Regard must also be had to the type of agreement, for example whether it is secured or not (see 5.3.5), the length of the loan – with higher interest acceptable over shorter periods (*Woodstead Finance Ltd v Petrou* (1986) 136 NLJ 188), the circumstances in which the loan was granted (see 5.3.4/5) and the rates charged by other lenders.

With regard to rates charged by other lenders, it is not clear whether comparisons should be made with the market as a whole or to credit realistically available to the debtor. In *Barcabe Ltd v Edwards* [1983] CCLR 11 (see 5.4), *Castle Phillips v Williams* [1986] CCLR 13 (see 5.5) and *Shahabinia v Gyachi* [1989] Lexis, CA (see 5.4) the courts looked at interest rates in general. More often, however, courts have looked at similar types of credit, for example, in *Castle Phillips v Khan* (above at 5.2.1 and see 5.5), *Davies v Direct Loans Ltd* (above at 5.2.1 and see 5.5), *Ketley v Scott* (above at 5.2.1 and see 5.5) and *First National Securities Ltd v Bertrand* [1980] CCLR 5 (see 5.5). In the latter case the judge stated that 'prevailing interest rates are not admissible where in the circumstances they are not applicable'.

It can be seen that it will be difficult to set any benchmarks. Against what rate or rates should the agreement be compared? Were the charges influenced by the circumstances of the debtor and, if so, were they justified or exploitative? Each case will have to be looked at on its merits and the 'precedents' will often be of little assistance.

5.3.4   Factors in relation to the debtor

Under s138(3) the court must have regard to the personal circumstances of the debtor and the nature and extent of any pressure on the debtor.

The debtor's personal circumstances

The areas referred to in s138(3)(a) – the age, experience, business capacity and state of health of the debtor – are largely self-explanatory and would be relevant, for example, where the debtor is immature, mentally unstable, senile, lacking in business knowledge and/or in poor health, etc.

Where an agreement is made with a debtor in these circumstances it may be arguable that onerous terms were imposed by the creditor taking advantage of the debtor's lack of knowledge, etc, that there was an unfair bargaining position and/or that the debtor may have been acting under the influence of the creditor. However, from the creditor's side it could be argued that onerous terms were imposed because of the debtor's circumstances, ie, because the debtor, given the relevant circumstances, was seen as a high risk borrower, rather than it being a case of the creditor exploiting the debtor's position.

In *Castle Phillips v Wilkinson* [1992] CCLR 83 the defendants had little understanding of financial matters or ability and were persuaded to accept an interest rate of 48%, over three times the building society rate. The loan involved little risk as it was adequately secured (see 5.3.5) and was held to be extortionate. See also *Barcabe Ltd v Edwards* at 5.4.

Where debtors are in poor health, etc, or under financial pressure (see below), for example, under threat of loss of home, these factors make them more vulnerable to exploitation. However, as discussed above, it is these same factors that will often create debtors' need for credit and at the same time make them less credit-worthy and unable to borrow from more mainstream lenders due to the risk involved, low income or lack of prospects, etc.

Financial pressure on the debtor

Under s138(2)(b) the court must have regard to the financial pressure on the debtor at the time of making the agreement.

It is unlikely that a debtor who has borrowed for extravagant or non-essential purposes will succeed in an allegation of extortionate credit unless the requirements of s138(1) can be clearly met. However, where the debtor is facing serious consequences such as loss of home, disconnection of utility supplies, imprisonment for non-payment of local taxes, etc, the element of the pressure on the debtor is likely to carry more weight.

In *Ketley v Scott* (above at 5.2.1 and see 5.5) it was held that pressure must be 'real pressure'; it was not enough that the debtor faced losing a deposit of £2,250 for failing to meet a completion date in relation to the purchase of a property (the debtor was not faced with losing his home).

As discussed above, it may be the debtor's reasons for needing credit that make the loan a high risk rather than it being the case of exploitation of a debtor in serious difficulty.

It is impossible to lay down any clear rules but it is necessary to look at agreements and the circumstances surrounding them as a whole. Advisers need to try to assess whether, in particular cases, the debtor's circumstances have led to unfair exploitation with a creditor taking unfair advantage by imposing terms that go beyond what is reasonable for profit and protection, or whether it is a case of the terms of the agreement genuinely reflecting the risk of lending to someone in the debtor's particular circumstances.

It may perhaps be useful to look at the terms upon which the creditor lends to other borrowers, although many high cost creditors, eg, moneylenders who collect door-to-door, will usually lend at the same (high) rate to all borrowers regardless of their particular need for the loan or particular circumstances. It will be useful, however, if it can be shown that a creditor has lent to a particular debtor at a higher rate or on more onerous terms than that creditor's usual 'standard rate'.

In relation to 'standard rates', creditors may argue that a standard rate of charge makes no consideration of debtors' personal circumstances and is based on external factors. Goode submits that courts should 'seek to avoid a result in which the standard use of charges which are reasonable in themselves is jeopardised because of the prospect that particular debtors may, on account of their personal circumstances, find specific agreements burdensome' (Goode I (2920)). However, standard rate charges are common and it would seem to be unfair to individual debtors if such charges could not be challenged by particular debtors in relation to their particular circumstances. Section 138(3) clearly builds a subjective element into the extortionate credit equation and the court should be able to look at a standard rate of charge, albeit a prima facie reasonable one, subjectively from a debtor's position. In any event, a challenge to a standard rate charge could be made on the basis that it was, in itself, extortionate under s138(1)(a). It should be noted that it is not uncommon to see such standard charges at between 150% to 300% APR (see *Barcabe Ltd v Edwards* at 5.4).

5.3.5   *Factors in relation to the creditor*

Under s138(4) the court must have regard to a number of factors in relation to the creditor.

The degree of risk accepted by the creditor and the value of any security

The degree of risk involved in a loan will be one of the major considerations in deciding whether an agreement, its APR and the payments required under it are grossly exorbitant.

Under the Moneylenders Acts a secured agreement was viewed differently to an unsecured one, and a rate of interest excessive on a secured advance may not have been excessive on an unsecured one. There is no reason to think the position is any different under CCA 1974.

The nature of any security will also be relevant. An advance secured by personal security, whether given by the debtor or a third party such as a guarantor will, in general, be seen as giving rise to a greater risk than an advance secured by real security, eg, on land, against goods or under a bill of sale.

Under the Moneylenders Acts it was the risk at the time the loan was made that was to be assessed and not 'what the real risk is, as ascertained after the event' (*Carrington Ltd v Smith* [1906] 1 KB 179). However, in relation to extortionate credit under CCA 1974 it would appear that this might not be the case and that the security should be assessed in terms of its current value. In *Davies v Directloans Ltd* (above at 5.2.1 and see 5.5) the value considered was one on a current forced sale.

Where a loan is totally unsecured, especially where the financial position of the debtor is precarious, high rates may be justified provided the debtor fully understands the transaction and is not taken advantage of or exploited (see 5.3.4 and case-law at 5.4 and 5.5).

The creditor's relationship to the debtor must be considered by the court

It may be that a special relationship between the creditor and the debtor could have given rise to undue pressure or influence.

Where such a relationship gives rise to undue influence, whether actual or presumed, by law or fact, this may itself be grounds for setting aside the agreement – see *Barclays Bank v O'Brien* [1993] 4 All ER 417, and would certainly be relevant in extortionate credit cases.

A less formal relationship may also be relevant in extortionate credit cases where it can be shown that the debtor, perhaps with little knowledge or experience, or with reduced capacity, etc, relied upon the creditor and was taken advantage of. It may also be relevant where, for example, a creditor or credit-broker is masquerading as a money adviser or debt counsellor, a not unknown situation.

Each case will have to be considered on its own facts and it is important to remember that a creditor may be held responsible for the actions of a third party who may have a relationship to a debtor (see *Avon Finance Ltd v Bridger, Coldunell v Gallon* (at 5.3.2) and *Barclays Bank v O'Brien* (above)).

Colourable cash price

This factor was included to prevent a creditor inflating the price of goods subject to a credit agreement, ie, to a price higher than that charged to cash customers, in order to reduce the credit charge and, therefore, the APR.

5.3.6   Other relevant factors

Although the above factors cover a wide range of circumstances relevant to the making of credit agreements they are not exhaustive. Section 138(2)(c), therefore, allows the court to consider other relevant factors.

Under the Moneylenders Acts it was held that a lender's failure adequately to explain the details, terms and effects of an agreement was relevant to whether it was harsh and unconscionable and this is likely to be the case now.

Other relevant factors may include pressure by the debtor for an immediate loan, failure by a debtor to disclose financial information including details of other liabilities (*Ketley v Scott* above at 5.2.1 and see 5.5), whether the debtor had access to, had taken or had been advised to take independent advice, over-zealous 'selling' of loans, a practice not unknown among second mortgage lenders, eg, to finance double glazing sales, or 'moral pressure' on a debtor to help a family relation (see *Lloyds Bank v Bundy* [1975] QB 236; [1974] 3 All ER 757, CA).

5.3.7   Conclusions

As can be seen from the above, it will often be difficult to make any definite assessment of the likelihood of the success of an extortionate credit allegation. It will be a case of looking at the various factors involved and trying to balance them to achieve a view of the particular agreement as a whole.

Successful extortionate claims have been particularly difficult in relation to short-term unsecured loans and it appears that it is generally seen as acceptable for such lenders to charge very high APRs of between 100% to 300%. However, there has been more success in relation to secured loans, especially where it can clearly be shown that there is adequate security – see the case-law at 5.4 and 5.5.

It should be noted, however, that once a basis for an extortionate credit allegation has been established the burden of proof falls on the creditor who must then prove that the agreement is not extortionate (see 5.6.4).

5.4   Unsecured loans case-law

Since the CCA 1974 provisions came into effect, few cases have been brought and even fewer have been successful. The following brief survey illustrates this.

Barcabe Ltd v Edwards [1983] CCLR 11.   This case held that the interest rate of 100% (APR 319%) was prima facie extortionate for a loan over one year. The agreement was reopened and a rate of 40% substituted. Edwards took out a loan for £400 but changed jobs, suffered a drop in income and defaulted after four months. He had little business capacity and his wife could not read. Comparison was drawn with other firms charging interest rates of between 18% and 20%.

Arrowfield Finance v Kosmider [1984] CCLR 38.   This case held that the bargain was not extortionate as both parties were experienced businessmen. Over 12 years Kosmider received loans on demand, without security, for his business. He claimed them to be unfair dealing as he had no independent advice and the lender was his accountant.

Patel v Patel [1987] Lexis, HC.   In this case a rate of 48% was accepted on the grounds that there was no substantial imbalance of bargaining power, the debtor did not lack business capacity and was aware of the cost of the credit in advance, suggesting it to acquire the loan intended for property improvements.

Shahabinia v Gyachi [1989] Lexis, CA.   The debtor received three business loans at 78%, 104% and 156%. The High Court reopened the bargains and reduced the interest to 15%. The Court of Appeal substituted flat rates of 30% 'to do justice between parties'. As with the *Patel* case above, this involved loans between individuals, but comparison was made with the bench-mark of bank base rates.

5.5 Secured loans case-law

Because of the existence of property provided as security for a loan and available to the creditor to repossess and sell in order to recover the debt, it has sometimes proved easier to show such bargains to be extortionate. This has been true both before and after 1974.

Part v Bond (1903) 93 LT 49.   A widow borrowed £1,000 at 45%, secured by a second mortgage. The rate was reduced to 10%.

Poncione v Higgins (1904) 21 TLR 11.   A woman was loaned £100 at 300%, charged on property. The court reduced the rate to 5%.

Blair v Johnstone (1911) 111 LT 426.   An advance secured on land at 50% was so excessive as to be reopened and 20% substituted.

Jennings v Seeley, Kruse & Seeley (1924) 40 TLR 97.   Loans at 82.5%, with the security of promissory notes and a pledge of furniture of considerable worth, were harsh and unconscionable and 15% was substituted.

Verner-Jeffreys v Pinto [1929] 1 Ch 401.   A loan at 48%, secured by a bill of sale on furniture, was harsh and unconscionable.

First National Securities v Bertrand [1980] CCLR 5.   This case held that a bargain is not extortionate if it is simply excessive. Bertrand received an on-demand overdraft of £17,500 at 17.8% APR, secured on houses bought for letting to tenants. To get the loan he lied about his circumstances, forged accounts, inflated the rental income and falsified the value of one property. He was under no pressure and had sufficient business capacity.

Wills v Wood [1984] CCLR 7, CA.   A bargain cannot be reopened if a debtor has simply been unwise. The interest rate was only 12% but might have been extortionate if the lender had exploited the debtor by charging a higher rate.

Castle Phillips v Khan [1980] CCLR 1.   This case held that the bargain was not extortionate where the defendant was mature, not lacking in business experience, under no financial pressure and advised by solicitors. Khan had borrowed £3,000 for property speculation, secured and at an APR of 32%.

Ketley Ltd v Scott [1980] ICR 240; [1980] CCLR 37.   An application to reopen an agreement for a secured loan for £20,500 at 12% for three months (APR 48%) was refused. Scott knew the APR but did not disclose full details of his financial situation (or overdraft at the bank secured on his property). This, together with the fact that the debtor made an urgent request for an immediate loan within 24 hours, thus preventing the creditor making appropriate checks on his credit-worthiness, justified charges which otherwise might have been held to be extortionate as it involved the creditor taking a considerable risk. The issue of pressure on the debtor was also discussed – the debtor's home was not at risk but rather the forfeiture of a deposit of £2,250 which would be lost if he could not complete a house purchase in time. This was held to be insufficient pressure on the debtor.

Premier Finance Co Ltd v Gravesande [1985] CCLR 1.   A loan was held not to be extortionate because the defendant did not disclose the full situation and gave Premier very little time in which to gather full information. Gravesande was buying a property and received a completion notice. He needed a loan within less than a week in order to save his deposit and was loaned £19,000 at 3.5% per month secured on property.

Leamington Spa Building Society v Jindal (1985) Lexis, CA.   As in many cases, the court's judgment reflected the status of the lender. An APR of 18.75% was not extortionate because it was in line with Building Societies Association rates.

Castle Phillips Ltd v Williams [1986] CCLR 13, CA.   The bargain would have been extortionate because of the manner in which the costs were calculated and deducted. The interest rate was 48% (APR 67.7%). Mr Williams sought a second mortgage to clear first mortgage arrears. He borrowed £11,000 including £2,000 fees. Soon after this he split up with his wife and Mrs Williams could not keep up the payments. The bargain must be looked at 'in the round'. See also *Castle Phillips Ltd v Wilkinson* [1992] CCLR 83 at 5.3.4.

Davies v Directloans Ltd [1986] 2 All ER 783; [1986] 1 WLR 823.   A bargain is not extortionate where the borrower has been warned of the cost, where the creditor takes a risk and the rate is not out of line with that charged by other firms. Davies borrowed from Directloans for 12 months whilst finding mortgage finance. It was stressed that it was an expensive loan. Davies then fell ill, defaulted and possession proceedings were commenced. Davies was still, however, given a loan at 21% to buy the house when he could not find building society finance and this cleared his existing loan and arrears. He defaulted a year later and possession proceedings were begun again. Davies was not under financial pressure as, although he had spent money on renovating property and providing a deposit, the lender did not take advantage of this.

Woodstead Finance Ltd v Petrou [1986] CCLR 107; (1986) 136 NLJ 188, CA.   The bargain was not extortionate as Petrou understood details of the loan and the APR was normal for such a short-term loan. Petrou had taken out a secured loan for £25,000 over six months at 42% APR to fund a failing business.

Devogate v Jarvis (1987) unreported, Sevenoaks CC.   A secured consolidation loan to clear existing debts at 39% APR was reopened and reduced to 30% APR by the court on the grounds that it was adequately secured and that the risk was, therefore, very low. The debtors were in an unequal bargaining position in that their circumstances (ie, financial pressure) gave them no option but to accept.

Prestonwell Ltd v Capon (1988) Lexis, Corby CC.   This case concerned a secured loan of £18,000 at a flat rate of 42%, used to consolidate debts. The court halved the rate on the grounds that cheaper loans were obtainable, there was little risk, the debtors had little business capacity, were under financial pressure and had no access to proper legal advice, although the judge observed that he was not restricted to comparing the interest rate with others solely within that sector of the market.

Southern & District Finance v Barnes [1995] CCLR 62; (1995) *Times*, 19 April, CA.   This case, which dealt with the appeals of three cases, was primarily concerned with the issue of time orders, but in giving judgment on one of the cases, *Equity Home Loans v Lewis*, obiter comments were made in relation to extortionate credit. Mrs Lewis borrowed £4,000 from Equity Home Loans, secured on her home, with a total of £19,000 repayable over 15 years at 44.1% APR. In relation to this loan, the court stated that 'the facts of the case are extreme, with the loan bordering on the extortionate, although this has not been alleged', and talked about 'the extortionate rate prescribed' and 'a penal rate of interest'. As no allegation of extortionate credit was made, no such finding could be made, and the bargain could not, therefore, be reopened. The court did, however, make a time order providing for, *inter alia*, no further or additional interest to be added.

5.6   Jurisdiction and procedures

5.6.1   *Application*

Application can be made by a debtor or surety:

- To the county court by way of originating application under CCR
  1981 Ord 49 r4(14) on payment of the appropriate fee (s139(1)(a)).
  Reference in s139(1)(a) to the High Court is now redundant following amendment to the section by High Court and County Court
  Jurisdiction Order 1991 SI No 724 art 2(8).
- In any proceedings relating to the enforcement of the agreement to
  which the debtor and creditor are parties (s139(1)(b)).
- In any other proceedings in any other court where the amount paid
  or payable under the agreement is relevant (s139(1)(c)).

Applications under s139(1)(b) and (c), where these relate to proceedings in the county court, are on notice to the court on form N244 and
will be treated as a defence with the result that no default judgment
can then be entered (CCR 1981 Ord 49 r4(15)). Presumably the court
would also accept applications by way of a defence, for example, on
N9B in default actions or on N11 in possession actions.

Applications under s139 1(b) and (c), where these relate to proceedings in the High Court, are by way of notice served by the debtor or
surety on all parties and filed with the court (RSC Ord 83 r2(1)). This
will prevent any default judgment being entered and presumably as
above, the court would accept an application by way of a defence.

In Scotland application will be to a sheriff court, and in Northern
Ireland to a county court where it is a regulated agreement or the
High Court where the agreement is not regulated and the credit or
credit limit exceeds £1,000.

5.6.2   *Order only on a debtor's application*

It appears that s139 only permits the court to reopen an extortionate
credit bargain where there has been application by the debtor or
surety. However, in *First National Bank v Syed* [1991] 2 All ER 250;
[1991] CCLR 37, CA, Dillon LJ speculated, obiter, that it might be
arguable that the court could reopen an extortionate credit bargain of
its own motion although this point was not taken up in *Southern and
District Finance v Barnes* which clearly considered that one of the
cases under appeal involved an extortionate or near extortionate
agreement (see 5.5).

5.6.3 *No order after judgment*

Under s139(4) it appears that a credit bargain cannot be reopened after a judgment has been entered in relation to it. However, it may be possible for the court to reopen the agreement on appeal or perhaps if the case is one which it may set aside. In *Shireknight v Wareing* (1993) unreported, 28 May, CA, the view was expressed, obiter, that a mortgagee's order for possession might be set aside pursuant to an application under s139.

5.6.4 *The burden of proof*

Section 171(7) provides where extortionate credit is alleged by a debtor it is for the creditor to prove the contrary. However, it is not enough for the debtor to raise an unsupported allegation. The debtor must adduce sufficient evidence to establish the basis of the claim on the balance of probabilities. The initial onus is, therefore, on the debtor to prove the particular facts upon which s/he seeks to rely.

If the debtor fails to do this there is, in effect, no case for the creditor to answer. Where the debtor succeeds in proving the basis for the allegation, the burden of proof then falls on the creditor to prove that the agreement is not extortionate. If the debtor has established the basis of the claim and the subsequent evidence is evenly balanced, the debtor will succeed. Where, however, on the face of it there is nothing unusual in the transaction and the creditor has acted as an ordinary lender, the creditor will be deemed to have discharged the burden of proof (*Coldunell v Gallon* at 5.3.2 above).

5.6.5 *Powers of the court*

Following an application to reopen a credit bargain and the finding that it is extortionate, the court has discretion to reopen it if it finds it just but is under no obligation to do so. The court may not consider it just, for example, where there has been misconduct by the debtor.

The powers can operate retrospectively and apply to all credit agreements with individuals, whenever made, subject to a judgment not already having been entered. The fact that an agreement has been discharged does not prevent the court reopening it although the court may be reluctant to do so a long time afterwards. In *First National Bank v Syed* (at 5.6.2 above) it was stated, obiter, that no action would be taken where a case had been proceeding for a considerable length of time (18 months).

Where the court does reopen an agreement it may, under s139(2), set aside all or part of any obligation imposed by the agreement, require the creditor to repay sums received, direct the return of any property provided as security and alter the terms of the agreement, for example, by reducing the rate of interest.

5.7   Reform

The low success rate post-1974 and the comparative wealth of case-law prior to the change in the law makes it clear that there are problems with the extortionate credit provisions. These arise partly from the need for the debtor to apply, partly from the phraseology of the sections which focus the courts very much on individual circumstances and partly from the fact that most of the case-law relates to defendants who were using the provisions as a last resort.

For some time there has been discussion of solutions, including recommendations that there be a return to a ceiling or ceilings of interest rates. The DTI responded to these concerns by issuing, in September 1991, recommendations for the reform of ss137 and 138. The idea is that the term 'unjust credit transaction' should replace 'extortionate credit bargain'. It was suggested that the new factors to assess the legality of the bargain should be whether excessive payments were required, whether business activity was involved which was deceitful, oppressive or otherwise unfair or improper and whether the lender exercised care and responsibility in making the loan, including taking steps to check the debtor's credit-worthiness and ability to pay. The court would be given the power to reopen transactions of its own motion and would be required to notify the Office of Fair Trading whenever a bargain was found to be unjust. The Office of Fair Trading and trading standards departments would be enabled to start proceedings for a declaration in the public interest that a bargain was unjust. These changes may well make these sections work as was originally intended, which is the Office of Fair Trading's hope. Regulations will be drafted to implement these changes in due course, but is is not known when they will be brought into effect.

CHAPTER 6

Proposed reform and deregulation of the CCA 1974

Reform of consumer credit law was proposed by the government in 1988 as part of its deregulation initiative. These proposals led to a report by the DG of FT: 'Consumer Credit Deregulation – a review of the scope and operation of the Consumer Credit Act 1974', (OFT, June 1994).

6.1 Proposed changes

A number of main recommendations were made in the report, and a further consultation document containing some of these recommendations was issued by the DTI in August 1995: 'Deregulation of UK Consumer Credit Legislation'. Although this was, as stated above, a consultation document, it gave a very clear idea of how the government intends to proceed, although no time-scale was indicated.

6.1.1 Business lending

The DG of FT recommended the implementation of government proposals to remove all business lending and hiring, including all business-related ancillary credit activities, from the scope of the Act. It is proposed, however, that lending and hiring to individuals, as currently defined by s189 to include unincorporated businesses, should continue to be licensable activities (see 'Releasing Enterprise', DTI, Cmnd 512, November 1988). This means that a licence under Part III of the Act will still be required for lending to unincorporated businesses, up to the maximum regulated agreement monetary limit.

These recommendations have been further considered and put out to consultation in 'Deregulation of UK Consumer Credit Legislation' (DTI, August 1995). The DTI has stated that it 'shares the Director General's view', recognises that there is some evidence of abuse of   169 hire agreements affecting sole traders and considers that licensing 'appears to remain a necessary protection'.

It is proposed, therefore, subject to a change of mind following consultation, that a licensed credit or hire business could enter a non-regulated agreement with a customer for the sale or hire of a product intended for the customer's business use, but would have to enter a regulated agreement if the product was intended for private use or a mixture of private and business use. It is intended that the documentation of agreements should include, as an integral part, a declaration to be signed by customers when the agreement is being made for business purposes. These changes will probably be introduced by creating a new category of agreements exempt from regulation although, as stated above, the licensing requirements of Part III of the Act will still be retained. The extortionate credit provisions, which relate to all lending, would remain applicable. To avoid potential abuse, the DTI is considering providing that the 'business use' declaration shall be of no effect, ie, void, where customers can prove that they were not carrying on a business and did not intend to do so.

There are clearly likely to be problems for proprietors of small businesses where personal and business finances often become intertwined. There are fears that pressure may be put on small traders to sign the 'business use' declaration with consequential loss of protection under the Act. It is also often the case that in credit-related matters, small traders generally have little or no more knowledge of the pitfalls of credit than the average consumer. This argument was countered by the DTI's view that where people are in business, the law should presume a high degree of care, expertise and sophistication, and that people in business should be willing to succeed or fail according to their ability to make business contracts.

6.1.2   Monetary limits

Various changes in the monetary limits applicable under the Act were recommended by the DG of FT on the basis of revalorisation (ie, updating in line with inflation) based on the original 1974 figures.

Changes recommended include:

- raising the upper limit for regulated agreements to £25,000;
- raising the small credit or hire agreement upper limit to £150;
- raising the lower limit under s75 (connected lender liability – see 2.6.1) from £100 to £150, and lowering the upper limit from

£30,000 to £25,000, although it appears that the DTI favours
retaining the current lower limit (see Figure 9 at p172);[1]
- an increase in the fees payable by consumers and sureties when
  requesting account information or copies of agreements under
  ss77–79 and 107–109, from 50p to £1;
- an increase in the upper limit of hire payments which excludes the
  right of termination of a regulated hire agreement under s107(a)
  (see 2.7.4). Currently, hire agreements which provide for payments
  in excess of £900 in any one year are excluded from the statutory
  right of termination. It is proposed to increase this figure to £1,500;
- an increase from £1 to £2 in the fee payable by a consumer to
  obtain a copy of a credit reference file under s158(1).

A full list of the proposed changes, as envisaged in the DTI's consultation document is included in Figure 9.

6.1.3 Licensing

In the deregulation review of June 1994, the DG of FT considered the
government's recommendations to move ancillary credit licensing
from a positive regime to a negative one, to change the requirements
on licensees notifying changes to the OFT and on the specific categories of licence currently required.

The DG of FT recommended that no changes be made with reference to ancillary business and that the system should not be changed
from a positive basis to a negative one. It was stated that the majority
of the OFT's regulatory activity was concerned with ancillary areas,
ie, categories C (credit brokerage) and E (debt collection) (see 2.3.6).
The DG clearly stated that the sectors of the credit market proposed
for removal from positive licensing were those that most need it.

Regarding licence categories, the DG proposed that the different
categories of licence be replaced by one licence covering credit or hire
trading as a whole. The DG would, however, have the right to determine that a particular trader should not carry on a particular type of
business, and licence applicants could voluntarily request that a particular category of work be excluded from their licenses.

---

1 It was also proposed by the DG of FT ('Connected Lender Liability – A further
   report by the DG of FT on s75 CCA 1974' (OFT, May 1995)), that the monetary
   limits of s75 be defined in terms of the credit provided rather than the cash price
   of the item concerned, although it appears that DTI is not considering this
   change (see also 6.1.9).

FIGURE 9: MONETARY LIMITS AND AMOUNTS UNDER CCA 1974 – RECOMMENDED REVISIONS

Section	Description	Current amount	Recommended amount
8(2)	Upper limit for regulated credit agreements	£15,000	£25,000
15(1)(c)	Upper limit for regulated hire agreements	£15,000	£25,000
17(1)	Upper limit for small agreements	£50	£150
43(3)(a)	Exemption limit for certain advertisements	£15,000	£25,000
70(6)	Upper limit for broker's fee or commission on cancelled regulated agreement	£3	£5
75(3)(b)	Lower and upper cash limits for connected lender libilility	£100 & £30,000	£100* & £25,000
77(1) 78(1) 79(1)	Fees for information to debtor/hirer	£0.50	£1
84(1)	Upper limit of debtor's liability for loss to creditor following misuse of credit token	£50	£50
101(7)(a)	Upper limit of annual hire payments for right of termination of regulated hire agreement	£50	£50
107(1) 108(1) 109(1)	Fees for information of surety	£0.50	£1
110(1)	Fee for copy of security instrument	£0.50	£1
118(1)(b)	Upper limit for use of unsworn statement in place of lost pawn receipt	£25	£75
120(1)(a)	Upper limit of pawned property which passes to pawnee on failure to redeem within redemption period of six months	£25	£75
121(1)	Upper limit of pawned property where notice of intention to sell not required	£50	£100
155(1)	Upper limit for broker's fee or commission for services not leading to an agreement	£3	£5
158(1)	Fee to credit reference agency for copy of file on individual	£1	£2

*Note: in the DG of FT's May 1995 report, it was recommended these limits be related to the amount of credit granted rather than the total value of the transaction (see p171, n1).

With reference to notifications by licensees, at present they are required to notify the OFT where there are changes in certain personnel involved in their business, ie, when new persons are appointed as officers of the business or their controllers. These requirements are thought to put a considerable burden on licensees, with some 50,000 notifications per year, and while it is estimated that there are thousands of failures to notify, none have yet been prosecuted by the OFT. The DG, therefore, recommended that licensees should be 'freed of the burden' of having to notify personnel changes as and when they occur, although notification of a change of business address would still be required as it reflects normal business practice. It was recommended, however, that notification should still be required where a newly introduced officer or controller has been convicted of offences involving fraud, dishonesty, violence, contravention of consumer credit legislation or discrimination, with failure to do so remaining a criminal offence. In addition, the DG recommended that it should be a requirement that there should be notification where an existing officer or controller is convicted of one of the above offences, not currently a requirement.

The DG has also recommended that he be given the power to request information from a licensee at any stage during the currency of a licence, and that it should be an offence to give false or misleading information.

Concerning the licensing of business lending and hiring, although it is proposed to remove these areas from regulation, it is intended to retain the requirement that such lending and hiring should remain licensable (see 6.1.1).

It is not entirely clear which of these proposals the government intends to introduce. The DTI clearly agrees with the continuation of licensing for business lending and hiring as a form of regulation and the proposals on notification, but does not appear to intend that the DG of FT takes additional powers with regard to requesting information from licence-holders. No comments were made by the DTI in relation to the abolition of the licence categories although it appears that the DG's recommendations to leave ancillary licensing on a positive basis have been accepted.

6.1.4   Early settlement rebates

The DG of FT recommended that the method of calculating early settlement rebates should be more equitable to borrowers, that the rule of 78 (see 2.7.6) should be replaced by an actual reducing balance formula, that lenders should be compensated for their administrative costs by way of a fixed fee rather than by deferment of the settlement date and that the transparency of the system be improved.

For agreements where interest is charged periodically on the balance outstanding on the account, it was recommended that the amount of the rebate could be ascertained by adding together all charges which would become payable under the agreement after the settlement date, and subtracting from the total of these any settlement fee. However, for other cases, where charges are added to and repayments deducted from the balance due as and when they arise, an actual reducing balance formula could be used, with a simple formula for agreements where equal repayments are made at equal intervals, and a more complicated one for agreements where unequal payments are required.

The aim is that the formulae will apportion over the whole term of the loan charges which may be levied at a particular point in time. This would prevent some of the abuses of 'front loading' charges under agreements.

Various examples of the new formulae are given in the DTI's consultation document, with comparisons to the result that would be achieved using the rule of 78.

Under the present provisions, there is no entitlement to early settlement rebate on running-account credit agreements, eg, store cards, credit cards, etc. Generally, this will remain the position although it is proposed to provide for rebates 'where appropriate', for example, on 'budget accounts' under which a borrower pays a minimum monthly repayment during the agreement, with anti-avoidance provisions to prevent a lender specifying that charges would be recoverable at the beginning of an agreement, ie, 'front loading'. No details are given, however, of how it is intended to do this. To compensate lenders for their 'start-up' or administration costs, it is proposed that a settlement fee be introduced as an alternative to the deferred settlement date. The DG recommended a maximum fee of £100, although in the DTI's examples of rebate calculations a £50 figure was used. The DTI is unsure, however, whether a maximum fee can be introduced under CCA 1974, and instead proposes to define settlement fees by limiting them to the 'reasonable costs incurred by the creditor in taking such steps as are necessary to settle agreements early', with a requirement that agreements must state whether a settlement fee will be charged, with borrowers entitled to particulars of how a fee will be made up, including a statement that it will be limited only to reasonable costs incurred.[2]

6.1.5   Advertising

The DG of FT recommended that the regulations relating to credit and hire advertisements (see 2.4.1) should be replaced by new, simpler regulations which will do away with the simple, intermediate and full advertisement categories. New regulations are proposed to:

- Ensure that an APR is quoted whenever an advertisement indicates an interest rate or any figures relating to the cost of credit, based on current variable rates, where appropriate.
- Allow traders to advertise what they are offering in general terms without having to give further details, although where terms for a particular product are advertised or specific examples are given, sufficient information as to cost should be given, ie, the amount of credit offered, details of repayment amounts, timing, etc, and the interest rate and APR.
- Require, in relation to the advertisement of secured loans, that any conditions, eg, having to take out an insurance or endowment policy, should clearly be indicated. The current warning statement about the effects of non-payment of secured loans would be retained but only in printed advertising.

Similar changes were recommended for hire advertisements.

It is not clear whether and to what extent the government intends to take up the DG's proposals. Little mention of advertising is contained in the DTI's consultation document. It is merely stated that 'there may also be some modification of the Advertisement Regulations'.

6.1.6   Quotations

The DG of FT recommended that the Quotations Regs be revoked and that CCA 1974 s46, which makes it an offence to advertise false or misleading information, should be extended to include information provided in response to requests from prospective customers. It appears to be the intention to revoke the Quotations Regs with s46 to be amended 'later when an opportunity arose'.

---

2 It is intended that the current regulations will apply to agreements entered into before any change comes into force and to exclude any early settlement fee from the total charge for credit/APR.

6.1.7   Requirements as to copies of secured agreements

Under CCA 1974 ss58, 62 and 63, in some circumstances, borrowers entering secured regulated agreements are entitled to three copies of agreements. It is proposed that the maximum of three copies be reduced to two by making agreements which come under s58 exempt from the requirements of s62(2) to provide a second copy of an executed agreement (see 'Regulated secured agreements' at 2.5.9, p65). No comment is made on this proposal in the DTI's consultation document.

6.1.8   Cancellation rights

It is proposed that the cancellation provisions of s67 should not apply to credit agreements where antecedent negotiations take place on trade premises but the agreement is subsequently signed by the consumer away from trade premises (see 2.5.11).

A proposal to harmonise the cooling-off period under s68 to one of seven days has been deferred for further discussion and consultation.

6.1.9   Connected lender liability

The area of connected lender liability under s75 has been subject to considerable dispute and discussion. Full details can be found in 'Connected Lender Liability' (OFT, March 1994) and 'Connected Lender Liability – a further report' (OFT, May 1995), both of which are summarised at 2.6.1.

In brief, the DG has recommended that:[3]

– the monetary limits be amended (see 2.6.1 and 6.1.2);
– creditors and suppliers should remain jointly and severally liable under s75, but that claims against credit card issuers should be limited to the amount of the credit involved;
– where a card issuer meets a claim which is covered by a consumer's insurance or bonding scheme, the creditor should be entitled to subrogate the rights of the consumer against the insurer.

In any event, it appears from the DTI's consultation paper that no imminent changes are intended, although a voluntary agreement was

---

3 These proposals were published as part of the DG's proposals for reform of credit card law. It is not clear whether the proposals, other than the change in monetary limits, are intended to apply to s75 in general or only to credit card agreements.

reached between the OFT and the main credit card issuers with the effect that up until 31 December 1996 foreign transaction claims would be met up to the amount of credit on an *ex gratia* basis.[4] From 1 January 1997, the voluntary agreement lapsed with creditors now setting their own policies.

6.1.10   Total charge for credit and APRs

Various changes are proposed by the DG of FT, most of a technical nature, which are of little relevance to advisers. They relate to APRs on overdrafts, mortgages where the initial rate charged differs from the lender's standard variable rate, APRs in advertising for credit cards, APRs for running-account credit in general, with a simplification of the formulae for calculating APRs in the Consumer Credit (Total Charge for Credit) Regulations 1980 SI No 51.

6.1.11   Extortionate credit

See 5.7.

6.1.12   Timetable for changes

No timetable for any intended changes has been given by the government. The majority of the changes can be bought about via regulation/statutory instrument rather than primary legislation. The period for consultation on the DTI's proposal has expired, although the EU Commission is currently reviewing its two directives on consumer credit, and these reviews may impact on them. The announcement of specific changes is awaited at the time of writing.

---

4 If it is accepted that credit card issuers are fully liable for foreign transactions under the Act, the voluntary agreement should not limit consumers' statutory rights.

CHAPTER 7

Consumer protection

This chapter gives an introduction to contract law, with the aim of providing guidelines for advisers. Although it is not a comprehensive examination, it is intended to indicate to advisers where further specialist assistance may be required, and when there may be grounds for defending default actions commenced by creditors for consumer debt. The chapter shows where liability arises in contract law, what the remedies of the consumer may be, and also looks at protection available without the need for litigation.

7.1   Contract terms

In order to decide whether a contract has been breached, it is necessary to know what information, or 'terms' were included in the contract at the time it was made and entered into by the contracting parties. Some contractual terms may be derived from the contract documentation, from other similar contracts which have been entered into by the same parties, or from the negotiations that took place between the parties.

However, other contractual terms are derived from statute and assumed to be present in all contracts. These 'implied statutory terms' are considered below, and the adviser is referred to the appropriate section(s) of the relevant legislation.

7.1.1   Implied statutory terms

These are as to:

- *Title*: It is implied that the seller has the right to sell goods subject to a contract, and that the buyer of the goods has the right to quiet possession and freedom from encumbrances. For example, in *Rowland v Divall* [1923] 2 KB 500, the plaintiff bought a car from the defendant, whom it transpired was not the true owner. The true owner recovered the car. It was held that the plaintiff could recover the price he had paid from the defendant.

The relevant legislation here is Sale of Goods Act 1979 (SOGA 1979) s12.

For goods on hire, it is a term implied by the Supply of Goods and Services Act 1982 (SGSA 1982) s7 that the hirer has the right to 'transfer possession of the goods by way of hire for the period of the bailment and, in the case of an agreement to bail, he will have such a right at the time of the bailment'.

- *Sale by description*: It is implied that goods supplied shall correspond with the description that is given of them. This implication is applied very strongly in favour of the buyer, and it applies even where the buyer has seen the goods before purchase. Where sale is by sample, there is the implication that the rest of the goods supplied will correspond both with the sample and its description. The relevant legislation here is SOGA 1979 s15. Supply of Goods (Implied Terms) Act 1973 (SG (IT)A 1973) s9 and SGSA 1982 s10 extend this requirement to the description of goods on hire. The Sale and Supply of Goods Act 1994 (SSGA 1994) also introduced the buyer's right to a reasonable opportunity to compare the bulk of goods supplied with the sample given before acceptance of the goods is deemed to have occurred.

- *Quality*: It is implied that goods are of merchantable quality if they are sold in the course of a business. This will not apply to defects specifically drawn to the buyer's attention before the contract is made, nor will it apply if the buyer has examined the goods before the contract is made as regards defects which the examination ought to have revealed. The relevant legislation here is SOGA 1979 s14. SG(IT) 1973 s10 and SGSA 1982 s9 extend this requirement to goods on hire.

Goods are deemed to be merchantable if they are as fit for a purpose for which goods of that kind are commonly bought as it is reasonable to expect, having regard to any description applied to them, the price and all other relevant circumstances.

- *Fit for the purpose for which they are sold*: It is implied that goods that are sold in the course of business are reasonably fit for any purpose expressly, or by implication, made known to the seller by the buyer. This condition will not be implied if circumstances show that the buyer did not rely on the statements of the seller, or if it can be shown that there is some reason why it would have been unreasonable for the buyer to rely on the seller's skill or judgment.

The relevant legislation here is SG(IT)A 1973 ss9(5) and 10, and SGSA 1982 s9 extends this requirement to goods on hire.
– *Supply of services*: This is covered by SGSA 1982 Part II. It implies terms that the supplier of the service will carry out that service with reasonable care and skill, within a reasonable time, and for a reasonable price.

It may thus be seen that there are virtually identical contractual conditions implied by:

– Supply of Goods (Implied Terms) Act 1973.
– Sale of Goods Act 1979.
– Supply of Goods and Services Act 1982. This Act extended the provisions of the SOGA 1979 to contract goods which are supplied under contracts which do not meet the SOGA 1979 definition of sale (contracts for hire). It also provided a statutory protection of consumers under service contracts by codifying the existing law.

7.1.2   Effect of the Sale and Supply of Goods Act 1994

The above Acts were all substantially amended by the Sale and Supply of Goods Act 1994 (SSGA). Before amendment the previous legislation made distinction between a contractual condition and a warranty.

A condition is an essential element of a contract, breach of which goes to the 'root' of the contract and entitles the buyer to reject the goods and treat the contract as repudiated, in addition to claiming damages (see 7.3.2 below). A warranty is a less important contractual term, breach of which does not allow the buyer to repudiate the contract, as it can still continue in a modified form, but permits damages to be claimed.

The distinction between these two categories has never been wholly satisfactory. Each case must be decided on its merits by the courts, with the resultant danger that a party who has repudiated a contract due to a beach of condition may be held to have done so wrongly, where it is found that the term breached was only a warranty.

SSGA 1994 replaces the expressions 'condition' and 'warranty' with the expression 'term'. It would appear that the question of whether a breach of contract amounts to a breach of condition or a breach of warranty is now a matter for the courts to decide, subject to the legislation specifying the particular status of certain terms, eg, specifying as conditions the implied terms that the seller has good title, that goods correspond to the description, and that goods are of satisfactory quality (SOGA 1979 ss12 to 15, as amended by SSGA 1994 s7 and Sch 2).

This Act also introduces the idea of 'satisfactory quality' as an implied term. This largely replaces the idea of merchantable quality, and amends SOGA 1979 s14(2). It is an important concept because goods may be unsatisfactory without being unfit for sale. SSGA 1994 inserts s14(2B) into SOGA 1979 which states:

> . . . the quality of goods includes their state and condition and the following (among others) are in appropriate cases aspects of the quality of goods –
>
> (a) fitness for all the purposes for which goods of the kind in question are commonly supplied,
> (b) appearance and finish,
> (c) freedom from minor defects,
> (d) safety, and
> (e) durability.

SOGA 1979 s14(2) still does not apply to defects which were made known, or should have been apparent to the buyer before the contract was entered into.

7.2 Problems with contracts

If a contract runs smoothly and all parties to it are satisfied, it is not likely that the terms of the contract will become an issue. However, in cases of dissatisfaction, the information in the contract will determine what action the plaintiff can take, and what remedies are available. Before the nineteenth century, the doctrine of *laissez-faire* applied. This is the doctrine of freedom of contract, where each party enters into a contract on the basis of the negotiations s/he made with the other contracting parties. However, as society and business became more complex, it was common for contracts to be between individuals and large organisations, and the balance of power in negotiations was upset. Companies would often refuse to do business except on the basis of standard terms and contracts. Often, 'exclusion' or 'limitation' clauses were inserted into these standard terms. Individual customers, when faced with a 'take it or leave it' approach, had little option but to accept the standard contract however unsatisfactory it may have been. The courts did not initially see it as part of their role to interfere, even when an exclusion clause was blatantly unfair.

However, as the inequity of such clauses became more apparent, the courts tried to limit their effect by a series of interpretative rules. These included the *contra proferentem* rule and the doctrine of fundamental breach. This latter doctrine is the concept that once a contract has been brought to an end by a fundamental breach and, therefore, ceased to be valid, any exclusion clauses would also cease to apply. However, various cases made it clear that there is no reason why, even where a fundamental breach had occurred, it should not be covered by an exclusion clause, provided the clause was clear and specific (*Suisse Atlantique, etc v Rotterdamsche KCNW* [1967] 1 AC 361 and *Photo Productions v Securicor Transport* [1980] AC 827).

Eventually legislation was introduced to try to deal with the problems that were arising. The Misrepresentation Act 1967 gave the courts powers to bar certain types of exclusion clauses. The Unfair Contract Terms Act 1977 (UCTA) is also important as it lays down a statutory definition of which contract terms will be unfair and, therefore, invalid. These areas are considered in turn below.

7.2.1   Misrepresentation

A misrepresentation is a statement of fact made by one party to another which, whilst not forming a term of the contract, is nevertheless one of the factors that induces a party to enter into the contract in the first place. The state of mind, the intentions and the degree of care taken by the person making the representation are necessary to clarify a statement as misrepresentation, but only to determining the *type* of misrepresentation that has occurred (if any).

Representations are limited to statements of facts, and not statements of opinion, intention or law. The distinction is of importance because if a person alters his/her position on the basis of a representation, the mere fact that a misrepresentation has occurred will entitle the person to certain remedies. If, on the other hand, s/he tries to take action on what was an opinion, or a promise that the person making the representation may or may not be able to fulfil, s/he must show that such a promise forms part of a valid contract. However, the expression of an opinion may in certain circumstances constitute a misrepresentation, for example, where it can be proved that such an opinion was never held by the person expressing it, or that it was expressed upon a matter about which the speaker was entirely ignorant.

The general rule is that silence does not amount to misrepresentation, and there is no absolute duty for a contracting party to disclose facts that are within his/her own knowledge. Failure to disclose a material fact which might influence the mind of the contracting party does not give the right to avoid the contract even where it may be obvious that the other party had a wrong impression that would have been corrected by disclosure. However, although a party to a contract may be legally justified in remaining silent on the point, if s/he does make a representation, it must be a full and frank statement. A partial account may or may not amount to a misrepresentation, depending on the facts.

A misrepresentation does not render a contract voidable (see below) unless it was intended to cause, and has in fact caused, a party to enter into the contract. Not only must a misrepresentation have been made but it must have been one of the factors which induced the party to enter into the contract. A representation will not, therefore, be actionable if the plaintiff did not know of its existence, did not allow it to affect his/her judgment or was aware of its untruth.

7.2.2 Types of misrepresentation

Fraudulent misrepresentation

In *Derry v Peek* [1889] 14 Ap Cas 337, fraudulent misrepresentation was defined as a false statement 'made:

- knowingly; or
- without belief in its truth; or
- recklessly, careless whether it be true or false'.

If the person making a representation honestly believed his/her statement to be true, s/he cannot be held liable for fraud, no matter how ill advised, stupid, credulous or even negligent s/he may have been. Motive is irrelevant in an action of deceit. Once it has been proved that the representee has acted on a false representation which the representor did not believe to be true, liability ensues, although the party may not have been motivated by any dishonest motives. The representor is not liable, however, until the representee has acted on the representation and thereby suffered loss.

Negligent misrepresentation at common law

The leading judgment in this area was given by the House of Lords in *Hedley Byrne v Heller* [1964] AC 465. The plaintiffs had suffered a loss by extending credit to a certain firm. They had been induced to do so by a reference, carelessly given by the firm's bank, which in effect vouched for the firm's credit-worthiness. The bank escaped liability because of a disclaimer clause, but the House of Lords made it clear that, but for this, the bank could have owed a duty to the plaintiff.

The House of Lords said that a duty would arise where a 'special relationship' can be shown. This will be deemed to exist where the representor has, or reports to have, some special skills or knowledge, and knows, or should know, that the representee will rely on the representation. The main impact of this case was to clarify the category of negligent misrepresentation, the remedy for which lay in damages (see 7.3.2) although this has been somewhat superseded by the Misrepresentation Act 1967 (MA 1967).

Representations under the Misrepresentation Act 1967

MA 1967 s2(1) provides:

> Where a person has entered into a contract after a misrepresentation has been made to him by another party thereto, and as a result thereof he has suffered loss, then, if the person making the misrepresentation would be liable for damages in respect thereof had the misrepresentation been made fraudulently, that person shall be so liable notwithstanding that the misrepresentation was not made fraudulently unless he proves that he had reasonable grounds to believe, and did believe up to the time that the contract was made, that the facts represented were true.

This provision reverses the burden of proof. Once the representee has proved that there has been a misrepresentation which induced him/her to enter the contract, the onus is on the representor to prove his/her belief in the truth of the representation, and that reasonable grounds existed for such a belief. It also removes the necessity to show a special relationship or duty of care between the contracting parties.

Innocent misrepresentation

This is a misrepresentation made without fault, where the representor had made a false statement but could not have been reasonably expected to know or find out that it was false. Prior to MA 1967, the only remedy was rescission (see 7.3.1 below), however, s2(2) allows damages in lieu of rescission, subject to certain limitations:

- it is within the discretion of the court;
- the award of damages is in lieu of the right to rescind (note: the plaintiff can be entitled to both remedies for fraudulent or negligent misrepresentation).

7.2.3   Exclusion clauses

As noted above, parties to contracts may attempt to avoid liability for misrepresentation, faulty goods or other grounds for ending a contract by the insertion of exclusion clauses. In order to be binding, an exclusion clause must have been incorporated as a term of the contract. Although stringent tests and rules have been developed by the courts, there are two main ways in which it can be determined whether an exclusion clause is incorporated. These are:

- by the fact that advance notice was provided to the other party that the exclusion clause is to be a term of the contract;
- the signature of the party agreeing to be bound by the exclusion clause.

Notice may be given to the contracting party by:

- display;
- documentation;
- course of dealing.

If notice is by display, then the contracting party must be given ample opportunity to see the notice before entering the contract. For example, a doorstep seller could not rely on a notice displayed at the company's head office. The situation where notice is given by course of dealing will arise where parties have dealt together in the past on a number of occasions, to the extent that one party can be presumed to know the terms and conditions on which the other operates.

The case of notice being given in a signed agreement was considered in *Parker v South Eastern Railway* [1877] 2 CPD 416. Mellish LJ said:

> where an action is brought on a written agreement which is signed by the defendant, the agreement is proved by proving his signature, and, in the absence of fraud, it is wholly immaterial that he has not read the agreement and does not know its contents.

This situation may be mitigated if there has been a misrepresentation, if there is an independent oral undertaking, if a plea of *non est factum* (this is not my deed) can be upheld, or if there has been fraud.

The issue of notice by documentation is more complex, and deserves further consideration.

Where a clause is contained in a document, it is still essential that the clause is incorporated into the contract. A document offered to the party after the contract has been made cannot contain any terms of the contract and so cannot be binding upon the recipient. Even where the document is provided before the contract is concluded, the document must be one on which a person could reasonably expect to find terms and conditions. The test that the courts apply is that of the expectation of the 'reasonable man'.

Documentary notice must also be sufficient in all the circumstances of the case. Again, the test applied is that of the expectations of 'the reasonable man'. In *Thompson v L M S Railway* [1930] 1 KB 41, the plaintiff was injured when she stepped from a train that had stopped short of the platform. Her ticket contained terms which referred to timetables which limited liability. She could not read the words on the ticket because she was illiterate. However, the court held that she was bound by the clauses limiting liability. A 'reasonable man' would have been able to read the ticket and know that exclusion clauses in the railway timetable could be referred to and were, therefore, incorporated into the contract.

The more unusual or unreasonable a clause, the greater notice must be given of it. In *Thornton v Shoe Lane Parking* [1971] 2 QB 163, Lord Denning MR said that the relevant exclusion clauses were so wide and so destructive of rights that, in order to be effective, they would have to have had a red hand pointing to them and be printed in red ink. Megaw LJ said that where a restriction was not usual, the defendant must show that he had fairly brought to the notice of the other party the intention to attach an unusual condition. The remarks of the court in the *Shoe Lane* case appear to suggest that if the party cannot withdraw from their prior intention to conclude the contract when an exclusion clause is brought to their attention, the exclusion clause will not have been incorporated into the contract. Neither can an exclusion clause be deemed to be part of the contract if contractual dealings have already been concluded.

To summarise, five questions need to be asked in order to determine whether notice given in the form of documentation is valid:

- Is a document contractual?
- Has reasonably sufficient notice been given?
- Is the relevant clause unusual?
- Could acceptance of the contract have been avoided once the exclusion clause had been brought to the party's attention?
- Was notice given before the contractual dealing had been concluded?

It can thus be seen that contracting parties could attempt to use exclusion clauses in their contracts to limit their liability for any misrepresentation. However, MA 1967 s3, as amended by UCTA 1977 s8, provides that:

> If the contract includes a term which would exclude or restrict –
>
> a) any liability to which a party to a contract may be subject by reason of any misrepresentation made by him before the contract was made; or
> b) any remedy available to another party to the contract by reason of such a misrepresentation,
>
> that term shall be of no effect except in so far as it satisfies the requirement of reasonableness as stated in section 11(1) of the Unfair Contract Terms Act 1977; and it is for those claiming that the term satisfies that requirement to show that it does.

7.2.4   *Unfair Contract Terms Act 1977*

UCTA 1977 applies to contract terms and to notices which are non-contractual and which purport to exclude or restrict liability in tort.

UCTA 1977 applies widely, but not to all contracts. Schedule 1 to the Act contains a list of contracts to which large parts of the Act do not apply. To money advisers, the most relevant of these will be:

– contracts of insurance;
– contracts related to the creation, transfer or termination of interest in land;
– contracts relating to the creation or transfer of securities or of any rights therein.

However, problems arising with contracts such as these may be dealt with by the Unfair Contract Terms Regulations 1995 SI No 3159.

UCTA 1977 actually deals with exclusion clauses, and not *all* contract terms. It acts in two ways: either to make a term completely ineffective, or to apply a test of 'reasonableness' rather than one of fairness.

The following terms will be made ineffective:

– *Personal injury or death*: It is not possible to exclude or restrict liability in negligence for personal injury or death 'by reference to any contract terms or to a notice given to persons generally or to particular persons' (s2(1)).
– *In contracts of sale or hire purchase*: The implied statutory terms for such contracts (see 7.1.1) cannot be excluded (s6(1)).

The terms subjected to a test of reasonableness include:

- Loss or damage arising from negligence other than personal injury or death.
- Consumer contracts where standard terms are used. These are defined as contracts where one party is dealing in the course of business, the other is dealing as a private individual, and goods involved in the contract are of a type usually supplied for private use or consumption.

UCTA 1977 s3 provides that the person who deals with the consumer on the basis of his/her own written standard terms of business:

> cannot by reference to any contract terms –
> (a) when himself in breach of contract, exclude or restrict any liability of his in respect of a breach; or
> (b) claim to be entitled:
>   (i) to render a contract performance substantially different from that which was reasonably expected of him, or
>   (ii) in respect of the whole or any part of his contractual obligation, to render no performance at all, except in so far as the contract term satisfies the requirement of reasonableness.

It is for the person alleging that a term is unreasonable to prove that it is. UCTA 1977 Sch 2 lays down guidelines for the application of the test, although these are not the only factors to which a court may have regard when deciding what is reasonable. They include:

- the strength of the bargaining positions of the parties relative to each other;
- whether the goods were in anyway adapted to the special order of the customer;
- where the term excludes or restricts any relevant liability if some condition is not complied with, and whether it was reasonable at the time of the contract to expect that compliance with that condition would be practicable.

7.2.5   *Unfair Contract Terms Regulations 1995 SI No 3159*

These regulations were introduced on 1 July 1995 to implement an EU directive in the UK. It was recognised that contracts, particularly where standard forms are used, may well contain small print binding consumers to terms which unduly limit their rights, and which they are not usually in a position to challenge. They apply in situations where the consumer is unable to negotiate individual contract terms.

The regulations gave new functions to the DG of FT. S/he was given a duty to consider complaints about unfair terms in consumer contracts, and the power to apply to the courts for an injunction to prevent businesses from continuing to use them. This amounts to power to enforce compliance with the regulations. The OFT now has an Unfair Contract Terms Unit, and has expressed the hope that the regulations will encourage companies to review their standard forms of contracts and remove any terms that may be unfair.

A relevant consideration will be whether the consumer would have agreed to the terms if the bargaining power of the consumer and trader were equally balanced. The definition of an unfair term, as set out in the regulations is: 'any term which, contrary to the requirements of good faith causes a significant imbalance in the parties' rights and obligations under the contract to the detriment of the consumer'. UCTA 1977 suggests that this may include terms that:

- allow a trader to keep a deposit if the consumer decides to pull out of the contract without providing equal compensation if the trader decides to cancel;
- allow the trader to change the characteristics of a product or service unilaterally, without valid reason;
- prevent the consumer from taking legal action in the case of a dispute, eg, by insisting that the matter is taken to arbitration instead;
- irrevocably bind consumers to terms with which they had no real opportunity of becoming acquainted before entering into the contract.

An example of such a term might be one which imposes heavy penalties if a consumer cancels a holiday, but does not bind the tour operator to pay compensation if the holiday company cancels.

The new regulations apply to a wider range of terms than UCTA 1977, in that they go beyond exclusion clauses to cover any term in any contract between a business and a consumer for the sale of goods or supply of services. Contracts relating to insurance and to certain financial transactions, which were exempt from UCTA 1977, are now covered. The regulations also require that any written term of a contract should be expressed in plain, intelligible language. Where the meaning of a term is doubtful, the courts will interpret it in favour of the consumer.

However, two important types of standard terms, core terms and mandatory terms, are excluded from the regulations. Core terms are those which define the main subject matter of a contract or which set the price to be paid. They are not subject to a test of fairness, and thus the regulations cannot be used to argue that a contract does not represent value for money. This exclusion only applies to core terms which are written in plain, intelligible language. Those which are unduly difficult to understand can be deemed to be unfair. Mandatory terms are those which have to be included, or where their inclusion is specifically permitted, by law.

The ultimate 'weapon' against companies that use unfair contract terms is an application to the High Court for an injunction. The DG of FT can ask for a temporary injunction pending determination of the case. However, when a complaint is made, the OFT will first try to persuade the company to withdraw the term from its contracts, and the company will have the opportunity to give undertakings rather than be faced with proceedings for an injunction. Terms which advisers consider may be unfair can be referred to: Unfair Contract Terms Unit, OFT, Room 505, Field House, 15–25 Bream's Buildings, London EC4A 1PR, or to local trading standards departments.

The new regulations are not retrospective, and their main aim is to stop unfair terms being used in the future. However, the OFT suggests that where a similar term in a contract formed after 1 July 1995 has been found to be unfair, consumers may be able to use this as evidence in an action relating to a contract formed before this date. The OFT regularly publishes a bulletin about contract terms which have been found to be unfair. The second of these, 'Unfair Contract Terms – A bulletin issued by the OFT', published in September 1996, includes an article on plain and intelligible language and comprehensive details of 37 cases where action has been taken, including one involving the Northern Rock Building Society and a clause imposing penalties for the early redemption of mortgages. Copies of this and the first bulletin are available from the OFT, PO Box 172, East Molesey KT8 0XW.

7.3 Remedies

If a contract can be shown to be defective in some way, the parties have a number of options, and in some cases can apply to the courts for relief. The different types of remedies and the circumstances in which they may be available, will be considered below.

7.3.1 Rescission

Rescission is available for any of the categories of misrepresentation. The effect of misrepresentation is to make a contract *voidable*. It is not automatically void. The contract is valid unless and until it is set aside.

Rescission has the effect of cancelling the contract *ab initio*, or from the start, and aims to put the parties back in the position they would have been in had the contract never been entered into. For example, the injured party would be entitled to recover anything that had been paid or delivered under the contract, but would have to make restoration of anything obtained under the contract. Rescission is the only remedy available for innocent misrepresentation. However, for fraudulent or negligent misrepresentation, the injured party may also claim damages (see 7.3.2). There are, however, restrictions to the right to rescind for misrepresentation. These include:

— *Affirmation of the contract*: Affirmation is complete and binding when the injured party, with full knowledge of the facts of the misrepresentation and the right to rescind, declares an intention, or performs some act, from which a willingness to proceed with the contract could be reasonably inferred. This will be subject to the injured party's knowledge of the right to rescind; in *Peyman v Lanjani* [1995] Ch 457 the Court of Appeal held that the plaintiff did not know that he had the right of rescission, and could not, therefore, be said to have elected to affirm the contract.
— *Lapse of time*: This does not amount to affirmation of itself, but may be treated as evidence of affirmation. In particular, it would be relevant where the vendor has altered his/her position in the reasonable belief that rescission will not be enforced, or where third parties have been misled by the inactivity of the injured party. Lapse of time will usually be evidence of affirmation if it comes after the injured party has discovered that s/he is entitled to rescind. However in *Leaf v International Galleries* [1950] 2 KB 86; [1950] 1 All ER 693 it was held that a contract for the sale of goods could not be rescinded on the basis of non-fraudulent misrepresentation after a period of five years had elapsed, as 'it behoves the purchaser either to verify or, as the case may be, to disprove the representation within a reasonable time, or else to stand or fall by it'. This may not be a bar in cases of fraud, as it invokes the equitable doctrine of *laches*, or delay defeating equity.
— *Restitution is impossible*: As noted above, the object of rescission is to restore the parties to their former position. In some cases this will not be possible, for example, if the goods subject to the contract had deteriorated, eg, a mine that has been worked out (*Vigers v Pike* (1842) 8 Cl & Fin 562). Restoration will not be enforced if

the result would be unfair, but if the property's substantial identity remains, restitution will be ordered on the basis that the plaintiff pay compensation for the goods' deterioration.
- *Injury to third parties*: The right of rescission will be lost if, before rescission takes place, an innocent third party acquires an interest in the subject matter of the contract.

MA 1967 conferred a general power to award damages in lieu of rescission. Thus a victim of innocent misrepresentation may be awarded damages if the court, using its discretion, considers it equitable to do so.

7.3.2   Damages

Damages for misrepresentation

For fraudulent misrepresentation, damages are assessed as in tort cases. In tort, the purpose of an award of damages is to put the injured party in the position s/he would have been in had the contract been properly performed and the wrong had not been committed. Therefore, for misrepresentation, damages will be compensating the injured party for losses that would not have occurred had the statements made been true. Usually in tort actions, the award of damages is limited by the tests of 'remoteness', that is, the defendant will be liable only for damages that were reasonably foreseeable. However, in *Doyle v Oldby (Ironmongers) Ltd* [1969] 2 QB 158, Lord Denning MR indicated that in cases of fraudulent misrepresentation:

> the defendant should be bound to make reparation for all the actual damage directly flowing from the fraudulent inducement . . . It does not lie in the mouth of the fraudulent person to say that they could not have been reasonably foreseen.

This suggests that in cases of fraud, actual loss should be compensated, and this reasoning was followed by the Court of Appeal in *East v Maurer* [1991] 2 All ER 733.

The measure of damages under MA 1967 s2(1) (see 7.2.2) is not entirely clear, although the language used suggests a tortious measure was envisaged.

Damages for breach of contract

Again the underlining principle of damages for breach of contract is to put the injured party, as nearly as possible, into the position s/he would have been in had the promise been fulfilled. Damages amount to compensation not punishment.

Methods of compensation
There are several ways in which injured parties can be compensated for the loss; they are entitled to claim whichever form of compensation they feel is most appropriate to their cases. These include:

- *Loss of bargain*: Damages for loss of bargain are assessable by the court, and aim to put the plaintiff in the same situation as if the contract had been performed. In a contract for the sale of goods which are found to be defective, the plaintiff will be entitled to damages reflecting the difference between the price paid under the contract and the actual value of the defective goods.
- *Reliance loss*: If the plaintiff, in anticipation of the fact that the contract will be performed, incurs additional expenses, s/he may be entitled to a refund of those expenses if the contract is breached. For example, in *Anglia Television v Reed* [1972] 1 QB 60 Anglia incurred expenses in preparation for filming a television play. Reed was due to play the leading role, but subsequently dropped out. Anglia tried hard to find a substitute but failed and had to abandon the play. It was held that Reed should compensate Anglia for the expenses spent in preparation for filming.
- *Restitution*: Where a contract is made and the price is paid, but the goods are not delivered, then the injured party is entitled to recover the price paid plus interest thereon.

In each of these cases, it is up to the injured party to show that the loss has actually occurred and should therefore be compensated for. There is a further test of 'remoteness of damage'. This test was established via *Hadley v Baxendale* [1854] 9 Exch 341 in which the court held that:

> Where the parties made a contract which one of them has broken, the damages which the other party ought to receive in respect of such breach of contract should be such as may fairly and reasonably be considered as either arising naturally, ie, according to the usual course of things, from such breach of contract itself, or such as may be reasonably supposed to have been in the contemplation of both parties at the time they made the contract as a probable result of the breach.[1]

It can thus be seen that special circumstances, ie, situations arising outside the normal course of events, will have to be made clear at the time of the contract, and accepted by all parties.

1   See also 2.6.1.

7.3.3   Other possible remedies

Application for an injunction

Under the Unfair Contract Terms Regulations (see 7.2.5) the DG of FT can apply to the High Court for an injunction to prevent a company relying on standard contract terms that are deemed to be unfair. At the time of writing, it remains to be seen how the OFT and the courts will apply these terms.

Equitable remedies

Damages for breach of contract may not always be satisfactory as a remedy. For example, there may be no satisfactory financial substitute for that which the injured party had bargained for. In such cases the injured party can apply for an order for specific performance, asking the court to order the defendant to perform his/her side of the contract. A prohibitory injunction may also be relevant, eg, where an employee has agreed not to go into competition against his employer or to work for his employer's competitors.

Repudiation

This occurs when one of the parties of the contract indicates 'beyond reasonable doubt' s/he does not intend to honour his/her side of the contract. This gives injured parties the right to treat the contract as having been breached at that point, and thereby absolves them from performing their own duties under the contract. The innocent parties acquire an immediate cause of action. They need not enforce it; they can either wait until the day of performance arrives, or treat the contract as discharged and take immediate proceedings. A breach of contract caused by the repudiation of obligations not yet due for performance is called an anticipatory breach. The right to claim damages may arise, but this will be subject to certain tests, as discussed above.

7.4   Keeping it out of court – alternatives to litigation

Because of the time, expense and complexity involved in bringing a claim to court, many people with contract law problems may not wish to take this course of action.

7.4.1 'Self-help'

Many basic consumer issues, such as faulty or unsatisfactory goods, may be dealt with by consumers themselves, by raising the issue with the retailer. Some common problems with complaining in this manner include:

– *Receipts*: Vendors may say that they require a receipt before they will exchange goods or refund money. However, *proof of purchase* is all that is required, and other items, eg, stores' carrier bags, credit card vouchers, etc, may count as valid proof of purchase.
– *Liability*: Some vendors may say that a fault is the responsibility of the manufacturer. However, unless the client is making a claim under a guarantee, the contract is between the buyer and the vendor.
– *Presents*: As the contract is between the buyer and the vendor, shops have no obligation to refund on goods the client did not buy, ie, to make a refund to the recipient of the gift.

Where goods are faulty, the vendor should offer a refund as the goods are clearly unsatisfactory and not of merchantable quality. The buyer is not obliged to accept an exchange or a credit note. However, where the goods are simply unwanted, there is no obligation to refund. Advisers requiring further information are referred to *WHICH?* Magazine, January 1996.

Where the client has paid for goods or services with a credit card, the card company may be jointly and severally liable with the vendor (see 2.6.1). A creditor may also be liable for misrepresentations made by a dealer or supplier (see 2.5.1).

7.4.2 Consumer protection via trading standards

Whereas overall enforcement of the CCA 1974 lies with the DG of FT, enforcement at a local level will usually be carried out by the local trading standards department.

These departments can check consumer credit documentation, give information about consumer credit licensing procedures and whether particular creditors are licensed, check that the charges that creditors are making are in line with the APR and the contractual terms quoted in the credit agreement and check early settlement statements given by creditors. They can also take action against creditors for harassment offences under Administration of Justice Act 1970 s40. Serious breaches of the Act and other offences can result in the trader having his/her consumer credit licence revoked and, therefore being unable to continue in business.

In addition, these departments may have responsibilities, some statutory, for checking the quality, quantity, price, description and safety of goods and services. They may also deal with health matters, such as dirty shops and restaurants, unfit food and drink, etc, or there may be a separate environmental health department dealing with these issues.

7.4.3   Ombudsman schemes

There are a number of ombudsman schemes that may be of assistance with consumer problems. These include the Banking, Building Society and Insurance Ombudsman. They are of use when companies' own complaints procedures have been exhausted without the complaint having obtained a satisfactory response. Such schemes generally deal with complaints relating to maladministration. The decisions may or may not be binding on the company, depending which scheme is used, but where further action does have to be taken through the courts, an ombudsman's decision can be useful in deciding whether the company has acted in a 'reasonable manner'.

A full directory of ombudsmen schemes, with a brief description of their powers and duties, can be obtained free of charge from the British and Irish Ombudsmen Association, 21 Queen Anne's Gate, SW1H 9BY, tel: 0171 915 3296. Details of schemes' memberships can be obtained directly from the relevant ombudsman's office.

7.4.4   Trade associations

Many organisations have trade associations or other representative bodies which can be of some assistance in resolving disputes. Most of these have developed codes of practices in conjunction with the OFT. In addition, they are also overseen by the OFT through its general Consumer Credit Act supervisory work, and specifically through the credit licensing procedure. These associations include:

– *Finance and Leasing Association*: Formerly the Finance Houses Association and the Equipment Leasing Association, these bodies merged in 1992. The roles of their members need no explanation but their purpose is representing lenders' interests to government, monitoring economic and legal developments, collecting statistics on business and ensuring best practice in lending by promulgating codes of practice. The FLA code deals with business practice and complaints, and includes an arbitration scheme to resolve disputes. It is operated for the association by the Chartered Institute of Arbitrators. In debt situations, the code promises a sympathetic response to all debt cases, with a named and specially trained staff member dealing with each case. Full consideration will be taken of all the circumstances, with referral to advice services being made where appropriate. Details can be obtained from the FLA, 18 Upper Grosvenor Street, London W1X 9PB, tel: 0171 491 2783. Members include the Associates, Avco, Beneficial Bank, Chartered Trust, Citibank, First National Bank, Forward Trust, HFC Bank, Mercantile Credit, North West Securities and United Dominions Trust.

- *Consumer Credit Trade Association*: This association represents retailers engaged in consumer credit. The association has a code based on the FLA's with a similar arbitration scheme. Current membership comprises approximately 680 companies. Most of these are credit granters but a few are suppliers of services to the credit industry. Copies can be obtained from CCTA at Tennyson House, 159–63 Great Portland Street, London W1N, tel: 0171 636 7564.
- *Council of Mortgage Lenders/Building Societies Association*: The bodies this organisation represents include building societies and large secured lenders. It is a trade association which represents its members to government in the preparation of new legislation, etc, provides lenders with information, training and guidance on good practice, provides statistics and deals with media issues. It is not a regulatory body and cannot investigate complaints or intervene with members' businesses. Any complaints addressed to it are referred to the chief executive of the lender involved. Some leaflets are produced for consumers on general aspects of property purchase and on mortgage repayment problems. For more information and leaflet copies contact CML/BSA, 3 Savile Row, London W1X 1AF, tel: 0171 437 0655.
- *Consumer Credit Association*: This represents providers of door-to-door collectable credit. It was the first to develop and launch a code of practice in 1984. This was revised in 1988 along the lines of the FLA code. It deals with business practice and complaints, and the association operates its own internal arbitration scheme. The main points regarding default are to encourage early contact and a sympathetic response, with a named staff member to deal with all cases. In collecting debts, unreasonable pressure and harassment

will be avoided. Details and copies of the code can be obtained from CCA (UK) Ltd, Queens House, Queens Road, Chester CH1 3BQ, tel: 01244 312 044.

– *British Bankers Association*: This is the trade association represent-ing both UK and foreign banks present in the country. It has just over 300 members including all major banks. The BBA's main role is to express the banking industry's views on domestic and inter-national developments, both legal and economic. It also produces statistics, publications on good practice and relevant areas of law, and provides training and information for members. Its main rele-vance to consumers, besides its involvement in commenting on new legislation, has been its involvement in drawing up the Code of Banking Practice in conjunction with the Building Societies Associ-ation and others. Where consumers are in dispute with their lender, the BBA can refer the matter on to appropriate sources of advice and information. For more information contact British Bankers Association, 10 Lombard Street, London EC3V 9EL, tel: 0171 623 4001.

– *Finance Industry Standards Association*: This association limits its membership to firms lending on the security of property and its main purpose is to promote good practice and high standards in the advertising of such loans. A code of practice has been developed dealing with all advertising and promotional material, whether produced by lenders or their associated brokers. The main provisions of the code are that advertisments should comply both with the spirit as well as the letter of the law, that quoted APRs should be actually representative of generally available loans, that the presentation of information should not give undue prominence to certain aspects and that references to an applicant's present indebtedness should be restrained in tone and prominence. The General Secretary of the Association monitors all forms of adver-tising and investigates any breaches found or reported to the FISA. A direct approach is made to the member to rectify the problem but if this is not possible the management committee of the association will hear the case. Its decision is binding. A formal 'warning' may also be issued, the ultimate sanction for which is the withdrawal of business from that member. Copies may be obtained from FISA, 8 Parrys Court, Northgate, Sleaford NG34 7BN, tel: 01529 303 046.

Appendices

Flowcharts

References in the flowcharts that follow are to the Consumer Credit Act 1974, unless otherwise stated. The flowcharts to be found in this appendix are as follows:

FLOWCHART 1 – IDENTIFICATION OF TYPES OF AGREEMENT

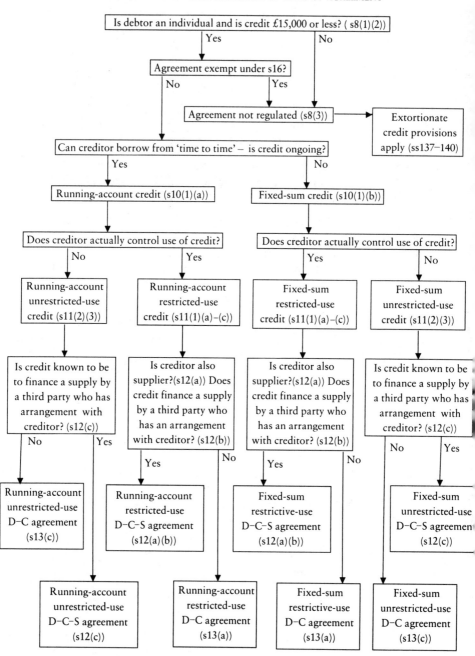

FLOWCHART 2 – CONSUMER CREDIT CHECKLIST

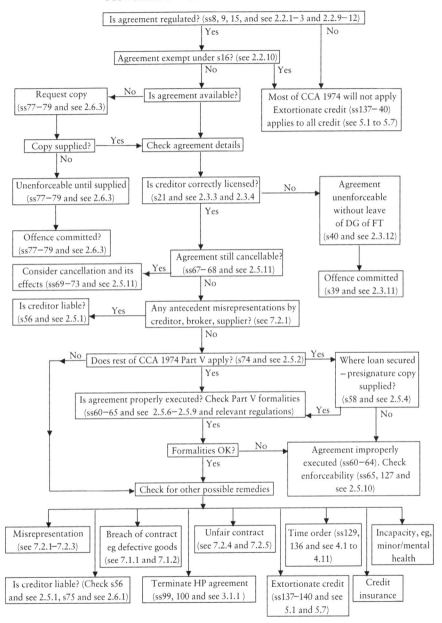

This chart is not intended to be exhaustive but is designed to direct advisers to the relevant sections of the Act and the text.

FLOWCHART 3 – COPIES OF AGREEMENTS AND NOTICES OF CANCELLATION RIGHTS

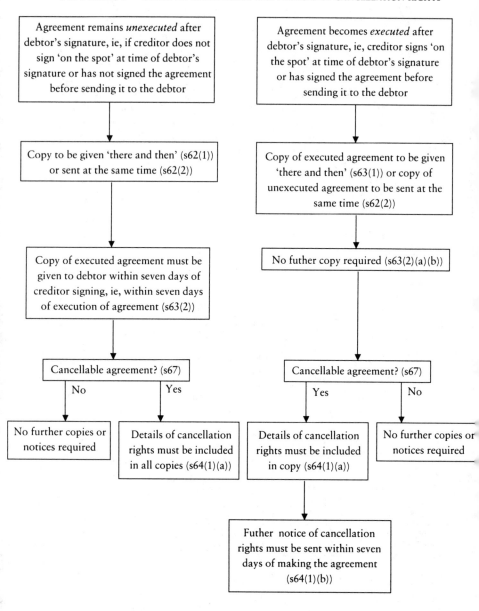

For full details of the requirements as to copies and notices of cancellation rights see 2.5.9.
For details of which agreements are cancellable see 2.5.11.

FLOWCHART 4 – NON-COMPLIANCE WITH COPY AND NOTICE PROVISIONS

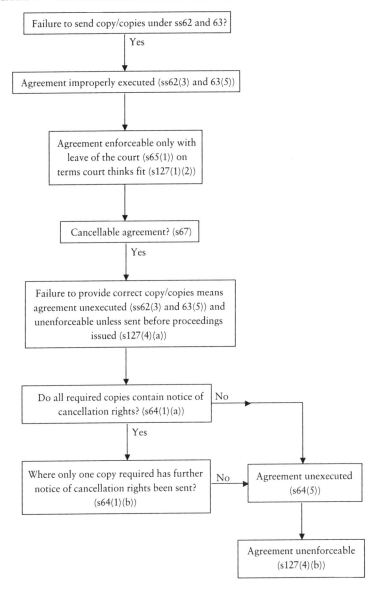

For full details of the provisions as to copies and notices of cancellation rights see 2.5.9.
For details of which agreements are cancellable see 2.5.11.
For further information on the enforceability of unexecuted agreements see 2.5.10.

Checklist: The formation of agreements under CCA 1974 Part V

- Is agreement regulated? (ss8, 9, 15, 16, 17, and see 2.2.1–2.2.3 and 2.2.9–2.2.12).
- Is it fully covered by Part V? (s74 and see 2.5.2).
- Is it in writing, legible and signed in the prescribed way? (s61 and see 2.5.8).
  - If not, agreement is unexecuted and unenforceable unless s127(3) applies (see 2.5.10)

- Does agreement contain all the relevant prescribed terms required by Agreement Regulations Sch 6? (ss60, 61, SI 1983 No 1553 and see 2.5.8).
  - If not, agreement is unexecuted and unenforceable unless s127(3) applies (ss65 and 127 and see 2.5.10).

- Does agreement contain all other relevant information (in the prescribed form where appropriate) required by the Agreement Regulations? (Schs 1 and 2 (credit agreements), 3 and 4 (hire agreements), 5 (prescribed signature box), 7 (details of APR) and see 2.5.8).
  - If not, agreement is unexecuted and only enforceable with the leave of the court and on the terms the court thinks fit (ss65 and 127 and see 2.5.8).

- Where agreement is cancellable (s67 and see 2.5.11) can it still be cancelled? Does the agreement (and all required copies) contain notice of the right to cancel? (ss62–64 and see 2.5.9).
  - Failure to include details of cancellation rights in an agreement (or copy) renders the agreement totally unenforceable (ss64(5), 127(4)(b) and see 2.5.10).
  - Failure to provide a copy of a cancellable agreement is, however, rectifiable under s127(4)(a) (see 2.5.10). Note: Where failure to send a required copy is rectified, it will of course start the 'cooling-off period' giving the consumer the right to cancel (see 2.5.10).
  - Where an agreement is cancellable and the consumer is entitled under ss62 and 63 to only one copy, a separate notice of cancellation rights must be sent under s64(1)(b) (see 2.5.9). Where a creditor fails to do this, the agreement will be totally unenforceable (s127(4)(b) and see 2.5.10).

- Where an agreement is/was not cancellable, have the correct copies been provided to the consumer? (ss62, 63 and see 2.5.9).
  - If not, the agreement is unexecuted and enforceable only with the leave of the court and on such terms as the court thinks fit (ss65, 127(1)(2) and see 2.5.10).

- Where an agreement is secured, has a pre-signature copy been provided for the consumer? (s58 and see 2.5.4).
  - If not, agreement is unexecuted and enforceable only with the leave of the court and on such terms as the court thinks fit (s61(2) and see 2.5.4, s127(1)(2) and see 2.5.10).

- Does agreement contain all the terms of the agreement made between creditor and consumer?
  - If not, agreement is unexecuted and enforceable only with the leave of the court and on such terms as the court thinks fit (s61(1)(b) and see 2.5.10).

Index

National Money Advice Training Unit

Birmingham Settlement's National Money Advice Training Unit provides a selection of handbooks written with specific money advice needs in mind. They are practical guides designed for easy, everyday use. Regular new editions ensure constant updating and improvement. All books are A4 paperback and illustrated with forms, etc.

Each handbook costs £6.55. All prices are inclusive of postage and packing. To order please photocopy and fill in the form below and return with a cheque for the full amount.

ORDER FORM				
Handbook	ISBN	Price	Quantity	Total
Debt Counselling (**New** 10th edition)	0 907272 51 7	£6.55		
Personal Insolvency (5th edition)	0 907272 45 2	£6.55		
Dealing with Distraint (6th edition)	0 907272 50 9	£6.55		
County Court Procedures (4th edition)	0 907272 49 5	£6.55		
Utility Debt & Disrepair (3rd edition)	0 907272 42 8	£6.55		
Self Employed & Debt (4th edition)	0 907272 41 X	£6.55		
			Grand Total	
PLEASE MAKE CHEQUES PAYABLE TO 'BIRMINGHAM SETTLEMENT'				

When completed, please return form to:

Course Administrator
National Money Advice Training Unit
Birmingham Settlement
318 Summer Lane,
Birmingham B19 3RL

Tel: 0121 359 3562   Fax: 0121 359 6357